A Generation at Risk

A Generation at Risk

Growing Up in an Era of Family Upheaval

Paul R. Amato

Alan Booth

Harvard University Press
Cambridge, Massachusetts
London, England

Second printing, 1998

Library of Congress Cataloging-in-Publication Data
Amato, Paul R.
    A generation at risk : growing up in an era of family upheaval /
Paul R. Amato, Alan Booth.
        p.   cm.
    Includes bibliographical references and index.
    ISBN 0-674-29283-9 (cloth : alk. paper)
    1. Parent and child—Longitudinal studies.   2. Child rearing—
Longitudinal studies.   3. Family—Longitudinal studies.   I. Booth,
Alan, 1935–   .   II. Title.
HQ755.85.A449   1997
306.874—dc21   97-11689

Acknowledgments

We thank Norval Glenn, Laura Spencer Loomis, Toby Parcel, Jessica Pellegrino, Sandra Rezac, Stacy Rogers, and Susan Welch for assistance and advice with various aspects of this book. We are also grateful to the numerous students with whom we have discussed our findings and interpretations. In particular, Scott Myers served as a coauthor of Chapter 5. In addition, we are indebted to the respondents who participated so generously in this study. The data set described in this book is based on the efforts of many people. John Edwards, David Johnson, Gay Kitson, F. Ivan Nye, and Lynn White helped to design the original study, and the staff of the Bureau of Sociological Research at the University of Nebraska–Lincoln carried out the interviews and prepared the computer files for data analysis. The study was supported by the Pennsylvania State University Population Research Institute, the University of Nebraska–Lincoln Research Council, grant no. 5 R01 AG04146 from the National Institute on Aging, and grant no. 1-HD28263 from the National Institute of Child Health and Human Development.

Contents

Figures

A Generation at Risk

CHAPTER ONE

Family, Social Change, and Transition to Adulthood

During the last three decades, remarkable transformations have occurred in the American family, including changes in economic well-being, gender roles, family relationships, and family structure. Many families have experienced economic hardship because of a decline in men's income in real dollars, periods of high unemployment, and an increase in under-employment. As married men's economic situations have deteriorated, married women have increased their labor-force participation, with mothers of young children showing a particularly dramatic change. But as mothers have moved into the paid labor force, fathers have only slightly increased their participation in child care and housework. Changing expectations about gender roles within the family mean that husbands and wives today must negotiate rights and responsibilities that previous generations took for granted, thus increasing the potential for marital tension. Along with these changes, the divorce rate has increased to an all-time high. The growing social acceptance of divorce has introduced an element of instability into *all* marriages; even happily married people can no longer assume the lifelong commitment of their spouses.

The ways in which these changes have affected children is the topic of this book. In particular, we focus on the transition to adulthood—a time when offspring leave home, finish their educations, assume full-time employment, form stable intimate relationships, and (for many) become parents. Social scientists have not studied young adults as often as other age groups, such as adolescents or the elderly. Yet, people's experiences in early

1

adulthood have profound implications for their accomplishments and well-being in later life. Many people entering adulthood today grew up in families that are strikingly different from the families in which their parents were raised. However, it is not clear what impact these changes have had on young people's lives. Indeed, the media refer to those reaching adulthood in the 1990s as "Generation X" because we know so little about them.

People hold clashing opinions about how changes in the American family have affected children. Some scholars argue that declining economic opportunities, increases in the proportion of dual-earner couples (and the work-family conflict that often accompanies these arrangements), and the rise in single-parent households represent a deterioration of the family as an institution, with problematic consequences for children (Bellah et al., 1985; Blankenhorn, 1995; Blankenhorn, Bayme, and Elshtain, 1990; Popenoe, 1988, 1993; Popenoe, Elshtain, and Blankenhorn, 1996; Zill and Nord, 1994). In contrast, other scholars argue that families are becoming more diverse but are not becoming weaker (Coontz, 1992; Demo, 1992; Skolnick, 1991; Stacey, 1990). Indeed, these latter scholars believe that children are resilient, and that many changes in family life, such as the movement toward more egalitarian marriage, have benefited children. A number of studies have tried to address these issues by focusing on how certain family characteristics are related to particular child outcomes. For example, studies have examined the impact of economic hardship, maternal employment, and parental divorce on the likelihood that young people will engage in delinquent behavior, drop out of high school, or marry relatively early. But no previous study has provided a comprehensive picture of how multiple dimensions of major family change are related to a broad range of outcomes among offspring.

How have changes in family life—including changes in economic circumstances, gender roles, marital relationships, and family structure—affected young people? To answer this general question, we draw on a national longitudinal study of married persons interviewed in 1980, 1983, 1988, and 1992. In 1992, we interviewed offspring who were 19 years old or older and had resided with their parents (the original respondents) in 1980 when the study began. We also obtained updated demographic information from offspring in 1995. The availability of detailed knowledge about children's families in the 1980s makes it possible for us to estimate the impact of family circumstances (and changes in family circumstances) on children as they make the transition to adulthood in the 1990s.

Our data set is well-designed for this task. Most surveys consist of interviews with one person on a single occasion. However, it is difficult to disentangle the direction of influence with cross-sectional data obtained from a single source; all one can conclude is that two variables are associated in some manner. Our study, however, is longitudinal, with parents providing information on independent variables in the 1980s and with children providing information on dependent variables in the 1990s. This strategy gives our study several advantages over prior research. First, the longitudinal design means that information on presumed causes is collected *prior to* information on presumed effects. In addition, not having to rely on retrospective accounts eliminates the errors that people often make when they are asked to recall the past. And using different sources for independent and dependent variables avoids problems due to same-source bias, that is, the tendency for people's feelings to distort their perceptions of events. Although these advantages do not guarantee our ability to make accurate causal inferences in every instance, they allow us to draw stronger conclusions about the long-term effects of family characteristics on offspring than do most previous studies.

Furthermore, because we have data over a fifteen-year period from two generations, we are able to place our work squarely in a *life course* perspective.

The Life Course

The life course perspective has emerged as a key theoretical orientation in family studies, and it provides an organizing framework in this book (Bengtson and Allen, 1994; Clausen, 1993; Elder, 1994; Rossi and Rossi, 1990). According to Elder (1994), the life course perspective has four central themes.

First, this perspective emphasizes the interdependence of lives over time. People do not live in isolation; instead, their decisions and circumstances affect the lives of others—especially other family members. Researchers working from this perspective have been particularly interested in family influence across generations. It is assumed, for example, that events in the family of origin, such as spells of economic hardship or divorce, have consequences for offspring's role transitions, such as school completion and early employment. Some life course research has focused on the manner in which family and individual traits are passed on from one generation to the next. It is well known that parents' socioeconomic status tends to be transmitted to children. But parents also influence children's personalities, attitudes, values, self-concepts, social skills, and lifestyles. Because offspring carry these traits forward into their adult lives, interpersonal outcomes such as marital quality, divorce, and parent-child relationships are also, to a certain extent, transmitted across generations (Belsky and Pensky, 1988; Caspi and Elder, 1988; Simons et al., 1993). Characteristics of the family of origin, therefore, continue to have consequences for children long after they have grown and left the parental home. Much of our attention in this book is devoted to understanding the links between parents' and children's lives over time.

Second, the life course perspective focuses attention on the timing and sequencing of events. A key assumption is that the impact of an event depends on a person's age and stage of life. For example, a spell of economic hardship, the movement of a mother into paid employment, or a parental divorce may have different consequences for children depending on what their ages are and whether they are still residing at home with parents. In this book, we consider how the effects of family circumstances vary with offspring's ages. We also consider the impact of events in relation to conditions that precede or follow the event. For example, the consequences of divorce may depend on whether it is preceded by a period of intense interparental conflict. Similarly, postdivorce factors, such as custody arrangements, the level of cooperation between former spouses, moving, and parental remarriage, may determine the impact of marital dissolution on children.

Third, this perspective views individuals as active rather than passive. This assumption is contrary to a deterministic view that sees parents and larger social forces as irrevocably shaping offspring's outcomes. Although people are influenced by childhood experiences, they also continue to change and develop throughout their lives. For example, some children who grow up in dysfunctional families replicate these problematic relationships when they enter adulthood and form their own families. In contrast, other offspring grow up in dysfunctional families but manage to enjoy healthy and satisfying family relationships in adulthood. Although a problematic family of origin is a disadvantage, its long-term impact is contingent on a variety of factors, including children's innate temperaments, other resources or stressors in the environment, the unique experiences that offspring have in adolescence and early adulthood, and characteristics of offspring's intimate partners (Amato, 1987a; Rutter, 1988; Rutter and Madge, 1976).

Because children are active, they make choices within the constraints and opportunities provided by their family backgrounds, stage in the life course, and historical milieus. For example, it is well known that contact between noncustodial fathers and their children following divorce tends to decline over time (Furstenberg and Nord, 1985; Seltzer and Bianchi, 1988). Not sharing a residence, strained family relationships prior to divorce, and the tension that often lingers between ex-spouses make it difficult for children to maintain close relationships with noncustodial fathers. Yet, when offspring reach adulthood, they have the option of seeking out their noncustodial fathers and attempting to reestablish relationships. Furthermore, many family processes and events can be seen as joint outcomes of parent-child interaction. The lack of contact that often characterizes children and noncustodial fathers may be as much a result of children's disinclination to see fathers as fathers' reluctance to visit children.

In general, the assumption of linked lives through time, combined with the assumption that people are active, suggests that there is both continuity and discontinuity across generations. This means that the influence of the family of origin is pervasive at all stages of the life course. But because of the many contingencies in people's lives, the average long-term effects of family-of-origin circumstances on offspring are likely to be modest rather than strong.

Fourth, the life course perspective leads us to consider families in their historical context. In our study, parents and children lived through dramatically different periods in recent American history, representing contrasting economic, demographic, and cultural milieus. The constraints and opportunities present in the 1990s are shaping the trajectories of young people in our study just as the constraints and opportunities of the 1960s shaped the trajectories of their parents as young adults. In this book, we interpret the behavior of these two generations—parents and offspring—in relation to events and trends occurring in the larger society.

Parents and Children in Historical Context

CHANGES IN SOCIOECONOMIC CONDITIONS

Typical fathers and mothers in our sample were born in 1940 and 1942, respectively. These men and women spent most of their childhoods during the period between the end of World War II and the beginning of the 1960s. This was a period of rising economic prosperity. From World War II through the 1960s, the United States economy expanded, unemployment remained low, and real incomes rose (Hernandez, 1993, chap. 7; U.S. Bureau of the Census, 1991). Economic growth, coupled with federal programs to combat poverty, lowered the level of family hardship; between 1959 and 1970, family poverty declined from 18.5% to 10% of all families (U.S. Bureau of the Census, 1993, Table 744).

After the turbulence and uncertainty of the Depression and World War II, people sought personal satisfaction and security in home and family life (Cherlin, 1992). Rising economic prosperity made it possible for many people to pursue these goals by purchasing homes and raising families in the growing suburbs of American cities. The pro-family ethos that marked the two decades following the war was reflected in a number of trends: the age at first marriage declined, the marriage rate increased, the number of children born per woman increased, and the divorce rate stabilized (Cherlin, 1992). Most of the parents in our sample started their own families toward the end of this period. The typical parents in our sample married in 1962—at age 22 for fathers and age 20 for mothers. They had their first child four years later, in 1966. These couples formed their families after living through two decades of remarkable prosperity and social stability.

Along with economic security, the educational levels of Americans increased. In 1950, among people 25 to 29 years of age, 53% were high-school graduates and 8% were college graduates. By 1970, the corresponding figures were 74% and 16%. This rise continued for another decade, with corresponding figures for 1980 of 84.5% and 22%. (After the 1980s, relatively little change occurred.) This increase was even more striking among African Americans, with the gap in educational attainment between blacks and whites narrowing substantially. (See U.S. Bureau of the Census, 1992, Table 219.)

Although educational levels continued to rise during the 1970s, the postwar period of relative affluence did not last. During the recessions of the 1970s and the early 1980s, the economic well-being of many families declined. In contrast to earlier decades of economic growth, between 1970 and 1982 the median income of male workers (in constant dollars) dropped by nearly 16% (U.S. Bureau of the Census, 1993, Table 729). Furthermore, unemployment reached nearly 10% of the labor force in 1982, the highest rate since the Great Depression of the 1930s (U.S. Bureau of the Census,

1993, Table 608). The loss of jobs during this time impacted disproportionately on men—especially African Americans (Wilson, 1987). The movement of many wives into the paid labor force helped to offset declines in husbands' wages in many households. Nevertheless, the poverty rate for families began to increase in the second half of the 1970s, from a low of 8.8% in 1974 to 12.2% in 1982 (U.S. Bureau of the Census, 1993, Table 744). Furthermore, rising educational levels, combined with declining employment opportunities, forced many people to accept jobs for which they were overqualified, or to accept part-time jobs, resulting in an inefficient use of human resources and frustration on the part of workers.

In the decade following 1982, median income remained fairly flat for married men but increased for married women. As a result, median family income increased somewhat, and the family poverty rate declined slightly (Zill and Nord, 1994). But these changes in averages mask the fact that economic resources became more unequally distributed during the 1980s, with people at the top of the income distribution earning more and those at the bottom earning less (Danziger and Gottschalk, 1993; Eggebeen and Lichter, 1991; Hernandez, 1993, chap. 7). During this decade, the share of total U.S. money income earned by the wealthiest 5% of the population increased by 12%, whereas the share earned by the poorest fifth of the population declined by 13% (U.S. Bureau of the Census, 1993, Table 722). Increases in women's earnings contributed to the increase in inequality, because these increases tended to be concentrated in families with high incomes (Karoly and Burtless, 1995). At the same time, poverty was increasingly concentrated in families with children, especially those headed by single mothers (Hernandez, 1993, chap. 7; McLanahan and Booth, 1989).

We have no information on the economic well-being of our sample of families in the 1970s. However, our data show that these families were caught up in the economic uncertainty that marked the 1980s. Between 1980 and 1988, 29% of the fathers in our study were unemployed for one month or longer, and one out of twenty married couples relied on public assistance. During this same period, the median annual income of fathers declined by about $3,000 (in constant 1992 dollars). But because mothers' incomes increased by about the same amount (because of greater labor force participation combined with a modest rise in wages), median family income changed little. However, 36% of couples experienced a *decrease* in total family income of over $10,000, whereas 19% experienced an *increase* of over $10,000. Similarly, between 1980 and 1988, 29% of parents reported that their economic situation had deteriorated during at least one time period between interviews, whereas 26% reported that their economic situation consistently improved between each of the interviews. These findings reveal considerable variability in economic well-being during the 1980s, with some families in our study experiencing declines into hardship and others seeing their standard of living improve.

CHANGES IN GENDER RELATIONS

Major changes in gender roles and attitudes have occurred since the early 1960s—the period when many of the parents in our sample married. Married women have been steadily increasing their labor force participation for the last century (Davis, 1984). However, during the time when men's wages were stagnant or declining, women's wages increased, as did the demand for female labor in the service sector of the economy. As a result, the percentage of married women with children in the labor force increased from 28 to 54 between 1960 and 1980 and to 68 in 1992 (U.S. Bureau of the Census, 1993, Table 633). Although economic motivations were important, women also entered the labor force because of declines in family size, increased educational attainment, and changing attitudes about women's employment (Davis, 1984; Hernandez, 1993, chap. 10; Leibowitz and Klerman, 1995). A comparable trend occurred in our sample. When we first interviewed parents in 1980, 61% of married mothers were in the labor force; this percentage rose to 71% in 1992.

The massive movement of married mothers into the paid labor force challenged the traditional division of labor in the home and placed pressure on fathers to become more involved in child rearing and housework. Surveys show that people in the 1980s were more likely than in the 1960s to agree that it is appropriate for wives to have their own careers, that employed women can be good mothers, that husbands of employed wives should do more housework and child care, and that wives should have equal say in making important family decisions (Thornton, 1989). The belief that fathers should be more involved with children is based on two assumptions: it is more equitable to mothers, *and* it benefits the children (Hochschild, 1989). Consistent with these shifts in attitudes, time budget studies show that fathers have increased the amount of time devoted to family work—especially in relation to child care (Lamb, 1987; Pleck, 1985). Nevertheless, even when mothers are employed full-time, they spend about twice as much time in housework and child care as do fathers (Hochschild, 1989; Lennon and Rosenfield, 1994; Pleck, 1985).

Although gender relations have become more egalitarian in recent years, countervailing trends have also occurred. Beginning in the 1970s and continuing through the 1980s and 1990s, the religious and political right became an important force in American life. Advocates of this view argue that men and women should play distinct roles in the family, based on their innate biological capacities. (For popular examples, see Davidson, 1989; Falwell, 1981; Gilder, 1986; Schafly, 1977.) Faludi (1991) argued that this movement represents a backlash against the gains made by feminists. Some individuals, influenced by this movement, abandoned the liberal views that were dominant in the 1960s and 1970s and became more conservative in their thinking. In contrast to the 1950s, when a broad consensus existed about the appropriate roles of women and men, today people's views are polarized, with some advocating egalitarianism and role-sharing and others advocating male leadership in the family and separate spheres of activity for men and women.

We see reflections of these larger social transformations among the parents in our study. The attitudes of fathers and mothers in our sample toward gender issues became more egalitarian, in general, between 1980 and 1992. For example, the percentage of fathers who agreed with the statement "Even though a wife works outside the home, the husband should be the main breadwinner and the wife should have the responsibility for home and children" declined from 57% in 1980 to 43% in 1992. Among mothers, the corresponding percentages declined from 43 to 24. At the same time, an increase occurred in the proportion of housework carried out by fathers. In 1980, 22% of fathers did "about half" of the housework, compared with 35% in 1992. Interestingly, although some surveys show differences in the reports of husbands and wives, spouses in our study reported similar figures. However, a minority of respondents (about one in seven) became more conventional in their attitudes during this period. For example, when presented with the statement "When jobs are scarce, a woman whose husband can support her ought *not* to have a job," 13% of respondents disagreed in 1980 but changed their minds and agreed in 1992.

CHANGES IN FAMILY STRUCTURE AND MARITAL QUALITY

Divorce and Remarriage. A third major change to occur in family life has been the increase in marital dissolution. The divorce rate in the United

States increased gradually during the first half of this century, surged following World War II, then declined and remained stable throughout the 1950s. The divorce rate began to increase again during the early 1960s—the period when many of the parents in our sample first married—and doubled between 1966 and 1976 (Cherlin, 1992). The divorce rate leveled off again during the 1980s, but at a historically high level. Currently, about one-half of all first marriages end in divorce (Cherlin, 1992).

The high rate of marital disruption, coupled with an increase in the proportion of children born outside of marriage, resulted in a substantial increase in single-parent households, usually mother-headed. In 1992, 26% of children under the age of 18 lived with a single parent; 16% lived this way because of parental divorce or separation (U.S. Bureau of the Census, 1993, Table 80). However, a snapshot of the population at one point in time underestimates the proportion of children who will ever experience parental divorce. In fact, about 40% of all children in the United States will experience a parental divorce prior to the age of 18 (Bumpass, Thompson, and McDonald, 1984).

The rate of remarriage following divorce declined during the 1970s and 1980s, with many individuals preferring to enter into cohabiting unions rather than second marriages (Cherlin, 1992). Nevertheless, remarriage is still very common, with three-fourths of divorced men and two-thirds of divorced women eventually remarrying (Sweet and Bumpass, 1987). Consequently, living in a stepfamily is a common experience for children. Currently, one child in ten lives with a stepparent, and about one-third of children will live with a stepparent prior to reaching the age of 18 (Glick, 1989). Because remarriage is still the norm, and because divorce rates are higher in second marriages than in first marriages, many children experience multiple parental divorces.

The increase in divorce that spread through the United States since the 1960s also affected the families in our sample. Among the parents in our sample, 9% experienced the divorce of their own parents. In comparison, among the offspring in our sample, nearly one in five saw their parents' marriage end in divorce, either prior to our first interview in 1980 or during the course of the study. This means that offspring were twice as likely to experience parental divorce as were their own parents. Of those offspring whose parents divorced, slightly more than one-half saw their mothers remarry, and over two-thirds saw their fathers remarry. Of those parental remarriages, about one-third had ended in divorce by 1992.

Marital Quality. The increased rate of divorce since the 1960s can be interpreted in two ways. On the one hand, it may reflect the fact that it is easier now than in the past to leave unhappy marriages as a result of more tolerant community attitudes, the introduction of no-fault divorce laws in all fifty states, and the growing economic independence of women. In other words, marital dissolution has increased because the barriers to divorce have become weaker. On the other hand, the increase in divorce may reflect a deterioration in the quality of marriage itself.

There is general agreement that the barriers to marital dissolution have become weaker and that this accounts for at least part of the increase in the rate of divorce (Burns and Scott, 1995; Cherlin, 1992; White, 1991). The notion that marital quality has declined is more controversial. Nevertheless, some evidence supports this notion. For example, if divorce removes unhappy marriages from the pool of married couples, then remaining marriages should be happier now, on average, than in the past. However, Glenn (1991), using annual data from the General Social Survey, demonstrated that the percentage of people reporting that their marriages are "very happy" declined gradually from 1973 to 1988—the opposite of what one would expect if the rise in divorce were due entirely to weaker barriers. Two studies based on the data set described in this book yield similar conclusions. Using a pooled time-series analysis based on the full set of 1980 respondents, Johnson and Amato (1996) found evidence of a period decline in marital happiness throughout the 1980s for marriages of all durations. And Rogers and Amato (in press) found that when matched on marital duration, a cohort of couples married in the 1980s reported less interaction, more conflict, and more relationship problems than did a cohort of couples married in the 1970s.

Additional indirect evidence comes from research on the link between marital status and personal happiness. In general, married people tend to be happier with their lives than single people. However, studies by Glenn and Weaver (1988) and Lee, Seccombe, and Shehan (1991) indicate that the "happiness gap" was lower in the 1980s than in the 1970s. This decline is due to the fact that never-married men and women reported increasing levels of personal happiness during the 1980s, whereas young married women reported lower levels of personal happiness. Consistent with this observation, people today increasingly are postponing marriage, avoiding marriage altogether, not remarrying following divorce, cohabiting rather than marrying, and having children outside of marriage (Cherlin, 1992).

Although most single young adults hold positive views about marriage, it seems likely that some are turning away from marriage because they perceive it to offer fewer advantages today than in the past.

A decline in marital quality over the last few decades is likely for several reasons. First, changes in gender arrangements mean that husbands and wives now have to negotiate work and family roles that were previously taken for granted. Research shows that disagreement over the household division of labor is a cause of dissatisfaction in many marriages (Hochschild, 1989; Pina and Bengtson, 1993; Vannoy-Hiller and Philliber, 1989; Yogev and Brett, 1985). This is particularly true when wives hold egalitarian, non-traditional attitudes (Greenstein, 1996). Consistent with these findings, divorced men and women often report that conflict over gender roles was a factor in the dissolution of their marriages (Kitson and Sussman, 1982).

Second, the declining economic position of young married men in the 1970s increased the degree of hardship experienced by many couples. Economic hardship, in turn, increases marital conflict (especially arguments over money) and the likelihood of marital disruption (Voydanoff, 1991; White, 1991). Hernandez (1993, pp. 390–391) estimated that economic recessions were responsible for about one-half of the increase in mother-only families formed through separation and divorce between the late 1960s and the late 1980s.

Third, changes in attitudes and values may have helped to undermine marital quality. Some observers have suggested that people have higher standards for marriage today than in the past (Booth, Johnson, and White, 1984; White and Booth, 1991). If people's standards are rising, then, all things being equal, an increasing number of people will find that their relationships do not live up to their expectations. A study based on college students in the 1960s and 1990s (Barich and Bielby, 1996) supports the notion that standards for evaluating marriage have changed. Compared with students in the 1960s, students now have higher expectations that marriage will meet their needs for companionship, personality development, and emotional security. In contrast, students now have lower expectations that marriage will meet their needs for children, a steady sexual relationship, and maintenance of a home. If marriage is increasingly defined as an arrangement for satisfying emotional needs, then people may be more likely now than in the past to abandon relationships that do not promote personal growth, in spite of other advantages of the marriage.

Similarly, support for the norm of lifelong marriage is less strong now than in the past (Bellah, Madsen, Sullivan, Swidler, and Tipton, 1985; Glenn, 1996). Although the belief that one can readily leave a marriage represents a weakened barrier to divorce, it may also lead spouses to invest less effort in resolving disagreements and making the sacrifices necessary for ensuring marital success, thus eroding relationship quality. Taken together, these considerations suggest that marriage today is a more difficult and less secure arrangement than it was several decades ago.

THE DIFFERENT HISTORICAL CONTEXTS OF PARENTS AND CHILDREN

The life course perspective sensitizes us to the fact that succeeding cohorts of youth enter adulthood in markedly different circumstances. As noted before, the parents in our study grew up in a distinct historical period—a time when families were relatively prosperous, the nuclear family was the norm, men were the main breadwinners, and most marriages lasted a lifetime. The majority of our parents finished school, began their first jobs, married, and started their families during this era. Consequently, their transitions to adulthood occurred within a predictable—if somewhat conformist and patriarchal—social environment. Growing up in a time of stability, parents in our sample probably were unable to anticipate the social upheavals that were to begin in the second half of the 1960s and affect their own families so dramatically.

For the offspring of these marriages, the story is quite different. The typical child in our sample was born in 1969, in the early stage of a period of sharp social change. During childhood and adolescence, some experienced declines into economic hardship, whereas others experienced rising affluence. Many children saw their mothers move into the paid labor force on a full-time basis. Although these employed mothers served as models of female achievement, many children witnessed conflict between their parents over gender roles and responsibilities inside and outside the home. In contrast, some children in our sample grew up in traditional male breadwinner families not unlike those of an earlier generation. Many children also experienced the divorce of their parents, as well as the remarriage of one or both parents. Other children grew up in relatively stable families —happy or otherwise. The childhood experiences of the young adults in our sample, therefore, reflect the growing diversity in family life in the United States that emerged during the 1970s and 1980s.

We interviewed these children in 1992 when their median age was 23. For these youth, the social milieu in the 1990s is quite different from that of the early 1960s when their parents were of similar age. Compared with their parents, these young people are entering adulthood with fewer career opportunities and less economic security. Structural changes in the economy during the last couple of decades have resulted in the disappearance of many well-paid unionized jobs in the manufacturing sector. Consequently, youth without a college education are seriously disadvantaged in starting wages (Murphy and Welch, 1993). Yet the costs of higher education are increasing faster than inflation, making a college degree unobtainable for many. Although it is easier for women to enter the labor force now, many women are clustered in low-paying, temporary jobs in the service sector. Indeed, earnings of men and women under age 25 fell 9% and 4%, respectively, between 1983 and 1992 (Zill and Nord, 1994), and the cohort of young adults born in the late 1960s faces a greater risk of living in poverty than any birth cohort since the late 1930s (Browne, 1995). Young unmarried adults have been leaving the parental home at increasingly early ages during much of this century (Goldscheider and Goldscheider, 1994). But declining job prospects and wages, as well as the soaring cost of housing during the 1980s, have made it more difficult for young people to establish residential independence from parents. As a result, youth in the 1980s and 1990s have been relatively slow to leave the parental home. And among those who do leave, "nest-returning" is common (Goldscheider and Goldscheider, 1994).

The life course perspective assumes that changing historical contexts affect the nature of young adults' intimate relationships. Consistent with this assumption, the median age at marriage declined throughout the first half of this century, reaching a low in the 1950s of 20 for women and 22 for men. By midcentury, most people married at a relatively young age, the great majority of people married eventually, and most marriages lasted a lifetime (Cherlin, 1992). Cohabitation and divorce were not uncommon, but most people did not experience these relationship statuses. Typical parents in our sample married in the early 1960s, just as this period of family history was coming to a close.

During the 1960s and 1970s, the pattern of mate selection began to alter in fundamental ways. Young people increasingly postponed marriage, with the median age at first marriage eventually rising to 24 for women and 26 for men (U.S. Bureau of Statistics, 1992, Table 130). Although the great majority of young people still desire marriage, an increasing proportion—especially African Americans—do not marry at all (Cherlin, 1992).

What accounts for this movement away from marriage? Part of the explanation is benign: Because of increases in college attendance, many young people are postponing marriage until their educations are completed. Other reasons, however, reflect underlying problems. For example, economic security promotes marriage, and young men who have steady jobs, earn high incomes, or own their own houses are more likely to marry than are other men (Lloyd and South, 1996). However, increasing numbers of young men—especially those without college degrees—do not experience these secure economic circumstances. Changes in gender relations have also complicated the mate-selection process. Many career-oriented women are reluctant to marry men who cannot sustain an egalitarian relationship. Similarly, many young men are confused about what to expect from a marriage partner. And the continuing high divorce rate presents a sobering reality check for young couples contemplating marriage.

For these reasons, young adults are postponing marriage, with many preferring instead to live as single, independent adults or in less-committed cohabiting relationships. Indeed, increases in cohabitation have offset much of the decline in marriage (Bumpass, Sweet, and Cherlin, 1991). However, cohabiting relationships tend to be unstable, with most couples either marrying or dissolving their relationships within two years (Bumpass, Sweet, and Cherlin, 1991). Even among couples who marry, the high divorce rate means that many people return to the marriage market within a few years. However, during the same time that people are extending the proportion of their lives that they spend as single adults, the rise of AIDS and other sexually transmitted diseases has made it more complicated to satisfy sexual needs outside of long-term monogamous unions.

In short, the predictable sequence of education, stable employment, marriage, and parenthood that marked earlier cohorts of young adults has given way to an increasing diversity of life paths. For these young adults, the options are broader—and the outcomes less certain—than those available to their parents. Yet, we know very little about the experiences of youth entering adulthood in the 1990s.

The Present Study

Our primary task in this book reflects a central goal of life course analysis: to understand how the family-of-origin affects offspring's well-being in young adulthood. Given the recent historical changes just described, we focus on three family-of-origin characteristics: parents' socioeconomic resources, parents' gender nontraditionalism, and parents' marital quality and divorce. Socioeconomic resources include parents' education, income, unemployment, welfare use, and perceptions of economic improvement or decline. Gender nontraditionalism includes mothers' hours of paid employment, the proportion of housework and child care done by fathers, and parents' gender role attitudes. Parents' marital quality includes measures of happiness, interaction, conflict, and divorce proneness, as well as divorce. Our notion of offspring well-being encompasses many aspects of life: relations with parents, the formation (and breaking) of intimate relationships, the quality of intimate relationships, social integration, socioeconomic attainment, and psychological well-being. By studying a variety of outcomes, we are able to develop a comprehensive profile of well-being in early adulthood.

Our approach to understanding offspring's well-being incorporates comparisons between different families at the same time and changes within families over time. To address differences between families, we examine the consequences of a particular family characteristic (such as parental income) in 1980, the first year of our survey. This part of our analysis compares offspring whose families were high or low on the characteristic. We then consider changes in family characteristics (such as changes in parental income) between 1980 and 1988. This part of our analysis compares the same offspring at two points in time. Change is a known stressor (Holmes and Rahe, 1968), especially if events are unpleasant (Norris and Murrell, 1987). But transitions out of unpleasant circumstances tend to improve people's sense of well-being (Wheaton, 1990). By examining changes that occurred during this eight-year period, we are able to estimate the extent to which shifts in family life during the 1980s affected offspring's lives, either negatively or positively, in the 1990s.

THE ROLE OF PARENTAL SUPPORT AND CONTROL

In addition to assessing the impact of parents' economic resources, gender nontraditionalism, marital quality, and family structure, we search for mechanisms through which these factors influence offspring's outcomes. We believe that the effects of these family-of-origin characteristics can be understood by using a *mediation model*. This model assumes that broad family factors (such as economic hardship and parents' marital quality) affect children largely through their impact on parent-child interaction. Examples of studies of family life that have used a mediation model include Conger et al.

(1994), Felner et al. (1995), Harnish, Dodge and Valente (1995), McLoyd et al. (1994), and Patterson, Reid, and Dishion (1992).

In trying to understand the key aspects of parent-child interaction, researchers and theorists have repeatedly made reference to two general dimensions. In an early study, Shaefer (1959) used a factor analysis of parental behaviors to arrive at two dimensions: (a) warmth versus hostility and (b) control versus autonomy. Later, Becker (1964) classified studies of parent-child relationships using two similar dimensions: (a) warmth and acceptance versus hostility and rejection, and (b) restrictiveness versus permissiveness. Similarly, in their comprehensive research review, Maccoby and Martin (1983) organized parent-child interaction along two dimensions: (a) accepting, responsive, and child-centered versus rejecting, unresponsive, and parent-centered, and (b) demanding and controlling versus undemanding and noncontrolling. Parker, Tupling, and Brown (1979), Rohner (1986), and Rollins and Thomas (1979) proposed similar two-dimensional schemes for understanding parent-child relations. In an Australian study, Amato (1990) found that similar dimensions also underlie young children's and adolescents' perceptions of their families.

Authors vary in the particular labels they give to these two dimensions. However, these two dimensions consistently refer to aspects of parental support (affection, responsiveness, praise, encouragement, everyday help, and guidance) and parental control (rule formation, rule enforcement, and supervision). Although one can draw subtle distinctions between labels, a consensus exists that these two broad dimensions summarize many aspects of parent-child interaction. Furthermore, the amount of support parents provide to children and the level of control parents exercise over their children appear to have important consequences for children's development and well-being.

Research has repeatedly demonstrated that a high level of parental support is associated with a variety of positive outcomes among children and adolescents, including psychological adjustment, academic achievement, high self-esteem, an internal locus of control, social competence, and the exhibition of considerate and altruistic behavior. Furthermore, a moderately high level of parental control—provided that it is does not involve coercive methods of discipline, such as hitting—is associated with desirable outcomes among children and adolescents. However, if parental control is excessive, then its consequences for children and adolescents are problematic. In other words, the association between parental control and offspring's outcomes appears to be curvilinear, with the best outcomes occurring when control is neither too low nor too high. (For reviews of this literature, see Gecas and Seff, 1991; Rollins and Thomas, 1979; and Maccoby and Martin, 1983. For recent applications, see Kurdek and Fine, 1994; and Lamborn, Mounts, Steinberg, and Dornbusch, 1991.) Support and control can also be viewed as aspects of Coleman's (1988) concept of social capital, that is, family relationships that facilitate children's development of human capital.

Why does parental support benefit children? Parental affection and re- sponsiveness convey to children a basic sense of security. Praise and en- couragement reinforce children's self-conceptions of worth and competence. Practical assistance and advice foster the learning of everyday skills. And guidance promotes the formation of long-term goals. In relation to parental control, both the setting and enforcing of rules teach children that their attempts to affect the environment must occur within a set of socially con- structed boundaries. In addition, by explaining the reasons behind rules, adults help children to internalize social norms and engage in self-regulation. Finally, through supervision, parents not only keep their children out of trouble but also communicate that they care what happens to them. Of course, parents need to exercise less control as children grow older. If parents are too restrictive, then children do not have opportunities to develop new forms of competence, profit from their own mistakes, and learn to accept responsibility for their own decisions.

In this book, we are concerned with the extent to which parental support and control mediate the impact of family-of-origin characteristics on aspects of offspring's well-being. For example, economic hardship appears to affect children, at least partly through its impact on the parent-child relationship. The stress associated with trying to make ends meet leads some parents to show less affection toward children, engage in harsher forms of discipline, and decrease the amount of supervision that they exercise. These parental behaviors, in turn, increase the risk of negative outcomes such as psycho- logical maladjustment, behavior problems, school failure, and delinquency among adolescents (Conger et al., 1992, 1993; Lempers, Clark-Lempers, and Simons, 1989; McLoyd, 1989; McLoyd and Wilson, 1991; Sampson and Laub, 1994). These problems among adolescents are likely to foreshadow future difficulties in young adulthood.

Of course, not all family-of-origin characteristics influence children through parental support and control. For example, although poverty can affect parent-child interaction negatively, it also can be a direct stressor for children. Poverty increases problems associated with inadequate nutrition, living in substandard housing, and growing up in unsafe neighborhoods. A lack of economic resources also places constraints on children's ability to succeed academically. Poor parents, compared with affluent parents, are less able to provide commodities such as books and computers; enriching experiences such as private lessons and travel; and financial support for tertiary education. The presence (or absence) of these economic resources can affect children regardless of the level of support and control that parents exercise.

Observational learning and modeling are also important mechanisms of influence. For example, observing maternal employment may lead children to adopt nontraditional attitudes about gender roles. Daughters, in particular, may be inspired to emulate their mothers' occupational achievements. Similarly, the observing of severe interparental conflict may teach children that aggression is an acceptable (or at least tolerable) way of dealing with disagreements, with detrimental consequences for the children's future intimate relationships.

We do not assume, therefore, that all family-of-origin characteristics affect children through parental support and control. Indeed, given that a variety of mechanisms of influence exist, one of our goals is to evaluate the extent to which parental support and control mediate the estimated effects of the independent variables. It is possible, for example, that parental support and control mediate the impact of some family characteristics but not others, and we leave this possibility open as an empirical question. Nevertheless, in terms of guiding our research, the mediation model based on parental support and control (a micro perspective) effectively augments life course concepts (a macro perspective).

TWO QUESTIONS ABOUT GENDER

Woven throughout the analysis are two questions that repeatedly appear in the literature and about which there is considerable disagreement: what is the father's role vis-à-vis the mother in influencing offspring's well-being? Does the family of origin affect sons and daughters differently?

The Role of Fathers.   Concerns about the impact of fathers are particularly salient today for two reasons. First, as noted earlier, many people have come to believe that fathers should be more involved in providing care to their children (Thornton, 1989). Rotundo (1985) referred to this as "androgynous fatherhood," although LaRossa (1988) pointed out that changes have occurred more in people's beliefs than in behavior. The second major change has been an increase in mother-only families, due to a rise in both divorce and nonmarital birth. As a result, men are spending decreasing proportions of their lives coresiding with children (Eggebeen and Uhlenberg, 1985). Furthermore, many nonresident fathers have relatively little contact with their children and either fail to pay child support or pay less than they should (Furstenberg, Nord, Peterson, and Zill, 1983; Seltzer and Bianchi, 1988). Taken together, these two trends yield a glaring contradiction: as the public is increasingly embracing the idea that fathers should take on a greater share of child-rearing responsibility, changes in family structure mean that many fathers are less involved with children today than were fathers in previous generations.

How important are fathers in children's lives? Several lines of research support the notion that fathers are important resources for children. Some studies show that father involvement and nurturance are positively associated with children's intellectual development, psychological adjustment, and social competence. (For reviews, see Lamb, 1981, 1987; Radin, 1981; Radin and Russell, 1983; and Snarey, 1993, chap. 6.) Other studies show that the absence of the father from the child's household is associated with lower scores on measures of cognitive ability (Hetherington, Camara, and Featherman, 1983); an increased risk of delinquency and deviant behavior (Dornbusch, Carlsmith, Bushwall, Ritter, Leiderman, Hastorf, and Gross, 1985; Matsueda and Heimer, 1987; Sampson, 1987); and lowered educational attainment (Amato and Keith, 1991b; Keith and Finlay, 1988; McLanahan and Sandefur, 1994). A third type of evidence comes from studies showing that most young children and adolescents feel close to their fathers, admire their fathers, and frequently mention their fathers as sources of practical help, advice, and moral support (Amato, 1987a; Rutter, 1979; Snarey, 1993).

In contrast, several groups of studies suggest that fathers play peripheral roles in their children's lives. One body of research suggests that father absence has few consequences for children once economic factors are taken into account (Crockett, Eggebeen, and Hawkins, 1993; Svanum, Bringle, and McLaughlin, 1982). A second set of studies show that contact between children and noncustodial fathers does *not* improve children's outcomes— a finding that appears to contradict the notion that fathers are key resources for children (Furstenberg, Morgan, and Allison, 1987; King, 1994). Finally, in studies of two-parent families, it is not clear whether fathers make an independent contribution to children's outcomes beyond that of mothers. It is likely that families in which fathers are highly involved are also those in which mothers are especially competent, caring, and encouraging of their husband's participation in child care. As such, the extra attention of fathers may be largely redundant once one takes into account the mother's involvement.

In this book, attention to fathers surfaces at many points. For example, in studying parents' economic resources, we consider the impact of fathers' and mothers' educations and incomes separately. We also focus on fathers when we examine their share of housework and child care—two variables that serve as key indicators of gender nontraditionalism.

Sons versus Daughters.   Sons and daughters experience family life differently. Mothers do not distinguish strongly between sons and daughters, but fathers tend to give more attention to sons—a tendency that grows more pronounced as children get older (Amato, 1987a; Harris and Morgan, 1991, Lamb, 1981; Marsiglio, 1991). For this reason, adolescent daughters tend to be especially close to their mothers but less close to their fathers (Amato, 1987a; Rossi and Rossi, 1990; Troll and Bengtson, 1979). Parents tend to punish sons more harshly than daughters (Amato, 1987a; Newson and Newson, 1976). This discrepancy may be due to the fact that boys tend to misbehave more than girls (Maccoby and Martin, 1983). Alternatively, it may be that parents are reluctant to use coercive forms of punishment on girls because parents see them as more vulnerable than boys. In addition, daughters do more household chores than sons (Amato, 1987a; Mott, 1994). Furthermore, these chores are strongly gender-typed, with girls doing tasks like cooking or drying dishes and boys doing tasks like mowing the lawn or washing the car. These findings indicate that sons and daughters growing up in the same family have different experiences of childhood.

Parents' socioeconomic resources tend to have different implications for sons and daughters. For example, some studies show that fathers' education has a greater influence on sons' educational attainment, whereas mothers' education has a greater impact on daughters' educational attainment (Marini, 1978; Rossi, and Rossi, 1990; Sewell, Hauser, and Wolf, 1980; Teachman, 1987). Parents' gender traditionalism also appears to have different consequences for sons and daughters. In particular, mothers' employment tends to be associated with increased occupational aspirations and higher self-esteem among daughters, but not among sons (Hoffman, 1989; Mischel and Fuhr, 1988; Spitze, 1988). Changes in family structure may also affect boys and girls differently. Some studies find that parental divorce increases behavior problems more among young boys than among young girls (Hetherington, Cox, and Cox, 1982; Wallerstein and Kelly, 1980). However, parental divorce may have more severe detrimental consequences for the educational attainment of daughters than sons (Amato and Keith, 1991b).

Given that family-of-origin characteristics appear to have different implications for sons and daughters, we consider whether parents' economic resources, gender nontraditionalism, marital quality, and divorce have different consequences for male and female offspring. This goal is accomplished by routinely examining interactions between family-of-origin variables and offspring's gender in predicting outcomes.

THE IMPORTANCE OF CHILDREN'S AGES

One of the assumptions of the life course perspective is that the impact of events depends on when they occur in people's lives. In 1980, although all offspring in our study lived at home with their interviewed parents, their ages ranged from 7 to 28 (with a median age of 11). It seems likely that the impact of many family events and transitions (such as a parental divorce or a period of welfare use) varies depending on whether children are in their first, second, or third decade of life.

Some family characteristics, however, show considerable stability over time. For example, Alwin and Thornton (1984) show that socioeconomic characteristics of families tend to change little throughout the years of childhood. Furthermore, their work indicates that the associations between family socioeconomic characteristics and offspring's outcomes are similar in direction and magnitude regardless of whether they are measured in early childhood or adolescence. This suggests that although it may be important to assess the consequences of family *changes* in relation to children's ages, it may not be necessary to consider children's ages when assessing the role of relatively stable family characteristics.

Nevertheless, to be on the safe side, we take into account children's ages when we estimate the effects of all family-of-origin characteristics. We do this by (a) controlling for children's ages in all analyses, and (b) examining interactions between family-of-origin variables and children's ages in predicting all outcomes.

Outline of the Book

The chapters that follow present the results of our study of offspring during the early years of adulthood. Chapter 2 presents details of the methodology of the study, including information on our sample, measurement of key independent variables, and general analytic strategy. The next five chapters present the substantive results of our research, beginning with material on close family relationships. Chapter 3 examines offspring's current relations with parents—outcomes that are a natural outgrowth of earlier family-of-origin experiences. We consider multiple relationship dimensions, such as affection, frequency of contact, and exchanges of assistance. Chapter 4 turns to offspring's intimate ties outside of the family of origin. This chapter looks at the formation of close relationships through dating, cohabitation, and marriage; we examine the occurrence and timing, as well as the quality and stability, of these relationships.

The next two chapters move away from close family relationships to focus on the integration of young adults into the larger society. Chapter 5 looks at two dimensions of social integration: behavioral integration (organizational membership and church involvement) and psychological integration (feelings of community attachment and the number of friends and kin to whom offspring feel close). Chapter 6 deals with another aspect of young adults' ties to the larger society: socioeconomic attainment. This chapter focuses on education, occupational status, earned income, and experiences of economic hardship.

Chapter 7 addresses a "bottom line" outcome: psychological well-being. Regardless of their success in other domains, unhappy, troubled youth are unlikely to meet their role expectations and contribute in a positive way to their families and communities. For these reasons, psychological well-being is of central interest. In this chapter, we consider four dimensions of psychological well-being: feelings of distress, self-esteem, happiness, and life satisfaction.

Finally, in Chapter 8, we summarize our findings and draw conclusions about the importance of family-of-origin characteristics for young people's well-being. In doing so, we consider how social change during the last three decades has affected the transition to adulthood and how the experiences of youth today differ from those of previous generations. We also discuss several general themes that emerge from our research: the role of parental support and control, the importance of fathers, and differences in the consequences of family life for sons and daughters.

Chapters 3 through 7 are divided into sections dealing with (a) parents' socioeconomic resources, (b) parents' gender nontraditionalism, and (c) parents' marital quality and divorce. Within each of these sections, we review pertinent literature and then present the results from our study. Although we deal with each set of independent variables in sequence, at the end of each chapter we provide a summary of the main findings and comment on their general implications. This way of organizing the book should allow readers to find material of interest relatively quickly.

Study Design,

Measures,

and Analysis

 The information on which this book is based comes from
the Study of Marital Instability Over the Life Course (Booth, Amato, Johnson, and Edwards, 1993). We began the investigation by contacting a na-
tionally representative sample of married persons and interviewing them
over the telephone. The plan was to interview these same individuals every
three or four years to monitor family change and to learn about the factors
that lead to fluctuations in marital quality and to divorce. Funding for the
study allowed us to interview these individuals in 1980, 1983, 1988, and
1992. In 1992, we decided to expand the research to include adult offspring
of the study participants. The purpose of the expansion was to assess the
long-term impact of family life on children who had lived with their interviewed parents in 1980 and had reached the age of majority (19 years) by
1992. We contacted the offspring again in 1995 to get updated information
on cohabitation, marital and parental status, educational achievement, and
occupational attainment.

The Sample of Parents and Offspring

SELECTING THE SAMPLE

The target population in 1980 consisted of all husbands and wives in households in the contiguous United States in which both spouses were present
and were under the age of 55 and who had access to a telephone. As 96%
of the adult population in the United States in 1980 had access to a tele-

phone, the use of telephone interviews rather than personal interviews had little effect on the overall representativeness of the sample.

Interviewers used random digit dialing to select the sample. An additional random procedure picked a couple if more than one married pair lived in the household. Still another random procedure determined whether the husband or wife would participate in the study. The final sample consisted of 2,033 married individuals. A Spanish-speaking interviewer carried out interviews with Hispanic respondents who were not fluent in English.

We asked everyone who was interviewed in 1992 to provide the names and telephone numbers of offspring who had resided in their households in 1980 but who were 19 years or older at the time of the 1992 survey. In families in which there was more than one eligible child, we obtained the names, addresses, and telephone numbers of two children. In households with three or more eligible children, we chose two children at random; we then randomly selected one of the two children to participate in the study. When it was not possible to interview the first selected child, we interviewed the second child, assuming that it was better to obtain information on one child than none. Six percent of the interviews were with offspring other than the first selected one.

In 1995, we carried out a short follow-up survey of offspring. This involved a mailed questionnaire containing fifteen items dealing with living arrangements, marital status, cohabitation, education, income, and occupation. We conducted telephone interviews with those who did not return the questionnaire or did not respond to a second mailing.

Response Rates. In 1980, 17% of targeted individuals could not be reached after twenty callbacks at different times of the day and on different days. Of those individuals contacted, 78% gave complete interviews, 4% gave partial interviews, and 18% refused to take part in the study. The reinterview rate was 78% in 1983, 84% in 1988, and 89% in 1992, yielding 1,193 completed interviews in 1992. These response rates are comparable to those obtained in studies using in-person interviews. (For a more complete description of the sampling procedures and a comparison with other studies, see Booth and Johnson, 1985.)

Among the respondents interviewed in 1992, 625 had children 19 years of age or older who had resided in the parental home in 1980. Fourteen percent of these parents elected not to give us the names and telephone numbers of offspring. Of the 537 offspring about whom we had contact information, we obtained interviews with 88% for a total sample of 471 offspring.

For the 1995 follow-up of offspring, 430 of the 471 offspring either returned a questionnaire by mail or completed a telephone interview, resulting in a response rate of 91%.

Maximizing Response Rates over Time. To keep the sample representative, it was necessary to keep people in the study year after year. We tried to accomplish this in a variety of ways. At the close of each interview, we asked for the names of three people who would know the respondents' whereabouts in case they moved; most respondents gave us the names of such people. These contacts proved to be invaluable in later follow-ups. We used them not only when people moved but also when people changed telephone numbers or lost their telephone services. To maintain respondents' interest in the research, we sent letters once a year describing some of the study's findings and asking them to contact us if they planned to move. The letters were sent with "address correction requested" so that the post office would provide us with new addresses if respondents had moved. In doing subsequent interviews, when respondents could not be located, we assigned trackers to consult city directories and public utility lists in an effort to obtain current telephone numbers. We did not exclude respondents who relocated outside the United States, although most of these people completed a printed copy of the interview schedule by mail.

When people refused to be reinterviewed, a different interviewer called back and made a second attempt, because another person, with a different approach, is often effective in turning refusals into completed interviews. We gave all reluctant respondents an opportunity to complete the interview schedule by mail as an alternative to a telephone interview. Finally, if it was clear that an interview was not going to occur, we sent a letter with a mail-back postcard. The letter informed respondents that they would not be contacted again, but asked if they would complete a few marital status questions on a stamped postcard and return it. In this way, we were able to obtain information on marital status from some individuals who dropped out of the study; this was useful in estimating divorce rates for different groups in the sample. (We counted these individuals as nonrespondents in the response rates cited previously.) Although some attrition is inevitable in a panel study, the use of these techniques helped to maximize the number of people who remained in the study over the twelve-year period.

Representativeness of the Sample. To determine the representativeness of the original 1980 sample of married people, we compared it with 1980 census data. The sample was similar to the national distribution of married individuals under age 55 in terms of the husband's age, wife's age, race, household size, renter/homeowner status, region of the country, and presence of children. The sample had the same biases in sex, education, and metropolitan status found in most survey research. Compared with the national population of married individuals, the sample was more likely to be female (59% of the sample versus 52% of the population), better educated (30% of the sample with a bachelor of arts degree versus 24% of the population), and living in nonmetropolitan areas (37% of the sample versus 26% of the population). The latter disparity occurred in all areas but the South.

To understand how attrition affected our sample of offspring, we compared the 1980 characteristics of all individuals in the sample who had children eligible for an interview in 1992 (those with a child over the age of 6 living in the household in 1980) with the 1980 characteristics of the parents of interviewed offspring in 1992. These results appear in Table 2.1 in the Appendix. In general, the parents of interviewed offspring in 1992 are very similar to the parents in the 1980 sample. Attrition is apparent in a few categories: African Americans, renters, and those in households in which husbands did not have a college education. However, in all categories the differences are relatively modest. Thus, in demographic terms, the findings of our study are generalizable to the 1980 sample, and therefore, to the larger population from which we drew our original sample.

Although sample attrition in demographic categories was minor, it might have been greater in families experiencing serious relationship problems. To check on this possibility, we carried out analyses in which we predicted attrition between 1980 and 1992 from a series of 1980 variables that measured various family processes, including parents' perceptions of their closeness to children, the quality of the parents' marital relationship, and whether a divorce occurred between 1980 and 1992. Attrition was significantly higher among parents who reported a relatively low level of marital interaction. But other variables, including other dimensions of the marital relationship, parental divorce, and the quality of parent-child relationships, did not predict attrition. It appears, therefore, that parents and children from discordant families were as likely to appear in our final sample as were parents and children from harmonious families. Consequently, the final

1992 sample of parent-child dyads does not appear to underrepresent families who were functioning poorly in 1980.

CHARACTERISTICS OF PARENTS AND OFFSPRING

Characteristics of the Parents.   The 1992 interview with parents provides the following information. Parents' ages ranged from 38 to 67, with a mean of 50 for mothers and 52 for fathers. We interviewed more mothers than fathers (62% versus 38%). Only 2% of the interviewed parents in 1992 were stepparents; the rest were biological (or adoptive) parents. In the great majority of cases (93%), both parents were white, reflecting the relatively small proportion of married-couple families among African Americans. The typical parent had thirteen years of education, with fathers averaging about one more year than mothers. About one-fourth of the parents were college graduates. The median income of parents (fathers and mothers combined) was about $45,000 in 1992, although the means were higher because of skewness in the income distributions. In 1980, when the study began, virtually all fathers and 61% of mothers were in the labor force. By 1992, 9% of fathers had retired, whereas the percentage of mothers in the labor force had increased to 71%.

Characteristics of the Offspring.   The following information comes from the 1992 interview with the offspring. The ages of offspring ranged from 19 to 40, with a median age of 23; 85% of offspring were 30 or younger. Daughters made up about half of the sample (51%). About one-fourth were living at home with parents, although half of these had returned home after living away from their parents for a period of time. One-fourth of the sample were college graduates, although 13% were still continuing their educations. In terms of marital status, most had never married, although 35% were married and 6% were divorced or separated. Of those who were married, 92% were in first marriages. Twenty-nine percent of the offspring had children of their own. In relation to parental divorce, most (81%) had continuously married parents; 10% lived with a stepparent because of divorce in 1980, and another 9% experienced a parental divorce between 1980 and 1992.

Between 1992 and 1995, the offspring sample changed in predictable ways. For example, those with college degrees increased from 25% to 36%, those married increased from 35% to 45%, and those with children increased from 29% to 40%.

In 1980 (during our first interview with parents), offspring ranged in age from 7 to 28. Most of our analyses in this book involve the full sample of offspring, including the small number of offspring who were in their twenties in 1980. We include this latter group because they were still living in the parental home in 1980 and, therefore, were susceptible to parental influence. However, in all analyses, we control for offspring's ages and look for interactions between 1980 family characteristics and offspring's ages. In other analyses in which we predict offspring transitions such as marriage and divorce, we omit those older offspring who experienced these transitions *prior to* the first parental interview in 1980. We note this omission in the text, when appropriate.

Measurement of Variables

Several principles guided our selection and construction of questions for the interviews. We used existing measures whenever possible so that our results could be compared with those of other studies and so that we could take advantage of the work that has gone into the development of the items. In some cases, no suitable measures existed, so we devised our own items. An example is our measure of divorce proneness. We pretested all items and scales for clarity, reliability, variability, and missing data before including them in the interviews. Also, we retained the precise wording of items from year to year so that we could assess change reliably.

A summary of the major variables that appear in our study is shown in the accompanying chart. The independent and control variables come from the parents' interviews, and the mediating variables (parental support and control) come from the offspring's interviews. Detailed information on these variables appears in Table 2.2 in the Appendix. All of the dependent variables come from the offspring's interviews, and we provide details on these variables in the relevant chapters. In general, the strategy of using parents to provide data on independent variables and using offspring to provide data an dependent variables allows us to avoid problems associated with same-source bias.

PARENTS' SOCIOECONOMIC RESOURCES

The parents' education is measured as the number of years of education completed by the father and the mother in 1980. In some analyses we examine mothers' and fathers' educations separately, whereas in other analyses we combine the two into a single variable by taking the mean. We

Variables used in analyses

Independent variables	Control variables	Mediating variables	Dependent variables
Economic resources	Parental race	Mother support	Parent-child relations
Parental education	Parental gender	Father support	Coresidence/distance
Parental income 1980	Offspring gender	Parental control	Contact
Income change 1980– 1988	Offspring age		Affection
	Number of siblings		Perceived consensus
Parental welfare use 1980–1988	Stepfamily in 1980		Perceived support
			Help received
Paternal unemploy- ment 1980–1988			Help given
Perceived economic change 1980–1988			Intimate ties
			Dating partner
			Cohabitation
Gender nontraditionalism			Marriage
Mothers' hours of employment 1980			
Mothers' employment change 1980–1988			Relationship quality
			Happiness
Fathers' share of housework 1980			Interaction
			Conflict
Fathers' housework change 1980–1988			Problems
			Instability
Fathers' share of child care 1980			
			Social integration
Parents' gender role attitudes 1980			Church involvement
			Clubs, organizations
Parents' attitude change 1980–1988			Close relatives
			Close friends
			Community attachment
Parents' marital quality/divorce			
Marital happiness 1980			Socioeconomic status
Marital happiness change 1980–1988			Education
			Occupational status
Marital interaction 1980			Income
Marital interaction change 1980–1988			Economic adversity
Marital conflict 1980			Psychological well-being
Marital conflict change 1980– 1988			Distress symptoms
			Self-esteem
Divorce proneness 1980			Happiness
Divorce proneness change 1980–1988			Life satisfaction
Divorce			

obtained information on income with a series of categorical items that asked whether family income was below or above particular levels. Respondents selected from an increasingly narrow range of categories until they were at the one that included their income. (Using categories in this manner yields higher response rates than asking directly for total income.) In some analyses, we examine mothers' and fathers' incomes separately, whereas in other analyses we combine the two by taking the sum. In preliminary analyses, we computed an income-to-needs ratio based on household composition. However, because this variable yielded results that were very similar to those based on income alone, we dispensed with this refinement in subsequent analyses.

To assess changes in economic resources over time, we compare parental income in 1980 and 1988. In doing so, we correct for inflation by expressing income in constant 1992 dollars. To assess periods of public assistance, we asked in 1983, "Have you received income from any public assistance program—for example, medicaid, food stamps, or welfare—since the fall of 1980?" We asked the same question in 1988 in relation to public assistance since the fall of 1983. Nine percent of parents used some form of public assistance between 1980 and 1988. We also included items that dealt with the unemployment of fathers (for at least one month) in the 1983 and 1988 interviews; 29% of fathers experienced a spell of unemployment between 1980 and 1988. To tap subjective aspects of changes in financial well-being, we asked the following question in 1980, 1983, and 1988: "During the last few years, has your financial situation been getting better, getting worse, or has it stayed the same?" Twenty-six percent of parents reported, at each interview, that their situation had consistently gotten better. In contrast, 29% of parents reported, on at least one occasion, that their situation had gotten worse. We represented these two outcomes—always better versus ever worse—as two dummy variables in our analyses, with all other parents serving as the omitted reference category.

NONTRADITIONAL GENDER RELATIONS

We created four indicators of family-of-origin gender nontraditionalism: the number of hours that the mothers were employed for pay outside the household, the proportion of household work done by the fathers, the proportion of child care done by the fathers, and the gender role attitudes of the parents. Some of our analyses focus on the actual number of hours mothers are employed, whereas other analyses divide mothers into four categories: those employed "over-time" (45 hours per week or more), full-time (35–44 hours per week), part-time (1–34 hours per week), and not at all. Information on mothers' hours of employment was available in both 1980 and 1988. In a few analyses we also include items reflecting mothers' reasons for being employed, as well as whether they engaged in shift work, worked irregular hours, and were satisfied with their jobs. We describe these items in later chapters, when appropriate.

The proportion of household work done by fathers is based on this inquiry: "In every family there are a lot of routine tasks that have to be done—cleaning the house, doing the laundry, cleaning up after meals, cooking dinners, and so on. How much of this kind of work usually is done by you—all of it, most of it, about half of it, less than half of it, or none of it?" Depending on who was being interviewed, we coded the item so that it reflected the amount of work done by the father. We asked this question in both 1980 and 1988. The proportion of child care done by fathers is based on this question: "How much of the looking after children is usually done by you—all of it, most of it, about half of it, less than half of it, or none of it?" Depending on who was being interviewed, we coded the item so that it reflected the amount of work done by the father. We asked this question in 1980 only. Not surprisingly, relatively few men did the majority of housework or child care; however, 41% of men did "about half" of the child care. This high figure is probably due to the fact that few men lived with infants or toddlers; most children in these households were either in primary school or high school. Although some research finds that fathers and mothers give different estimates of the amount of time spent in family work (with men claiming more time than women acknowledge), mothers and fathers in our study provided similar accounts. Nevertheless, we always controlled for the source of information (mothers versus fathers) when analyzing these data.

We assessed parents' gender role attitudes with a scale that included items dealing with men's and women's family and work roles. Examples of items include the following: "A woman's most important task in life is being a mother," "A husband should share equally in household chores if his wife works full time," and "The husband should be the main breadwinner while the wife has the main responsibility for child care." Parents responded to each statement with options ranging from "strongly disagree" to "strongly agree." Appropriate items were coded so that higher scores indicated *less* traditional, more egalitarian attitudes. Scale scores were available in both 1980 and 1988.

We do not have gender role attitudes for the parent who was not interviewed, so this aspect of nontraditionalism is based on the attitudes of only
one spouse. However, we assume that the attitudes of fathers and mothers
are positively correlated. To test this idea, we located two items in the
National Survey of Families and Households (Sweet, Bumpass, and Call,
1988) that are very similar in content to items on our attitude scale. One
item dealt with husbands being breadwinners and the other with husbands
and wives sharing domestic tasks equally. Because data in the National
Survey of Families and Households are available from both spouses, we were
able to examine the correlation between husbands' and wives' scores on the
two-item scale. The correlation is .45 ($p <. 001$), but with the correlation
corrected for attenuation because of unreliability (alpha = .64 for respondents and .66 for spouses), our estimate of the true correlation is .70. This
finding supports our assumption that spouses tend to be similar in gender
attitudes. Therefore, we do not distinguish between fathers' and mothers'
reports for the analyses reported herein, although we always control for the
gender of the interviewed parent and, when appropriate, test for interactions between attitudes and gender in predicting offspring's outcomes.

To assess the feasibility of combining the measures into one nontraditionalism scale, we factor analyzed mothers' labor force participation, the
fathers' housework, and the parents' gender role attitudes, using a principal
components model. One factor emerged that accounted for 50% of the
variance in the variables, and all factor loadings were .6 or above. Consequently, we standardized the variables (using Z scores) and summed them
to form a general index of gender nontraditionalism. We use this index as
a control variable in many analyses. (For more information on the use of
this index, see Booth and Amato, 1994a.)

PARENTS' MARITAL QUALITY AND DIVORCE

We used four measures of marital quality that have been shown to be con-
ceptually and empirically distinct dimensions (Johnson, White, Edwards,
and Booth, 1986). These are marital happiness, marital interaction, marital
disagreement, and divorce proneness. We assessed each of these dimensions
in 1980 and 1988.

Parents' marital happiness is an ten-item scale. For example, we asked
respondents whether they are very happy, pretty happy, or not too happy
with the amount of understanding received, the amount of love and affection received, the extent to which the respondent and spouse agree about

things, their sexual relationship, the spouse as someone who takes care of things around the home, the spouse as someone to do things with, and the spouse's faithfulness. The higher the score on this scale, the greater the parents' marital happiness.

Parents' marital interaction is derived from the parents' reports of how often (almost always, usually, occasionally, never) they engage jointly in five different activities—eating the main meal, shopping, visiting friends, working on projects around the house, and going out (e.g., playing cards, seeing movies, bowling). Higher scores on this scale signify greater marital interaction.

Like parents' marital interaction, parents' marital conflict is a collective property of the marriage. This measure taps the extent of disagreement, frequency of serious quarrels, and occurrence of physical violence. Higher scores on this scale indicate greater marital conflict.

Parents' divorce proneness, which is defined as the propensity to divorce, includes both a cognitive component (thinking the marriage is in trouble, considering the idea of getting a divorce), and actions (talking to friends or spouse about the possibility of divorce; consulting with clergy, a counselor, or an attorney; or filing a petition). The scale consists of thirteen items that tap both the frequency and the timing of the indicators. Because the scale is positively skewed, the measure was logged to normalize the distribution. Those who score high on the scale are nine times more likely to divorce than those who score low on the scale (Booth, Johnson, White, and Edwards, 1985).

We assessed marital dissolution at two time periods: before 1980 and between 1980 and 1992. Pre-1980 divorce means that the offspring experienced divorce at an earlier age (median age of 5) and were living in a stepfamily at the time of the first parental interview in 1980. Forty-seven offspring were in this category. In addition, forty-two offspring experienced the divorce of their biological parents between the 1980 and 1992 interviews. Of these offspring, eight experienced divorce between the ages of 9 and 12, twenty-four experienced divorce as teenagers, and ten experienced divorce in their early twenties, although some in the latter group were still living with parents at the time of the divorce. In some analyses we use these two variables separately, whereas in other analyses we combine them into an "any divorce" category.

In cases of divorce, we have additional information (which we obtained from either the parents or the children) on children's age at divorce, the

level of post-divorce conflict between parents, changes in residence following divorce, custodial arrangements, contact with noncustodial parents, and
parental remarriage. We present information on these variables, when appropriate, in the relevant chapters.

CONTROL VARIABLES

In all analyses, we adjust for variables that may be correlated with both our
independent and dependent variables. Control variables include the interviewed parent's race and gender, as well as the offspring's gender, age, and
number of siblings. Because offspring's and parents' ages are highly correlated ($r = .82$), it is not necessary (or advisable) to control for the latter
because of problems that may arise from multicollinearity. In most analyses,
we also control for whether children lived in a stepfamily in 1980.

When estimating the effects of parental socioeconomic resources, we use
the control variables just noted. When measures of the parents' gender
nontraditionalism serve as independent variables, we add controls for parental education and family income. However, because mothers' employment directly affects family income, we control for husbands' income rather
than family income when estimating the effects of maternal employment.
In analyses in which parents' marital quality and divorce are the main independent variables, we control for parents' socioeconomic resources and
gender nontraditionalism. To simplify these analyses, we use the summary
index (that combines mothers' employment, fathers' share of household
work, and parents' gender role attitudes) as the control variable. This procedure implies a rough causal ordering of variables, that is, we assume that
parents' socioeconomic resources (for example, education) affect parents'
gender nontraditionalism (for example, gender role attitudes) and that both
of these sets of variables affect parents' marital quality and the likelihood
of divorce. Of course, there are probable exceptions to this ordering of
variables. Nevertheless, this simple assumption allows us to proceed with
key analyses without getting bogged down in testing dozens of alternative
models.

MEDIATING VARIABLES

Although we were not able to measure parental support and control when
children were growing up, we included a series of retrospective questions in
the 1992 offspring interview schedule. These questions asked young adults
to recall parental behaviors during their teenage years. We used the teen

years, rather than early childhood, as a reference point because this period is closer to the time of the interviews. Consequently, recollections of parental behavior during adolescence are likely to be more accurate than are recollections of earlier periods of childhood. In addition, we assume that parent-child relationships in adolescence often have stronger implications for outcomes in adulthood than do parent-child relationships earlier in life.

We did not have information on parental support and control from parents. Fortunately, several previous studies have collected information on parent-child relationships from two generations, and these studies consistently indicate positive, significant, and moderate (but not large) correlations between parents' and children's reports. For example, Draughn and Waggenspack (1986) found a correlation of .41 between fathers' and college daughters' ratings of supportiveness. In a study of parental support and control, Gecas and Schwalbe (1986) found correlations that ranged from .24 (mothers' and sons' reports) to .41 (fathers' and daughters' reports). Finally, Paulson, Hill, and Holmbeck (1991) found that correlations for a measure of parent-child emotional closeness ranged from .33 (for fathers and early adolescent sons) to .58 (for mothers and early adolescent daughters). These correlations indicate that children and parents generally agree on parental behavior, although there is some difference of opinion as well. Adolescents' ratings of parental support and discipline are also significantly associated with trained observers' reports of parental behavior (Simons et al., 1993).

To assess parental support and control during adolescence, we used questions similar to those employed by other survey researchers (Barber, Chadwick, and Oerter, 1992; Barnes and Farrell, 1992; Gecas and Schwalbe, 1986). To measure maternal support, we asked offspring how often their mothers helped them with homework, helped them with personal problems, talked with them, and showed affection toward them when they were teenagers. We also asked offspring to rate, overall, how close they felt to their mothers when the offspring were teenagers. We used a parallel set of questions to assess paternal support.

Consistent with previous studies (Amato, 1987a; Rossi and Rossi, 1990; Rutter, 1979), most offspring report moderate to high levels of support from parents during the teenage years. In addition, perceptions of mother support and father support are positively and significantly correlated. In other words, offspring who report a high (or low) level of support from their mothers during adolescence also tend to report a high (or low) level of support from fathers. Nevertheless, levels of support are significantly higher for mothers than fathers. For example, 37% of offspring say that their mothers helped them often with homework, and 44% say that they often had talks with their mothers. The comparable figures for fathers are 12% and 23%, respectively. In terms of overall closeness, offspring are more likely to say that they were very close to their mothers than to their fathers (33% versus 25%); correspondingly, they are less likely to say that they were not very close to their mothers than to their fathers (16% versus 30%). If we consider only offspring whose parents remained continuously married, the gap in support between mothers and fathers is not as large, but still significant. Daughters and sons do not differ significantly in the amount of support that they report having received from mothers or fathers.

To measure parental control, we asked four questions about parents when their offspring were teenagers. These questions dealt with the number of rules offspring had to follow (for example, rules about staying out late, doing chores, and watching television), how closely offspring were supervised, how many important decisions offspring made for themselves, and how strict their families were, overall. Our measure of parental control correlates at virtually zero with our measures of maternal and paternal support, suggesting that support and control are independent dimensions of parent-child relations.

Most offspring report a moderate level of parental control. For example, 48% report that their parents had some rules, compared with 31% who report many rules. Similarly, 53% say that their parents supervised their behavior somewhat closely, compared with 32% who say very closely. Daughters report significantly more control than do sons. This report is consistent with the notion that parents are more protective of daughters than of sons, presumably because daughters are perceived as more vulnerable and because the risk of a premarital pregnancy is usually more consequential for daughters.

Preliminary analyses support our decision to explore the role of parental support and control in mediating the effects of family-of-origin characteristics on children. As we anticipated, offspring's recollections of parental support and control are related significantly to many of our independent variables (as reported by parents). For example, both maternal and paternal support tend to be especially high when mothers are well-educated, parents experience increases in income over time, mothers are employed part-time (as opposed to full-time or not at all), fathers are highly involved in child care, and parents have high-quality marriages that do not end in divorce. In addition, a high level of parental control is significantly linked with high paternal education, mothers not working long over-time hours, fathers taking on a substantial share of housework, parents' shifts toward more traditional gender attitudes, and high marital quality among parents.

Analytic Procedures

STATISTICAL METHODS

We use regression techniques for most of our analyses. Ordinary least squares is appropriate when the outcome is an ordered variable (for example, a scale of affection for fathers), whereas logistic regression is appropriate when the outcome is a dichotomous variable (for example, whether offspring have a steady dating partner). For time-varying events, such as cohabitation, marriage, and divorce, we use discrete-time hazard models estimated with logistic regression (Allison, 1984). For these outcomes, we create person-year files based on the number of years that the offspring in our sample were "at risk" for experiencing a transition. All these techniques allow us to control for potentially confounding variables and estimate the unique effects (as well as many of the indirect effects) of the family-of-origin variables under study.

ANALYTIC STRATEGY

Each chapter includes separate sections dealing with (a) parents' socioeconomic resources, (b) parents' gender nontraditionalism, and (c) parents' marital quality and divorce. Within each of these sections, we begin by focusing on the parental variables measured in 1980. For example, in estimating the impact of parents' socioeconomic resources, we use parental education and income in 1980 as independent variables, and offspring's outcomes in 1992 as dependent variables. We then estimate the effect of *changes* in parental variables between 1980 and 1988 on offspring's outcomes in 1992. In most cases, we do this by including the same variables for both time periods in the equations. For example, to assess the impact of changes in parental income, we include income in 1980 and 1988 (in constant dollars) in the equation simultaneously. The coefficient for the 1988 variable (with the 1980 variable in the equation) reflects the impact of changes in income during this period. Preliminary work revealed that using absolute changes in actual dollars and using percentage changes yield similar results for most outcomes, so we stick with the former in all analyses in this book. Other variables, such as parents' perceptions of improvements or declines in financial well-being between interviews, assess change directly and do not require prior information on the variable.

Our analysis strategy allows us to answer two questions. First, what are the consequences for offspring in 1992 of parental characteristics measured twelve years earlier, when all offspring lived in the interviewed parents' households? Second, what are the consequences for offspring in 1992 of parental characteristics that changed during the 1980s? We use 1988 as the end point for assessing family change, rather than 1992, for two reasons. First, our strategy provides a clear time ordering, with changes in the family of origin between 1980–1988 occurring *prior to* offspring's outcomes in 1992; this allows firmer conclusions about the causal ordering of variables. Second, in 1988, the median age of offspring was 19. At this time, approximately one-half of the children had not yet left the parental home. Thus, the years between 1980 and 1988 reflect a time when most children were living in the parental household and were still economically dependent on parents. By 1992, however, most of the children were living away from home and were often economically independent of parents. Consequently, family changes between 1988 and 1992 are of less relevance in explaining outcomes for most offspring. The one exception involves parental divorce: to capture as many cases of divorce as possible, we include parental divorces between 1988 and 1992, along with other cases of divorce, as predictors.

Moderator Variables.   At many points in the following chapters, we note that the associations between parental and offspring variables are moderated by offspring's gender, age, coresidence with parents in 1988 or 1992, or living in a stepfamily in 1980. When we make these statements, we mean that we tested for interactions by creating multiplicative terms between the moderating variables (offspring's gender, age, and so on) and the independent variables and then entered them into the equations. In fact, we checked for interactions (using the moderator variables just mentioned) in all of the analyses described in this book. When these interactions are statistically significant, we describe how the estimated effects differ for the two categories of offspring, for example, those who resided with parents in 1988 and those who did not. But when these interactions are not statistically significant, we usually make no reference to them. Readers should assume, therefore, that if we do not mention interaction effects, it is because they were statistically insignificant and not because we did not check for them.

Mediating Variables.   At many points in this book, we discuss the role that certain variables (such as parental support and control) play in mediating associations between independent and dependent variables. Our usual strategy is to start with the regression coefficient that represents the best estimate of the effect of the independent variable on the dependent variable (that is, the coefficient derived from a model that includes appropriate control variables to rule out the possibility of spuriousness). We then enter the potentially mediating variable in the equation and examine the extent to which the original regression coefficient declines in the new model. We assume that the more the coefficient declines, the more the third variable mediates the estimated effect of the independent variable on the dependent variable. Also, we take special note of occasions in which the original association is no longer statistically significant following the introduction of the mediating variable.

MISSING DATA

The amount of missing data is small for all of our independent and control variables. For example, family income is often a variable that yields a large amount of missing data in survey research. However, in our study, only 3% of cases are missing data on parents' income. One way of dealing with missing data is to exclude from the analyses any cases that lack information on any variable. This solution is problematic in the present study. Because the number of offspring in our data set is not large, especially when we focus on subgroups of interest (such as those who experienced a parental divorce), we are reluctant to throw out *any* cases if we can avoid it. In preliminary analyses for several diverse outcomes, we used three methods of dealing with missing cases: listwise deletion (in which we omitted cases with any missing data), simple mean substitution (in which missing data on independent variables are replaced with the mean), and mean substitution with dummy variables that reflected whether data were missing for predictors. These analyses yielded results that were virtually identical, presumably because of the small amount of missing data. Therefore, for the sake of simplicity, and to minimize loss of cases, we rely on simple mean substitution to handle most missing data problems.

We never use mean substitution, however, when data are "missing" out of logical necessity. For example, scores on marital quality scales in 1988 are absent when parents divorced between 1980 and 1988. Readers should also be aware that we do not substitute missing data for dependent variables; instead, we throw out any case that has missing data on an outcome for a given analysis. For this reason, the number of cases varies slightly from one outcome to the next. But because the amount of missing data is small for almost all outcomes (rarely more than a few percent), the sample sizes usually vary by no more than a few cases.

EFFECT SIZES AND SIGNIFICANCE TESTS

For ease of presentation, we show our key results in each chapter graphically. When dependent variables have an inherent meaning (for example, the number of years of education), we present the results using the original metric. However, when dependent variables are scale scores (such as affection for parents or self-esteem), we standardize the distributions to have means of zero and standard deviations of 1 before presentation. Given that the unit of measurement in most scales is arbitrary, this procedure results in little loss of information. More importantly, standardized scores allow us to report effect sizes, that is, differences between groups as a proportion of the standard deviation of the dependent variable. Because it provides a common metric, the use of effect sizes helps us to make comparisons about the estimated effect of a variable (say, parental divorce) on offspring outcomes that involve different scales of measurement. It also provides a convenient way of interpreting the strength of associations. We assess effect sizes using the following conventions: those .24 or less (that is, less than one-fourth of a standard deviation difference between groups) are *weak*; those between .25 and .49 are *moderate*; and those .50 or more are *strong*.

We present full details on the key findings (including the regression equations) in the Appendix. In describing our results in the text, however, we omit most statistics and simply describe how variables are associated. *Readers should assume that if we say that two variables are associated, it means that the association is statistically significant at the .05 level of probability or less.* Occasionally, we state that two variables are marginally associated, meaning that the association is marginally statistically significant ($p > .05$ but $< .10$). We rely mainly on two-tailed tests of statistical significance. The exception involves parents' marital quality and divorce. For these variables, previous literature is consistent about the direction of associations. For example, it is difficult to construct an argument that persistent marital conflict is good for children; consequently, in analyses involving these variables, we use one-tailed tests.

Given that our study involves a large number of independent and dependent variables, it is likely that some statistically "significant" results are really due to chance rather than to a substantive association between variables. When conducting multiple significance tests, there are several conventions available to decrease the risk of making this error. One possibility is to adjust the criterion level for significance to a lower probability value, based on the number of tests conducted. Another strategy is to use a multivariate method (such as MANOVA) and to pool dependent variables and test for overall significance before examining particular dependent variables. These methods are useful in a single study that tests a relatively small number of hypotheses; however, there is no standard technique for dealing with the problem of multiple significance tests in a study as broad as the present one.

To avoid confusing statistical with substantive significance in the present study, we focus on general patterns of significant results. To illustrate this logic, if multiple outcomes are available (for example, four dimensions of offspring's psychological well-being) but only one shows a significant association with a particular independent variable, then we usually dismiss this as a chance finding. However, if multiple dependent variables show a consistent pattern of significant results, especially if the pattern is congruent with theory or previous research, then we report this as a "real" finding. In deciding whether a meaningful pattern of results is present, we consider associations that are only marginally significant ($p < .10$) to be relevant, provided that other fully significant associations are also present. This use is especially appropriate when we examine subgroups (such as married offspring) for whom the number of cases is not large, and hence, the power of statistical tests to reject the null hypothesis is weak.

Conclusion

Our data set is uniquely suited to investigate the impact of family-of-origin characteristics on young adult offspring. Our study (1) has data from both parents and offspring; (2) examines associations between family characteristics in 1980 and offspring's outcomes twelve to fifteen years later; (3) allows us to examine the implications of *changes* in family characteristics during the 1980s for offspring; (4) includes a broad range of social-psychological and demographic variables for parents and offspring; and (5) covers a critical period in the life course (the early years of adulthood) for a rarely studied group of people: those reaching adulthood in the 1990s. In the following chapters, we present the results of our investigation of the links between family-of-origin characteristics and aspects of well-being among young adult offspring.

Relationships

with Parents

Relationships with parents usually continue long past the time children reach adulthood, leave home, and form their own families. Most young adults find that parents are a continuing source of companionship and support. However, some young adults, after leaving home, have little contact with parents; and others harbor feelings of resentment toward parents from childhoods that were less than idyllic. The nature of these relationships has important implications, as feelings of affection facilitate exchanges of assistance between parents and adult children (Hogan, Eggebeen, and Clogg, 1993). Parents often provide critical support when offspring are establishing their own households and families; offspring, in turn, often provide critical support when parents are in their later years. Close and supportive links between adult children and their parents also promote the psychological well-being of both generations (Amato, 1994; Barnett, Marshall, and Pleck, 1992; Roberts and Bengtson, 1993; Snarey, 1993; Umberson, 1992). These benefits appear to be long-lasting: in a longitudinal study, Roberts and Bengtson (1996) found that affection for parents during late adolescence and early adulthood predicted offspring's self-esteem twenty years later.

In this chapter, we focus on the ties that offspring have with their parents during the transition to adulthood. The life course perspective, with its assumption of linked lives over time, suggests that young adults' relationships with parents reflect earlier family-of-origin experiences. This perspective also suggests that the bonds between parents and young adult offspring set the tone for parent-child relations throughout the remainder of the life course. Yet, we know relatively little about the ways in which early family experiences affect young adults' ties with parents. Learning more about this process is essential if we wish to understand the implications of changes in family life during the last several decades for the nature and quality of intergenerational relations.

This chapter examines the ways in which parents' economic resources, gender nontraditionalism, marital quality, and family structure in 1980— as well as changes in these variables between 1980 and 1988—are associated with various dimensions of parent-child relationships in 1992. The mediation model suggests that these family-of-origin characteristics affect offspring largely through their impact on parental support and control when offspring are growing up. In line with this assumption, we assess the extent to which parental support and control during adolescence mediate the associations between family-of-origin characteristics and the young adult offspring's relations with their parents.

Measuring Relationships with Parents

The parent-child relationship includes multiple dimensions, such as affection, agreement, contact, and helping. It also includes factors that provide opportunities for interaction, such as coresidence or distance between parents' and children's residences. To capture the complexity of offspring's ties with parents, we asked about each of these relationship dimensions.

We measured children's feelings of affection for mothers and fathers with one item dealing with the overall closeness of the relationship and five items from Bengtson and Schrader's (1982) positive affect scale. The five items referred to parental understanding, trust, respect, fairness, and affection. The mean ratings served as measures of *affection for mothers* and *affection for fathers*. The higher the score on these scales, the closer children felt to parents. (Details on these and other measures of parent-child relationships are available in Table 3.1 in the Appendix.) Overall, children report positive feelings for both parents—a finding consistent with previous research (Troll and Bengtson, 1979). However, ratings are higher for mothers than for fathers. For example, 64% of offspring describe themselves as "very close" to their mothers, compared with 43% who describe themselves as "very close" to their fathers. Sons and daughters do not differ in their ratings of affection for either parent. The fact that children feel closer to mothers than to fathers has been noted by other investigators (Amato, 1987a;

Thornton, Orbuch, and Axinn, 1995; Rossi and Rossi, 1990) and is consistent with the data in Chapter 2 regarding children's recollections of maternal and paternal support.

Offspring also rated the extent to which they shared similar or dissimilar views with their parents with regard to their "general outlook on life." We used this item, repeated for mothers and fathers, to reflect perceptions of *consensus with mothers* and *consensus with fathers*. This measure is included because previous research shows that consensus is only moderately correlated with measures of affection for parents (Troll and Bengtson, 1979). High ratings on this variable reflect high perceived agreement. Little difference is apparent in children's perceptions of agreement with mothers and fathers: 73% report similar or very similar views for mothers, compared with 71% for fathers. Sons and daughters do not differ in their perceptions of consensus with either parent.

Coresidence with parents reflects another dimension of the parent-child relationship. In our sample, 21% of offspring live with both parents, 3% live with mothers only, and 1% live with fathers only. If we omit married offspring from our calculations, then 40% live with one or both parents. Because so few offspring live with one parent only, in most analyses we combine children who live with one or both parents into a single group. However, when we turn our attention to parental divorce, our focus is on whether offspring live with mothers or fathers.

For offspring who do not live with parents, we asked about the distance between parents' and children's households. *Distance from parents* is a critical relationship dimension, as it reflects opportunities for interaction and assistance to occur. Because most parents live together, we use a single measure (distance from parents) in most analyses. In cases in which parents live apart and when divorce is not the focus of our analysis, we take the mean number of miles between children and each of the two parental households as our measure of distance. However, when we consider the impact of parental divorce on children, we examine distance from mothers and fathers separately. The distances in our sample range from less than one mile to 10,000 miles, but most are quite short, with the median distance being 30 miles. The finding that most adult offspring live close to their parents is consistent with prior research (Rossi and Rossi, 1990; Troll and Bengtson, 1979). In our sample, daughters live farther from parents (about 20 miles) than do sons. Because the distribution of distances is positively skewed, we used a logarithmic transformation (base 10) to normalize it prior to statistical analysis.

Offspring who do not live with parents told us the number of days since they last had *contact with mothers* and *contact with fathers*, including seeing, talking on the telephone, or receiving a letter. Consistent with previous research (Rossi and Rossi, 1990; Troll and Bengtson, 1979), the majority of offspring had been in contact with parents relatively recently. However, even in cases in which parents live together, children often have more recent contact with one parent than the other. Most children in our sample had recent contact with mothers, with three-fourths having had contact within the previous two days. In comparison, only 45% had contact with their fathers during the previous two days. Daughters talked with their mothers more recently than had sons, although daughters and sons did not differ in the length of time since they last communicated with their fathers. Because the distribution is positively skewed, we used a logarithmic transformation (base 10) to normalize it prior to statistical analysis. Note that when discussing results for contact and distance in the text and figures, we take the antilogs so that values of dependent variables appear in the original metric.

We also included three measures of assistance between the generations. Respondents with continuously married parents rated the likelihood that they would call on parents for help with (1) transportation, (2) home or car repairs, (3) other work around the house, (4) advice or encouragement, (5) child care, and (6) a loan or gift of $200 or more. The mean rating served as a measure of *perceived assistance from parents*, with high scores indicating a greater likelihood of asking for help. The child care item was omitted for offspring without children. When parents were divorced, we asked the questions separately for mothers and fathers.

To measure *receiving help* from parents, offspring reported whether, during the past month, they had received help from parents with (1) transportation, (2) home or car repairs, (3) other work around the house, (4) advice or encouragement, and (5) child care. Offspring also reported whether, during the previous two years, they had received a loan or gift of $200 or more from parents. To provide a summary index, we used the proportion of items on which help was received. The child care item was omitted for offspring without children. We based corresponding measures of *giving help* to parents on the same items, except that we omitted the question on child care. When parents were divorced, we asked these questions separately for mothers and fathers. Preliminary inspection of these variables revealed that daughters score marginally higher than sons on perceived help from parents, although sons and daughters do not differ in their reports of receiving or giving assistance.

These various dimensions of parent-child relationships tend to be positively correlated. For example, affection is positively and significantly associated with consensus, contact, perceived assistance, giving help, and receiving help. However, these correlations tend to be modest, ranging from .53 (affection for mothers and consensus with mothers) to .11 (affection for fathers and giving help to fathers). Furthermore, not all relationship dimensions are positively correlated. Affection for parents, for example, is not correlated with distance from parents. And affection for fathers (but not mothers) is significantly *negatively* associated with coresidence with parents ($r = -.14$). This latter finding indicates that offspring get along better with their fathers if they do not live with them. The fact that most of these measures are only modestly correlated suggests that it is necessary to study multiple relationship dimensions to understand fully the nature of parent-child ties.

To provide a preliminary assessment of the utility of the mediation model, we examined associations between our measures of parent-child relationships and offspring's recollections of parental support and control during adolescence. Maternal and paternal support are positively and significantly associated with most of the parent-child relationship variables, including affection for mothers and fathers, consensus with mothers and fathers, contact with parents, perceived assistance from parents, and help given to and received from parents. These findings are consistent with Rossi and Rossi (1990), who also found that retrospective ratings of parental affection during childhood are good predictors of closeness to parents in adulthood.

In addition, parental control is related in a curvilinear fashion to several relationship variables, including affection for mothers, affection for fathers, consensus with mothers, and perceived assistance from parents. The highest levels of affection, consensus, and perceived assistance are associated with a moderate level of parental control. In contrast, affection, consensus, and perceived assistance are relatively low when parental control is either very low or very high. Because recollections of parental support and control are associated with most of the parent-child relationship measures *and* with many of the key independent variables in our study (see Chapter 2), we assess the mediation model in our analyses that follow. In doing so, we consider both the additive and curvilinear effects of parental control.

Parents' Socioeconomic Resources and Offspring's Relationships with Parents

PREVIOUS STUDIES

Attention to the life course and the mediation model indicates that relationships between parents and adult children are, to a certain extent, a continuation of the parent-child relationships during childhood. For this reason, studies that focus on young children and adolescents are relevant to our interest in socioeconomic resources, and thus we review them along with studies of adult offspring. For the same reason, we refer to studies of children when assessing the probable impact of parents' gender nontraditionalism and marital quality.

Studies of Children.   Education is associated with the values that underlie parents' methods of child-rearing. Well-educated parents (especially if they hold high-status jobs that involve self-direction and complexity) tend to emphasize independence, achievement, and self-control, whereas poorly educated parents tend to emphasize conformity, obedience, and respect for authority (Gecas, 1979; Kohn, 1963, 1977). In line with these values, well-educated parents tend to react to children's misbehavior by pointing out the negative consequences of children's actions, whereas poorly educated parents tend to rely on coercive forms of discipline, such as yelling or hitting (Dodge, Pettit, and Bates, 1994; Gecas, 1979; Simons et al., 1993). Parental education is also associated with home environments characterized by greater parental involvement (Gecas, 1979; Marsiglio, 1991), parental warmth and support (Dodge, Pettit, and Bates, 1994; Felner et al., 1995; Simons et al., 1993), cognitive stimulation, safety, and cleanliness (Parcel and Menaghan, 1994, chap. 3). This pattern appears to hold in African American families as well as in white families (Ahmeduzzaman and Roopnarine, 1992). These findings suggest that the child-rearing practices of well-educated parents facilitate emotional closeness between children and parents more so than those of poorly educated parents.

Family income is also related to parent-child relations. In particular, the stress of trying to make ends meet under conditions of economic hardship tends to deplete parents' coping skills, leaving them irritable and more coercive in their dealings with children. In a study of children of the Great Depression, Elder and his colleagues (Elder, 1974; Elder, van Nguyen, and Caspi, 1985) found that economic deprivation resulting from unemployment was associated with fathers becoming less nurturant, more punitive, and more arbitrary in their treatment of children. Correspondingly, children described their unemployed fathers as being rejecting, indifferent, and unsupportive. Investigations using more recent data also show that long-term economic deprivation as well as abrupt declines into poverty are associated with low parental nurturance and harsh discipline of children (Conger et al., 1992, 1993; McLoyd, 1989; McLoyd and Wilson, 1991; Sampson and Laub, 1994; Voydanoff, 1991).

Many of these studies suggest that economic hardship has greater consequences for children's relationships with fathers than with mothers. Because men have traditionally been defined as primary breadwinners, poor fathers must deal not only with economic deprivation but also with a sense of failure in the provider role, thus leaving them irritable and oversensitive when interacting with children. However, economic hardship in mother-only families is also related to more punitive, more restrictive, and less effective maternal behavior (Colletta, 1979; Gelles, 1989).

Some studies suggest differences in the reactions of daughters and sons to economic hardship. Flanagan (1990) found that hardship increased conflict with parents more for sons than for daughters. In contrast, Elder, van Nguyen, and Caspi (1985) found that during the Great Depression, financial hardship increased fathers' rejection of daughters more than of sons, especially when daughters were not physically attractive. Using a different data set, Hook (1990) also found that daughters were more likely than sons to report increases in family tension during periods of economic uncertainty.

Studies of Adult Offspring.   Relatively few studies have considered how socioeconomic resources in the family of origin affect parent-child ties once children are grown. However, existing studies are generally consistent with those just described in suggesting that high parental education and income facilitate parent-child affection. Umberson (1992) found that parental education is positively associated with contact with mothers, whereas low parental income is associated with relationship strain with fathers. Another study indicated that parental education is positively related to children's feelings of intimacy with both parents (Cooney, Leather, and Hutchinson,

1995). Only one study (Rossi and Rossi, 1990) suggested that parental education *lowers* affection between children and parents. Consistent with studies suggesting positive effects of parental education, White (1994b) found that childhood poverty is linked with less closeness to mothers and fathers in later life.

Parents' socioeconomic resources also have implications for parent-child coresidence. Children with well-educated parents tend to marry later than do children with poorly educated parents (Avery, Goldscheider, and Speare, 1992; Goldscheider and Waite, 1991; Keith and Finlay, 1988), and delaying marriage increases the length of time during which children might reside in the parental home. However, parental education and income also increase the likelihood that offspring will establish residential independence prior to marriage (Goldscheider and Goldscheider, 1993, 1994; White, 1994a). According to Goldscheider and Goldscheider (1994), well-educated parents value independence and encourage their children's departure from the parental home. In addition, children from high-income families are likely to attend college, which usually results in their moving away from the parental home. These considerations suggest that parents' socioeconomic resources decrease the odds of parent-child coresidence, at least among unmarried offspring.

In addition, parental education is associated with greater distance (Bulcroft and Bulcroft, 1991) and fewer visits between adult children and parents (Bulcroft and Bulcroft, 1991; White, 1994b). This finding is consistent with a more general trend for middle-class kin to live farther apart than working-class kin (Logan and Spitze, 1994). However, because most studies find positive associations between parental education and parent-child affection, the associations between parental education, distance, and contact probably reveal less about emotional closeness than about the need for offspring to be geographically mobile to obtain college degrees and find suitable professional positions.

Research dealing with exchanges of assistance yields similar findings. Several studies based on the National Survey of Families and Households demonstrate that parental education and income have independent positive associations with exchanges of social and economic support between adult children and their parents (Eggebeen and Hogan, 1990; Hogan, Eggebeen, and Clogg, 1993; Hoyert, 1991; White 1992, 1994b). Other studies based on different data sets yield similar conclusions (Rossi and Rossi, 1990, pp. 424–437; Umberson, 1992).

HYPOTHESES

Our review of previous research suggests that high parental education and income are associated with greater parental nurturance and more effective parental control of children—factors that facilitate children's feelings of affection for parents. Studies of adult offspring also suggest that parents' education and income strengthen the ties between generations. These considerations lead us to hypothesize that parents' socioeconomic resources are positively associated with adult offspring's affection for parents, consensus with parents, contact with parents, and exchanges of assistance with parents. The mediation model suggests that parental support and control during adolescence can account for this pattern. Consequently, we hypothesize that controlling for parental support and control weakens or eliminates the associations between parents' socioeconomic resources and adult offspring's relationships with parents.

In relation to coresidence, we expect that among unmarried offspring, those from high-resource families are *less* likely to be living in the parental home than are those from low-resource families. Similarly, we predict that among offspring who no longer live with parents, those from high-resource families live farther from parents than do those from low-resource families. However, we do not assume that these patterns are due to lowered affection for parents. Instead, we assume that they are due to offspring's educational and occupational attainment.

Although previous studies are not entirely consistent, they suggest that the consequences of socioeconomic factors are more pronounced for children's relations with fathers than with mothers—a possibility we explore next. In addition, we examine the notion that economic hardship places more strain on father-daughter than on father-son relationships.

RESULTS

Because we are concerned with how parents' socioeconomic resources affect children's relations with biological parents (or in a few cases, adopted parents), we omit forty-five children who lived with stepparents in 1980 from the following analyses. Consequently, readers should note that parental education, parental income, and changes in parents' economic resources always refer to parents rather than to stepparents. For the same reason, we also omit children living in stepfamilies in 1980 from analyses reported in later sections of this chapter dealing with parents' gender nontraditionalism and marital quality.

Parental Education.   Several studies suggest that parental education increases affection, contact, and exchanges of assistance between adult children and their parents. But in our data, mothers' and fathers' years of education are not related to most dimensions of the parent-child relationship.
It doesn't matter whether parents are well or poorly educated: offspring feel
as close to them, agree with them as much, communicate with them as
frequently, and exchange assistance with them as often.

A few differences are apparent, however. Among unmarried offspring,
those with well-educated parents are less likely to be living at home with
parents than are those with poorly educated parents. This difference is true
regardless of whether we consider mothers' or fathers' educations, although
the association is stronger for mothers than for fathers, and only the former
variable is significant when both appear in the regression equation together.
The interactions between offspring's gender and maternal/paternal education are not significant, so the results hold for both daughters and sons.
(Readers can view the full regression equations dealing with parental education in Table 3.2 in the Appendix.)

Figure 3.1 shows the association between mothers' education and the
likelihood of living at home for unmarried offspring. To construct the figure,
we derived the predicted values from the logistic regression equation, with
all control variables set at the mean (if ordered) or mode (if categorical).
Note that the predicted probability of coresidence for daughters declines
from .52 when mothers have 10 years of education to .24 when mothers
have 16 years of education. A similar pattern is apparent for sons. Children
from well-educated families are *not* less likely to be living at home because
their parents send them to college. When we control for children's current
school enrollment and years of education, the association between parents'
education and living at home declines but little. Furthermore, affection for
parents cannot account for this association because affection is not related
to parental education. It seems, therefore, that well-educated parents encourage their children's residential independence, as Goldscheider and
Goldscheider (1994) suggested.

In addition, for offspring who no longer live at home, both mothers' and
fathers' years of education are positively associated with the *distance* between parents' and offspring's households. Once again, the absence of an
interaction with child gender indicates that the association holds for both
sons and daughters. Figure 3.1 shows the number of miles that children live
from parents by mothers' education. To keep the presentation consistent

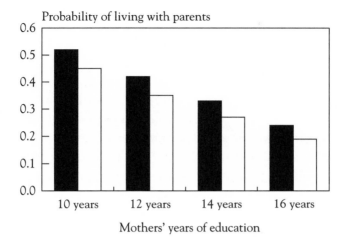

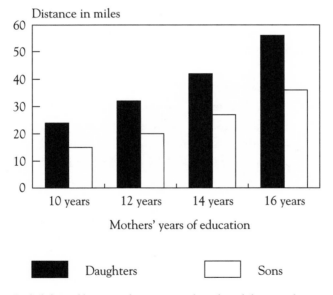

Figure 3.1   Probability of living with parents and predicted distance from parents in 1992 by mothers' years of education

with the first half of the figure, we used the ordinary least squares regression equation to predict these values, based on the same criteria just noted. Note that when mothers have ten years of education, daughters live 24 miles away, on average. But when mothers have sixteen years of education, daughters live 56 miles away, on average. A similar pattern is apparent for sons. The explanation for this trend is straightforward: The children of well-educated parents need to be mobile to attend college and obtain suitable occupations. When we control for offspring's education and occupational attainment, the association between parental education and distance disappears. However, it is important to note that even though children tend to live farther from well-educated parents, they feel as close to them, keep in touch with them as often, and are as likely to exchange assistance with them as are children with poorly educated parents.

Parental Income.   Previous literature suggests that economic hardship when children are growing up can erode the quality of interaction between children and parents. To assess this notion, we first examine mothers' and fathers' incomes in 1980—the first year of our survey when all the children were living at home with their parents. However, the equations (which include mothers' and fathers' educations as controls) reveal that dimensions of the parent-child relationship are not associated, in general, with parental income.

We also considered changes in parental income between 1980 and 1988. On the basis of previous research, we assumed that declines in real income erode parent-child relationships, whereas increases in real income benefit parent-child relationships. We carried out these analyses only on parents who remained continuously married between 1980 and 1988 so that income shifts are not confounded with parental divorce. Contrary to our expectations, shifts in parental income are not associated with affection, consensus, or contact in 1992. However, shifts in parental income are related to the perceived availability of help from parents and the amount of help children actually receive from parents. (See Table 3.3 in the Appendix for the full equations.)

Figure 3.2 shows the associations between income change and perceived help and help received. In this figure, we divide parents into those whose incomes declined by $10,000 or more between 1980 and 1988 (in constant 1992 dollars), those who experienced little change, and those whose incomes increased by $10,000 or more. These three groups represent 22%,

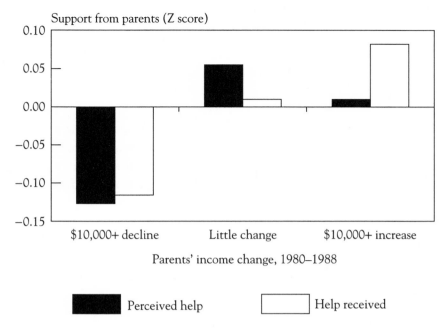

Figure 3.2 Support from parents in 1992 by changes in parents' income between 1980 and 1988 (in constant 1992 dollars)

49%, and 29% of our families, respectively. To facilitate interpretation of the figure, the two outcomes are adjusted to have means of zero and standard deviations of 1.

In relation to *perceived help,* offspring whose parents experienced a decline of $10,000 or more are less likely to ask parents for help than are offspring whose parents experienced little change or those whose parents experienced increases in income. The difference between those whose income declined substantially and those in the other two groups represents one-fifth and one-seventh of a standard deviation, respectively, reflecting weak but nontrivial effect sizes. Offspring whose parents increased their incomes, however, are not markedly different from those who experienced little change.

In relation to help received, both gains and losses of parental income appear to be consequential. The difference between the $10,000 increase and the $10,000 decrease groups represents one-fifth of a standard deviation, indicating a weak but nontrivial effect size. To gain more insight into this association, we disaggregated our measure of helping into its component parts. This step revealed that shifts in parental income are related significantly to two forms of helping: assistance with transportation and gifts or loans of $200 or more. Income changes are not related to receiving help with home or car repairs, help around the house, child care, advice, or emotional support.

Periods of parental welfare-use between 1980 and 1988 are not related to any dimensions of parent-child relationships. But consistent with the findings for shifts in income, offspring whose fathers were unemployed between 1980 and 1988 are less likely (at marginally significant levels) to ask parents for help or to receive help from parents. These associations persist when we control for income change between 1980 and 1988. Parents' perceptions of whether their economic situation had gotten better or worse during this period yield results similar to actual shifts in income.

Given that a decline in income and other indicators of economic hardship were *not* associated with affection or contact with parents, it seems that lowered perceptions of parents as sources of assistance reflect either the offspring's belief that their parents are unable to respond to requests for help, or the offspring's preference not to burden parents who may be experiencing hard times. This interpretation is consistent with the finding that income shifts are associated mainly with help with transportation and finances—forms of assistance that depend on access to automobiles (which are expensive) and cash. Also, consistent with this interpretation, we find no evidence that offspring's recollections of parental support or control during adolescence mediate the associations between economic decline during the 1980s and receiving assistance from parents in 1992.

SUMMARY

Our results suggest few effects of parents' socioeconomic resources on sons' and daughters' relationships with parents in early adulthood. In particular, we find no associations between parental education or income and children's affection for parents. This finding appears to contradict several previous studies of adult offspring (Cooney, Leather, and Hutchinson, 1995; Umberson, 1992, White, 1994b). However, studies are few in number and not always in agreement (Rossi and Rossi, 1990). The fact that offspring and parents are generally close, regardless of resources, suggests that parents do not allow economic problems (including declines in household income and periods of paternal unemployment) to affect their long-term relationships with children as much as some studies suggest. Alternatively, tension between parents and children due to economic hardship may dissipate as children enter adulthood and become more independent of parents. It is also possible that long-lasting negative effects occur only when economic hardship is extreme and prolonged, and we may not have a sufficient number of families in our sample who experienced severe conditions to detect such effects.

In other respects, however, our data are congruent with previous research. Consistent with several studies (Goldscheider and Goldscheider, 1993, 1994; White, 1994a), we find that parental education is associated with decreased coresidence between unmarried children and parents. And consistent with Bulcroft and Bulcroft (1991), we find that parental education is positively related to the distance between children's and parents' residences. These associations are not related to affection between parents and offspring; instead, they appear to reflect the different lifestyles and career trajectories of youth with highly and with poorly educated parents.

Our results are also in agreement with previous investigations in showing that parents' economic resources are related to children's perceptions of support and receipt of assistance from parents (Eggebeen and Hogan, 1990; Hogan, Eggebeen, and Clogg, 1993; Hoyert, 1991; Rossi and Rossi, 1990; Umberson, 1992; Voydanoff, 1991; White 1992). When parents experience increases in real income over time, the children are more likely to receive assistance from their parents. But when parents experience declines in real income, the children are less likely to ask for help or to receive it. Because these indicators of hardship are not related to offspring's current affection for parents, or to their recollections of parental support and control during adolescence, it seems reasonable to conclude that these events lower helping because they limit parents' ability to provide assistance.

Parents' Gender Nontraditionalism and Offspring's Relationships with Parents

PREVIOUS STUDIES

In this section, we consider three aspects of parents' gender nontraditionalism: maternal employment, fathers' share of housework and child care, and parents' attitudes toward gender roles.

Studies of Children. In relation to maternal employment, employed mothers spend less time with their children, overall, than do nonemployed mothers (Greenberger, O'Neil, and Nagel, 1994). But most of this difference is in time spent in the presence of children rather than in direct interaction (Nock and Kingston, 1988). Indeed, many mothers compensate for their absence from the home during work hours by increasing the amount of time they spend in intense interaction with children during nonwork hours (Mischel and Fuhr, 1988). In addition, fathers with employed wives tend to spend more time at home with children and engage in somewhat more child care than do fathers with nonemployed wives (Barnett and Baruch, 1987; O'Connell, 1993; Pleck, 1985). Maternal employment is also associated with greater father control and discipline of children, presumably to compensate for a decline in the amount of time that mothers engage in child supervision (Amato, 1987a). Overall, although maternal employment changes the pattern of family life, it appears to have few implications for the total amount of time that parents are directly involved with their children.

Similarly, most studies find no effects of mothers' employment on the quality of mother-child relationships (for example, see Armistead, Wierson, and Forehand, 1990). Some studies show that adolescent daughters identify more closely with and express greater admiration for employed than non-employed mothers, possibly because employed mothers have higher status in the family and in the larger society (Hoffman, 1989; Mischel and Fuhr, 1988; Richards and Duckett, 1991; Spitze, 1988). Key factors, however, are mothers' satisfaction with work roles and the amount of support and assistance they get from husbands. Relations between employed mothers and their children may be especially positive when mothers want to be employed, are satisfied with their jobs, and have supportive spouses. On the other hand, relations with children may be problematic when mothers prefer not to be employed, are dissatisfied with their jobs, or receive little support from spouses (Hoffman, 1989; Mischel and Fuhr, 1988; Spitze, 1988; Zaslow, Rabinovich, and Suwalsky, 1991). For similar reasons, mother-child interaction may be strained among full-time homemakers who wish to be employed.

Although most studies show few negative consequences of maternal employment, not all studies yield sanguine conclusions. In relation to parental time, Muller (1995) found that adolescents reported the lowest level of parental involvement in school activities (talking with children about school, visiting schools, and checking homework) and supervision of children after school when mothers were employed full-time. Another line of research (Baydar and Brooks-Gunn, 1991; Belsky, 1991; Belsky and Egge-been, 1991) suggests that the full-time employment of mothers during the child's first year of life increases the risk of insecure attachments to parents as well as the risk of behavior problems in later childhood. Finally, research shows that shift work and irregular work hours affect women's personal happiness and may have a negative impact on their family relationships (Menaghan and Parcel, 1991; White and Keith, 1990).

In relation to fathers' participation in housework and child care, a high level of father involvement may have problematic implications for children under some circumstances. For example, if mothers in dual-career families put pressure on reluctant fathers to increase their contributions to family work, then this pressure may increase the level of tension in the household (Crouter et al., 1987). However, fathers who willingly engage in housework and child care are likely to have closer relationships with their children than are other fathers (Gerson, 1993; Russell, 1983; Snarey, 1993).

We know of no studies that have considered how parents' attitudes about gender roles in the family might affect parent-child relationships. People who hold traditional beliefs assume that parents who enact conventional husband/breadwinner and wife/homemaker roles make more effective parents; those with nontraditional views disagree. However, these expectations are based on ideology rather than on research. We see no compelling reason for believing that parents' beliefs about gender directly influence the quality of parent-child ties one way or the other.

Studies of Adults. Few studies have considered the consequences of maternal employment, fathers' involvement in family work, and parents' gender role attitudes for relations between parents and adult children. In two Australian studies, Khoo, Krishnamoorthy, and Trlin (1984a, 1984b) found that maternal employment when children were growing up had few consequences for intergenerational relations when children reached adulthood. However, adult daughters (but not adult sons) were more likely to discuss intimate topics with employed mothers, suggesting greater closeness in the mother-daughter relationship. Another Australian study (Young, 1987) showed that daughters (but not sons) left home earlier when mothers were employed. Furthermore, both sons and daughters cited conflict as a reason for leaving more often when their mothers were employed, although it is not clear if offspring were referring to interparental conflict or parent-child conflict. Overall, we know little about the long-term consequences of parents' gender nontraditionalism for later parent-child ties.

HYPOTHESES

The life course perspective suggests that events in the family-of-origin can have a lasting influence on parent-child bonds. Nevertheless, previous research leads us to believe that maternal employment has, overall, few consequences for young adult offspring's relationships with their parents. However, maternal employment may be problematic under certain circumstances, such as when mothers are dissatisfied with their jobs, do shift work, work long hours, or experience conflict with their husbands over household responsibilities. We hypothesize that children experience closer relationships with their fathers when the fathers take on a relatively large share of household chores and child care, especially if this happens in a context of interparental harmony. By referring to the mediation model, we assume that parental support and control when children are adolescents account for the links between paternal involvement and later ties between offspring and fathers. Finally, we anticipate that parental attitudes about gender roles have few implications for parent-child relationships.

RESULTS

Maternal Employment. Consistent with previous literature indicating that maternal employment has few consequences for children's relationships with mothers, our data show that mothers' employment in 1980 is not associated with children's affection for mothers, consensus with mothers, contact with mothers, coresidence with parents, distance from parents, or exchanges of assistance with parents in 1992. However, contrary to our expectations, mothers' employment in 1980 is associated with several aspects of the *father-child* relationship in 1992. Offspring report more affection for fathers, more consensus with fathers, and (marginally) more recent contact with fathers when mothers were employed than when mothers were not employed. But among employed mothers, the number of hours of employment is negatively related to affection, consensus, and contact. Plotting a regression line reveals that offspring report the most positive relationships with fathers when their mothers worked part-time and the least positive relationships when their mothers worked more than a 40-hour week. (See Table 3.4 in the Appendix for the full regression equations.)

Several explanations for the negative association between mothers' hours of employment and offspring's closeness to fathers come to mind. Although some women may work long hours because they love their jobs, others may work long hours because fathers are poor breadwinners or have other problems that detract from family relationships. In fact, our data show that mothers are significantly more likely to work long hours when (a) fathers have been unemployed in the three years prior to 1980, (b) fathers score high on a measure of behavior problems that includes items dealing with being in trouble with the law and having a drug or alcohol problem, or (c) offspring recall a relatively low level of support from fathers during adolescence. With all of these variables (unemployment, behavior problems, and support) included in the statistical model, the negative associations between mothers' work hours and dimensions of the father-child relationship decline by one-half and are no longer significant. This finding is consistent with the notion that problematic characteristics of fathers account for both mothers' long hours of employment and poor father-child relationships in early adulthood.

Next, we limited our analysis to families in which mothers were employed in 1980 and considered some of the circumstances surrounding their employment. Several studies show that shift work, working irregular hours, and dissatisfaction with work conditions affect mothers' personal happiness and may have a negative impact on family relationships. We had indicators of all of these variables in our 1980 interview. However, we find no evidence that any of these aspects of mothers' employment in 1980 are associated with relationship outcomes.

Mothers' reasons for working yield more interesting results. In 1980, parents rated the importance of various reasons for the mother's employment. Our analysis shows that in 1992 offspring have a relatively low level of affection for their fathers if their mothers worked because they either (a) didn't like staying at home or (b) wanted to become more financially independent. These results did not depend on whether mothers or fathers provided the ratings.

Figure 3.3 shows the association between affection for fathers and endorsement of these two motives. Notice that the greatest difference in father affection is between "very important" and the other responses. For the *don't like staying at home* item, the difference between the "not important at all" and "very important" categories represents two-thirds of a standard deviation. For the *financial independence* item, the corresponding difference is over

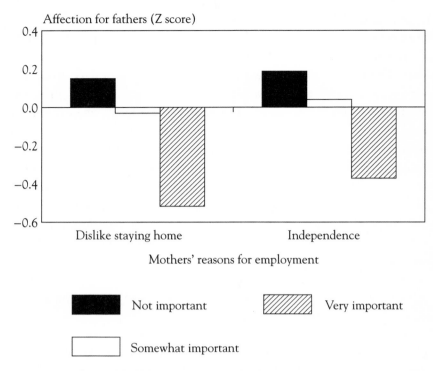

Figure 3.3 Affection for fathers in 1992 by mothers' reasons for employment in 1980

one-half of a standard deviation. Readers should note that these are large effect sizes.

Mothers who wish to get away from the home or who want to be financially independent may find that domestic labor does not provide a sufficient level of personal satisfaction. Some husbands, especially if they are traditional, may find this situation troublesome, thus increasing tension in the marriage. Alternatively, wives who anticipate an impending divorce may move into the labor force to achieve financial independence prior to marital dissolution. We assume, therefore, that maternal employment under these circumstances is related to low affection for the fathers because it is bound up with poor marital quality. In support of this explanation, when we control for parents' marital quality in 1980, the association between *desiring financial independence* and father-child affection declines to a nonsignificant level. Similarly, the coefficient for *not wanting to stay at home* declines by about one-fourth, although it remains significant. These results suggest that these two motives for maternal employment predict poor father-child re-lationships because they occur in poor-quality marriages.

Finally, we consider whether changes in mothers' hours of employment between 1980 and 1988 are related to parent-child relations in 1992. When we include mothers' hours of employment in both 1980 and 1988 in a series of regression models, two associations emerge: when mothers increased their hours of employment, offspring report more willingness to ask parents for assistance and more help received from parents. It seems likely that when mothers raise their hours of employment, the added financial security in-creases the flow of assistance from parents to young adult children. Indeed, controlling for increases in mothers' income substantially reduces the as-sociations between increases in mothers' hours of employment and helping.

Fathers' Share of Family Work. Although we hypothesized that paternal involvement in family work increases opportunities for close relationships to develop between fathers and children, we find no evidence that fathers' share of household chores in 1980 is related to aspects of parent-child re-lationships in 1992. However, as expected, fathers' share of child care in 1980 is positively associated with offspring's affection for fathers in 1992. This association does not depend on whether mothers or fathers provided the ratings of household labor. Inspection of adjusted means reveals that the gap in offsprings' affection for fathers who did no child care and those who did about half is three-fourths of a standard deviation—a very large effect size. On the basis of the mediation model, we assumed that father support during adolescence mediates the association between fathers' share of child care and later affection for fathers. Consistent with this assumption, adding offspring's recollections of father support to the equation reduces the coefficient by about half, leaving it nonsignificant. (See Table 3.5 in the Appendix for more details.)

Although we did not anticipate it, the fathers' share of child care in 1980 is also negatively associated with parent-child coresidence in 1992. When fathers did no child care, the probability that unmarried offspring live with their parents is .60; but when fathers did about half of the child care, the probability is only .28. It seems likely that fathers who are highly involved with children also hold nontraditional attitudes toward family life. As Gold-scheider and Goldscheider (1994) argue, parents with nontraditional atti-tudes often encourage their children to live away from home prior to mar-riage.

Gender Attitudes. As we anticipated, parents' gender attitudes in 1980 are not related, in general, to aspects of parent-child relationships in 1992. However, a shift in attitudes between 1980 and 1992 on the part of either mothers or fathers predicts the likelihood that unmarried children live with parents in 1992. To illustrate this trend, the probability of living with parents is .40 among offspring whose parents did not change attitudes appreciably, compared with .24 among those whose parents became more liberal and .56 among those whose parents became more conservative. This result is based on a shift of one-half standard deviation up or down the attitude scale. As we noted before, these findings are probably due to traditional parents wishing to keep their children at home prior to marriage and liberal parents encouraging their children's residential independence (Goldscheider and Goldscheider, 1994).

SUMMARY

Maternal employment appears to have no negative or positive long-term consequences for children's relationships with mothers, a finding that is consistent with most prior research (Hoffman, 1989; Mischel and Fuhr, 1988; Richards and Duckett, 1991; Spitze, 1988). However, the conditions of mothers' employment are related to the quality of later *father-child* relationships. For example, offspring report the most affection for their fathers if their mothers are employed part-time. But if mothers are employed "overtime" (more than 40 hours per week), or if they are working because they dislike staying at home or wish to be independent, children have relatively poor relationships with fathers.

Why might mothers' part-time employment benefit the father-child relationship? Although the answer is not clear, several other studies have shown that part-time employment among mothers is more likely than full-time employment to be linked with positive family outcomes (Hoffman, 1974, 1989). This result may be because mothers' part-time employment increases household income in a manner that avoids the work-family conflict that often results from full-time employment. Perhaps mothers' part-time employment encourages fathers to become more involved with their children, but does not place so much pressure on fathers that they experience it as an onerous demand.

We have more information about the link between mothers' long work hours and poor father-child relationships. This pattern is bound up with problematic aspects of the fathers' behavior, including unemployment, behavior problems, and low support for adolescent children. These findings suggest that mothers' long work hours are not a cause of poor father-child relationships; instead, long maternal work hours and lack of affection for fathers may both be due to problematic characteristics of fathers.

Consistent with several studies of fathers (Gerson, 1993; Russell, 1983; Snarey, 1993), young adult offspring report more affection for fathers who were highly involved in child care twelve years earlier. In line with the mediation model, paternal support during adolescence accounts for most of this association. This finding suggests an important consequence of father involvement: a close emotional bond with children that continues as offspring reach adulthood.

Finally, our results support the notion that unmarried children of non-traditional parents tend to leave home relatively early (Goldscheider and Goldscheider, 1993, 1994). In particular, when fathers are highly involved in child care or when parents adopt nontraditional gender attitudes, unmarried offspring are relatively unlikely to be living with their parents in 1992. We assume that unmarried children of nontraditional parents leave home relatively early because their parents encourage residential independence. Because well-educated individuals tend to hold nontraditional attitudes, this interpretation is consistent with the finding that parental education is associated with less coresidence between parents and unmarried offspring.

Parents' Marital Quality, Divorce, and Offspring's Relationships with Parents

PREVIOUS STUDIES

Studies of Children.   A number of studies have shown that interparental conflict is associated with problematic parent-child relationships (Davies and Cummings, 1994; Emery, 1982, 1988; Grych and Fincham, 1992; Hetherington and Clingempeel, 1992). This situation occurs for a number of reasons. Marital conflict makes family life stressful for children, leads parents to discipline their children more harshly and inconsistently, reduces parents' expressions of affection toward children, and decreases the extent to which parents are emotionally available. In addition, physical aggression between parents increases the risk of child abuse (Gelles, 1987).

Several studies suggest that marital conflict is more problematic for the father-child than the mother-child relationship. Belsky, Youngblade,

Rovine, and Volling (1991) found that a decline in marital quality over a three-year period was associated with fathers becoming more intrusive and less supportive of their young children; mothers, in contrast, revealed no comparable changes. Amato (1986), Brody and Pillegrini (1986), Harris and Morgan (1991), and Peterson and Zill (1986) also found that parents' marital conflict is linked more strongly to poor father-child than to poor mother-child relationships among both children and adolescents.

Parental divorce also appears to have a detrimental effect on the quality of children's relationships with custodial parents—usually mothers. This fact is not surprising, considering that marital dissolution is associated with increases in symptoms of psychological distress (Booth and Amato, 1992) and declines in income and social support for mothers (McLanahan and Booth, 1989). In a longitudinal study, Hetherington, Cox, and Cox (1982) found that recently divorced custodial mothers exhibited many of the same problematic behaviors characteristic of parents in high-conflict families. Although the quality of custodial mothers' parenting improved after two or three years, problems persisted in their relationships with sons. Hetherington and Clingempeel's (1992) study of young adolescents, however, suggested that puberty introduces new tension into relationships between single mothers and daughters. Consistent with these findings, an analysis of the National Survey of Families and Households showed that divorced and remarried mothers, compared with mothers in first marriages, reported fewer enjoyable times with their children, had more disagreements with their children, and were more likely to yell at or spank their children (Acock and Demo, 1994, chap. 5).

In relation to fathers, research consistently shows that contact between noncustodial fathers and children tends to decline over time, although this effect is less pronounced when children are adolescents at the time of divorce (Furstenberg and Nord, 1985; Seltzer, 1991). This decline in contact has several causes. A small number of mothers deliberately restrict fathers' access to children. Some men feel "pushed out of the picture" when custodial mothers remarry (Seltzer and Bianchi, 1988). Other men find that commitments to new spouses and stepchildren interfere with their relationships with their own children. More generally, many men appear to view fatherhood as a package deal, accepting responsibility for children only as long as they are married to the mother (Furstenberg and Harris, 1992).

Studies of Adults. A life course perspective suggests that disrupted relationships between parents and children due to interparental discord have the potential to persist well into adulthood. Although few studies have considered the long-term consequences of parents' marital conflict for relationships between parents and adult offspring, available studies support this conclusion. Amato and Booth (1991a) found that among adults whose parents remained continuously married, those who recalled their parents' marriage as being unhappy had relatively little contact with parents. Similarly, Rossi and Rossi (1990: 346–348) found that parents' reports of marital unhappiness were negatively related to children's affection for fathers but not for mothers. Finally, Cooney (1994) found that the recollections of young adults of their parents' marital conflict during adolescence were negatively associated with sons' feelings of intimacy with mothers and with sons' and daughters' feelings of intimacy with fathers. Although these three studies suggest that interparental discord erodes the quality of relationships between parents and adult children, they are all based on retrospective data. No longitudinal studies are available that match data on parents' marital conflict during childhood with data on children's relationships with parents when they reach adulthood.

Although studies of the long-term consequences of parents' marital discord are rare, studies dealing with the long-term consequences of divorce are more common. This literature suggests that the disruptive effects of divorce on parent-child relationships persist well into adulthood. Several studies of university students show that divorce is associated with lowered feelings of closeness to fathers, especially among daughters (Cooney, Smyer, Hagestad, and Klock, 1986; Fine, Moreland, and Schweibel, 1983; White, Brinkerhoff, and Booth, 1985). Research based on large, random samples of adults yield similar results. For example, Rossi and Rossi (1990, 346–348) found that marital disruption was associated with less affection between offspring and parents, with mothers reporting lower affection between children and fathers, and fathers reporting lower affection between children and mothers. Aquilino (1994) found that children who had been in mother custody following divorce, compared with those in continuously intact two-parent families, felt slightly less close to their mothers and considerably less close to their fathers. Zill, Morrison, and Coiro (1993) and Cooney (1994) also found that parental divorce was associated with lowered feelings of intimacy between young adults and their parents, especially fathers.

Divorce is also related to parent-child coresidence. Aquilino (1990, 1991), Goldscheider and Goldscheider (1989, 1993), and Cooney (1994) all found that young adults from single-parent and stepparent households achieved residential independence earlier than did those from continuously intact two-parent households. Furthermore, the relatively early home-leaving of children in divorced families appears to be due to low levels of family cohesion and harmony, rather than to other causes, such as leaving to attend college (Aquilino, 1990, 1991; Kiernan, 1992; White and Booth, 1985).

For offspring not living with parents, those from divorced families have less frequent contact with parents than do those from continuously intact two-parent families. Cooney (1994) found that adult children with divorced parents had less contact with fathers than did children with nondivorced parents, but no differences were apparent in contact with mothers. Amato and Booth (1991a) found that parents' marital dissolution was associated with decreased contact with both parents, although the association was stronger for fathers than mothers. In addition, Aquilino (1994), Amato and Booth (1991a), and Lye, Klepinger, Hyle, and Nelson (1995) all found that adult children of divorce had less contact with noncustodial parents than with custodial parents, regardless of parental gender.

Several national studies also indicate that adult children of divorce-exchange help with parents less often than do adult children of continuously married parents (Aquilino, 1994; Cooney and Uhlenberg, 1990; Umberson, 1992; White, 1992). This trend appears to hold for all types of aid, including financial assistance, practical help, and emotional support.

HYPOTHESES

Consistent with the life course perspective of continuity over time, the studies just reviewed suggest that parents' marital discord and divorce during childhood weaken the emotional bonds between offspring and parents in later life. Consequently, we hypothesize that low marital quality and divorce when children are growing up are associated with less affection, consensus, coresidence, contact, and assistance between parents and young adult off-spring. Furthermore, using the mediation model, we hypothesize that these observed associations decline substantially if we take into account parental support and control during adolescence.

The literature also indicates that divorce has a more adverse effect on children's ties to fathers than to mothers. Some of the studies just reviewed suggest that this may be because fathers rarely have custody of children following divorce. This explanation seems likely, given that living apart restricts opportunities for contact and for emotional bonds to grow between fathers and children. However, even in continuously intact families, a high level of conflict is associated with poor relationships between fathers and children. This finding suggests that some of the apparent "effects" of divorce on father-child relationships may actually begin prior to marital separation. In other words, interparental conflict may increase the likelihood of both divorce and poor father-child relationships, thus producing a spurious correlation. To address this issue, we use our longitudinal data to estimate the extent to which both divorce *and* predivorce conflict between parents affect later parent-child relationships.

Finally, a life course perspective suggests that we attend to the timing and context of events. For this reason, we examine children's ages at the time of divorce. We also consider the possibility that the consequences of marital disruption depend on circumstances after the divorce, such as custody arrangements, the extent of postdivorce conflict between parents, and whether parents remarry.

RESULTS

Parents' Marital Quality. To simplify the interpretation of our results, we restrict our initial analyses to 384 offspring who *never* experienced a parental divorce. Although we have data on four dimensions of parents' marital quality in 1980, two of these dimensions—marital happiness and divorce proneness—are consistently related to parent-child relationships in 1992. The direction of associations is as we expected: the happier that parents are with their marriage, the more affection offspring feel for their mothers and fathers, the greater the consensus between offspring and their mothers and fathers, and the more help offspring receive from and give to parents. Parental divorce-proneness is generally related to the same outcomes, but in the opposite direction; divorce proneness also predicts a marginally lower likelihood of seeing parents as sources of assistance. These findings hold for both sons and daughters and do not vary with offspring age. (See Table 3.6 in the Appendix for details.)

The associations between parents' divorce-proneness and affection for parents are shown in Figure 3.4. The "low," "medium," and "high" groups are based on natural cutting points in the distribution of divorce-proneness scores and represent 54%, 27%, and 19% of the total sample, respectively. It is clear from the figure that affection for parents is lowest when parents' marriages are very unstable (but continuously intact) and is highest when parents' marriages are stable. Also, although parents' divorce-proneness is related to affection for both parents, its consequences are somewhat stronger

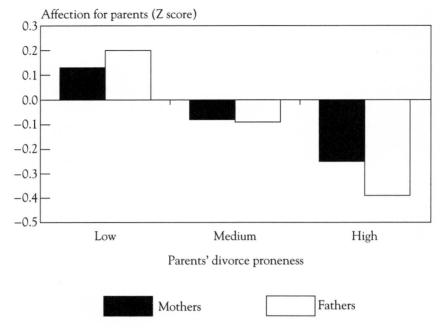

Affection for parents (Z score)

Figure 3.4   Affection for parents in 1992 by parents' divorce proneness in 1980

for fathers than mothers. The mean differences between stable and very unstable marriages represent over one-third of a standard deviation for mothers, and over one-half of a standard deviation for fathers, indicating moderate and strong effect sizes, respectively. The results for parents' marital happiness are similar to those shown in the figure.

Changes in parents' marital quality between 1980 and 1988 are also related to aspects of children's relationships with parents in 1992. For example, increases in marital happiness are positively associated with affection for mothers and affection for fathers. Similarly, increases in divorce proneness are negatively associated with affection for mothers, affection for fathers, and consensus with mothers. Further examination of means (after adjusting for all control variables) reveals that the highest level of affection for parents occurs when parents' marriages are consistently stable, whereas the lowest level of affection occurs when parents' marriages are consistently unstable. Shifts in instability (from low to high, or from high to low) are associated with intermediate levels of affection. The difference between the continuously unstable and continuously stable groups are moderately strong, and represent about one-third of a standard deviation for mother affection and nearly one-half of a standard deviation for father affection. This pattern of results suggests that the longer children are exposed to marital instability, the more detrimental the impact on later affection for parents. Results based on marital happiness lead to similar conclusions.

We also find that shifts in parents' marital happiness and instability between 1980 and 1988 are mainly associated with father-child affection when offspring lived at home with parents in 1988. This is reflected in interactions between the two marital quality variables and coresidence in 1988 in predicting father-child affection. It makes sense that shifts in parents' marital quality have the greatest impact on children who are still living at home when the changes are occurring.

Parental Divorce. The offspring in our sample who experienced parental divorce fall into two groups. Forty-seven offspring had experienced parental divorce and were living in a stepfamily at the time of the first parental interview in 1980. An additional forty-two children experienced the divorce of their biological parents between 1980 and 1992. Children in the first group were younger at the time of parental divorce, with a median age of 5, compared with a median age of 16 in the second group. All children in the first group were living in stepfamilies in 1980, whereas some of the children in the second group eventually lived in stepfamilies and others did not. Readers should keep these differences in mind as they examine the results that follow.

We begin by comparing children who experienced a parental divorce between 1980 and 1992 with those who never experienced a divorce. Marital dissolution between 1980 and 1992 is related to many dimensions of parent-child relationships; such as less affection for mothers among sons; a lower likelihood of coresidence with mothers; less affection for fathers among daughters; less consensus with fathers; a lower likelihood of coresidence with fathers; more days since the last contact with fathers for daughters; and marginally less willingness to ask parents for assistance. Consistent with our literature review, the divorce coefficients are somewhat stronger for fathers than for mothers. However, we also see a pattern in which later divorces appear to weaken opposite-gender dyads more than same-gender dyads, with mother-son and father-daughter relationships being affected more than father-son and mother-daughter relationships. (See the middle column of Table 3.7 in the Appendix.)

These gender differences are displayed in Figure 3.5. It is clear that di-

Figure 3.5   Affection for parents in 1992 by parental divorce between 1980 and 1992

vorce between 1980 and 1992 is associated with less affection on the part of sons for both parents, although the difference is greater for mothers than fathers. These differences represent effect sizes of nearly one-half and one-third of a standard deviation, respectively. In contrast, among daughters, divorce is associated with slightly higher affection for mothers (although this difference is not statistically significant) and dramatically lower affection for fathers. Comparable effect sizes are .23 and − .94, respectively. These results suggest that the mother-daughter relationship is particularly resilient to the disruption of divorce, whereas the father-daughter relationship is particularly vulnerable.

Earlier, we noted that when parents have unhappy and unstable marriages, children have comparatively low levels of affection for parents. This raises the question of whether parents' marital quality *prior to* marital disruption accounts for the link between divorce and problematic parent-child relationships. To test this idea, we look at associations between divorce and children's relations with parents, both prior to and after controlling for predivorce parents' marital quality. For these analyses, we omit children whose parents divorced prior to 1980 and were living in stepfamilies at the time of the first parental interview.

Controlling for parents' marital quality in 1980 does not have a dramatic impact on the associations between divorce between 1980 and 1992 and parent-child relationships in 1992. For example, including the four measures of parents' marital quality reduces the association between divorce and sons' affection for mothers by about one-fourth. A similar reduction occurs in the association between divorce and daughters' affection for fathers. However, the coefficients for divorce and affection for parents are still significant with all measures of predivorce parents' marital quality in the equations. Furthermore, the associations between divorce and daughters' contact with fathers, father-child consensus, living with mothers, living with fathers, and asking parents for help are virtually unchanged when we add controls for predivorce marital quality.

Typical results are presented in Figure 3.6. This figure shows simplified path models involving parents' marital happiness in 1980, parental divorce between 1980 and 1992, and children's affection for mothers and fathers in 1992. For sons, parents' marital happiness increases affection for fathers, but divorce is not associated with further declines in affection. In contrast, parental divorce and marital happiness have independent effects on sons' affection for mothers. In other words, parents' marital happiness appears to have a direct effect on sons' affection for mothers as well as an indirect effect through divorce. For daughters, both marital happiness and divorce appear to have independent effects on affection for fathers, whereas only parents' marital happiness is associated (weakly) with mother-child affection. Similar results occur if we use divorce proneness, rather than marital happiness, in these models.

What about the marital disruptions that occurred prior to 1980, when children were younger at the time of marital disruption and were living in stepfamilies in 1980? Results for this variable are similar to those just described, that is, divorce (and remarriage) is associated with less affection for parents, less consensus with parents, a lower likelihood of living with fathers, greater distances between fathers and children, and more days since the last contact with fathers. (See the first column in Table 3.7.) As with divorces between 1980 and 1992, those prior to 1980 had stronger and broader consequence for relations with fathers than with mothers. However, these early divorces do not suggest stronger effects on opposite-sex parent-child dyads. It may be that when marital disruption occurs earlier in life, relations with both parents are weakened. But by the time children are

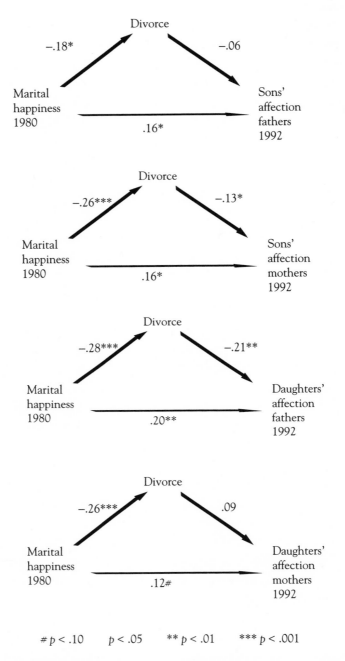

Figure 3.6   Path models relating parents' marital happiness in 1980, divorce between
1980 and 1992, and offspring's affection for parents in 1992

adolescents, they identify closely enough with the same-gender parent that divorce does not substantially weaken that particular relationship.

Overall, our findings suggest that low marital quality *and* marital dissolution have negative consequences for children's relationships with parents in early adulthood. To further illustrate this conclusion, we show adjusted means for mother-child and father-child affection for three groups of families: those in which parents were happily married and did not divorce, those in which parents were unhappily married and did not divorce, and those in which parents divorced. To form the first two groups, we averaged parents' marital happiness across 1980, 1983, and 1988. The third group consists of offspring whose parents divorced either prior to *or* after 1980. These results appear in Figure 3.7.

Figure 3.7 shows that even though parents' marital unhappiness is associated with lowered affection for parents in intact families, both sons and daughters have the lowest levels of affection for parents in divorced families. In other words, relations with parents appear to suffer, on average, more

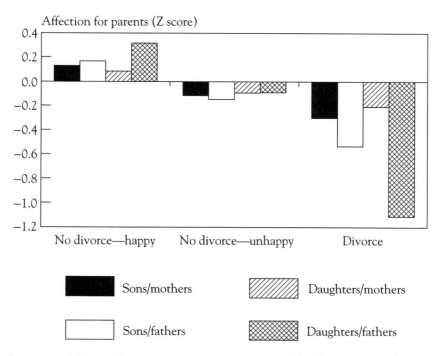

Figure 3.7 Affection for parents in 1992 in three types of families: continuously married and happy, continuously married and unhappy, and divorced

when parents divorce than when unhappily married parents stay together. Similar conclusions are reached if we use other dimensions of parents' marital quality rather than marital happiness. This finding suggests that parents who remain married in spite of marital problems do not put their relationships with children at risk as much as do parents who dissolve their marriages. The exception to this trend involves same-gender parent-child ties in divorces that occur when children are older.

Both the life course perspective and the mediation model suggest that the weak parent-child ties associated with parental discord and divorce are continuations of problematic relationships that originated when offspring were younger. Consistent with this assumption, controlling for maternal and paternal support during adolescence decreases the links between parents' marital quality/divorce and current affection for parents by more than one half, generally to nonsignificant levels. This finding is consistent with the assumption that parental support during childhood mediates the impact of parental discord and divorce on offsprings' affection for parents in adulthood. However, parental control does not appear to play a mediating role.

Although marital dissolution appears to have pervasive consequences for children, it is *not* related to offspring's reports of giving help to or receiving help from parents. Figure 3.8 demonstrates why this is the case. For each form of help, the first column in the figure shows the percentage of offspring from continuously intact families who received assistance; the second column shows the corresponding percentage of offspring from divorced families who received assistance. The second column is divided into three groups: those who received help from fathers only, those who received help from mothers only, and those who received help from both parents. For example, consider help with transportation. Among offspring from intact families, 44% received help from their parents during the previous month. Correspondingly, among offspring from divorced families, 25% received help from their mothers only, 6% received help from their fathers only, and 8% received help from both parents. The percentages for the divorce group add to 39, a figure not appreciably different from the figure for the intact group.

The point here is that divorce creates two households (rather than one) from which children can receive assistance. Once we combine those who receive help from mothers *or* fathers, the result is a net level of assistance comparable to that received by children from intact families. Note, however, that mothers are contributing the majority of assistance following divorce. Relatively few offspring receive any type of help from divorced fathers

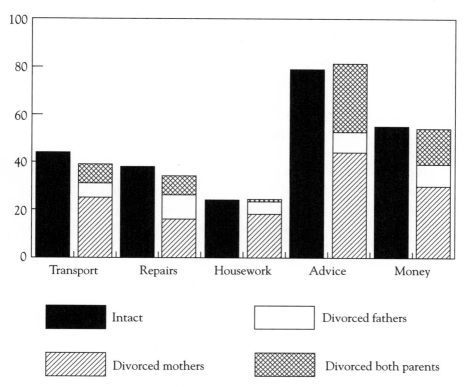

Figure 3.8 Percentage of offspring receiving various forms of assistance from parents by parental divorce

only. Nevertheless, none of the differences between those from intact and disrupted families in Figure 3.8 are significant. The results for help given are very similar to those shown in Figure 3.8.

Dimensions of Divorce. Before concluding, we also examine several dimensions of the divorce experience that might affect later parent-child relationships. Among the offspring who experienced a parental divorce, age at the time of disruption is one of the strongest predictors of relationships with fathers in adulthood. Age at divorce is positively associated with affection for fathers, consensus with fathers, living a shorter distance from fathers, and seeing fathers more recently. When divorce occurs early in children's lives, it is probably difficult for children to form strong bonds with nonresident fathers. In contrast, divorces at later ages, after children have had time to establish bonds with fathers, do not appear to be as problematic.

This interpretation is consistent with several previous studies of children (Furstenberg and Nord, 1985; Seltzer, 1991) and adults from divorced families (Zill, Morrison, and Coiro, 1993).

Mother custody is associated with less affection for fathers, greater distances between children and fathers, and longer periods of time since father contact. These findings are consistent with Aquilino (1994) and Amato and Booth (1991a), who found that relations between adult children of divorce and fathers were mainly problematic when mothers had custody.

We also had access to a four-item scale that measures offspring's reports of conflict between divorced parents over custody, visitation, child support payments, and the way that parents raised the child. High levels of conflict following divorce are related to less affection for fathers, less recent father contact, and a lower likelihood of living with fathers. These results are consistent with studies showing that conflict between parents following divorce is as problematic for parent-child relationships as is conflict prior to divorce (Johnston, 1994).

A few prior studies suggest that parental remarriage has implications for young adults' ties with parents. Aquilino (1994) found that remarriage decreased offspring's contact with custodial parents, regardless of the custodial parents' gender. In contrast, Zill, Morrison, and Coiro (1993) found that the remarriage of custodial parents (usually mothers) decreased contact with fathers in later life, but not with mothers. In the present study, the remarriage of mothers is not related to affection for or contact with either parent. However, maternal remarriage is related to children's giving less assistance to and receiving more assistance from their mothers' households. Single mothers are often resource-poor. Consequently, they may not be in a position to offer assistance to offspring. Indeed, their neediness may reverse the usual flow of assistance from children to mothers. Remarriage makes mothers better able to provide assistance to their children and lessens their need for help from their children. The notion that single mothers are resource-poor and receive more assistance than married mothers is congruent with the previous work of Rossi and Rossi (1990) and White (1992). Consistent with most other studies, remarriage among fathers is not related to later parent-child relationships in our data.

SUMMARY

Previous cross-sectional research suggests that interparental conflict when children are growing up negatively affects the quality of interaction between parents and children in later life (Amato and Booth, 1991a; Cooney, 1994; Rossi and Rossi, 1990, 346–348). These findings are congruent with the life course assumption that early family problems have long-term negative consequences for relationship trajectories. However, no previous study has been able to address this issue using parents' reports of marital quality when children are growing up and children's reports of parent-child relations in adulthood. Our study clearly shows that poor marital quality in 1980, when children were living at home with parents, is associated with problematic parent-child relationships twelve years later. Contrary to a number of studies of children and adolescents (Amato, 1986; Belsky, Youngblade, Rovine, and Volling, 1991; Brody and Pillegrini, 1986; Harris and Morgan, 1991; Peterson and Zill, 1986), we find that interparental discord affects children's relationships with mothers as well as with fathers, although we also find that these links are somewhat stronger for fathers than mothers. This difference in results may be due to several features of our study, including its focus on young adults, its longitudinal design, and the availability of data from both parents and children.

Consistent with a number of prior investigations, we find that parental divorce is associated with lower affection between children and parents (Aquilino, 1994; Cooney, 1994; Rossi and Rossi, 1990; Zill, Morrison, and Coiro, 1993); less coresidence with parents (Aquilino, 1990, 1991; Cooney, 1994; Goldscheider and Goldscheider, 1989, 1993); and less frequent contact with parents (Aquilino, 1994; Amato and Booth, 1991a; Lye, Klepinger, Hyle, and Nelson, 1995). Furthermore, as shown in several previous studies, we find that the consequences of marital dissolution tend to be stronger for fathers than mothers. The exception to this rule occurs in late divorces when children are adolescents or in early adulthood; in these cases, the mother-son relationship appears to suffer more than the father-son relationship.

Contrary to some previous studies, our study does not find that marital disruption is related to the frequency of help exchanged between parents and children (Aquilino, 1994; Cooney and Uhlenberg, 1990; Umberson, 1992; White, 1992), although it appears to decrease children's willingness to ask parents for assistance. Our failure to find that divorce lowers intergenerational assistance may be because previous studies did not take into account the fact that children of divorce have two households, rather than one, with which to exchange aid.

Overall, we see that low marital quality *and* divorce are problematic for children's later relationships with parents. These findings are broadly consistent with the life course perspective—with its emphasis on linked lives over time—and with the mediation model—with its emphasis on the role of early parent-child interaction in mediating the effects of family-of-origin characteristics on offspring in adulthood. Furthermore, as the life course perspective suggests, the consequences of divorce appear to vary with children's age at the time of marital dissolution, as well as with a variety of postdivorce circumstances. For example, loss of affection for fathers is greatest if divorces occur when children are young, when mothers have custody, and when a good deal of conflict occurs between parents following the divorce.

Conclusions

Young adulthood is a particularly important time for children and their parents, since the relationships they form during these years are likely to color their interactions throughout the rest of the life course. What are the implications of family-of-origin characteristics, and changes in these characteristics over time, for the bonds between young adult offspring and their parents?

Our study suggests that parental income, declines in income, paternal unemployment, and spells of welfare use have relatively few long-term consequences for children's relations with parents. This conclusion seems to contradict studies showing that economic hardship has a negative impact on parent-child relationships. However, most prior studies focused on young children or adolescents still living at home. Our results suggest that even if economic hardship strains family relationships when children are growing up, these tensions are largely ameliorated by the time that offspring reach adulthood. Of course, it may be only when families experience *extremes* of economic hardship that long-term ties are eroded. But even if this latter explanation is correct, our study still suggests that in the broad majority of families, periods of economic deprivation are not as problematic as some have argued. Our results are not completely sanguine, though, because we find that when parents experience declines in income or periods of unemployment, children receive less assistance from parents and are less inclined to ask parents for help. We conclude that this trend has more to do with parents' financial constraints, however, than with changes in affection.

The gender nontraditionalism of the family also appears to have few negative consequences for later parent-child relationships. Mothers' long hours of employment predict poor father-child relationships. But children have relatively strong ties with fathers when mothers are employed part-time (rather than not at all) and when fathers take on a substantial share of child care. Furthermore, when mothers increase their hours of employment over time, the flow of assistance from parents to offspring is greater. Overall, however, children's long-term bonds to parents appear to depend little on whether parents are traditional or nontraditional.

In contrast to the modest, infrequent, and sometimes contradictory results for parents' economic resources and gender nontraditionalism, we find evidence of consistent and moderately strong negative effects of parents' marital quality and divorce. Furthermore, low marital quality and divorce appear to have independent consequences: an unhappy marriage weakens parent-child ties, and divorce weakens them even further. Ties between older daughters and mothers appear to be modestly affected, but ties between older daughters and fathers appear to be especially vulnerable.

One of the goals of the life course perspective is to place current findings in a historical context. If we extrapolate our data across the last three decades, then our results suggest that the major changes that constitute the focus of our book—declines in economic resources, changes in gender relations, and increases in marital discord and divorce—have resulted in a net *decrease* in ties of affection, contact, and support between the generations. In particular, our data suggest the following scenario. Economic decline in recent years has lowered many parents' ability to provide assistance to adult children. Men's increased involvement in child care over this period has helped to strengthen their bonds with children, but change in this direction has been slow. Indeed, the reluctance of many men to share household labor equitably, combined with increases in women's hours of employment, has generated conflict and instability within many marriages. Moreover, increases in interparental conflict and divorce have had a negative and long-lasting impact on parent-child relationships. It is true that most children still feel a high level of affection for their parents and maintain frequent contact with them. Nevertheless, the combined impact of these trends—especially the increase in marital discord and divorce—may well represent a general weakening in the bonds of affection and assistance between the generations over the last several decades.

CHAPTER FOUR

Intimate

Relationships

Establishing satisfying long-term intimate relationships is one of the main challenges of early adulthood. Emotionally close and supportive relationships are critical because they contribute to people's sense of well-being and mental health. In the United States, as well as in a variety of other societies, married individuals report greater happiness, exhibit fewer signs of depression and anxiety, engage in less risk-taking behavior, and live longer than do single individuals (Gove, Hughes, and Style, 1983; Lillard and Waite, 1995; Mastekaasa, 1994; Ross, 1995; Waite, 1995). Marriage is advantageous because people provide emotional support to their spouses and discourage their spouses from engaging in risky behavior. Marriage also provides economic benefits to men as well as to women; compared with single people, married people have higher household incomes and benefit from economies of scale (Lillard and Waite, 1995; Ross, 1991, 1995). Although people with a high level of psychological and economic well-being are more likely to be selected into marriage, research strongly suggests that marriage *causes* many of these benefits (Waite, 1995).

Of course, marriage is not always a blessing. Bernard (1982) argued that marriage tends to benefit women's mental health more than men's; this perception is related to the fact that wives report more problems in their marriages and receive less emotional support from their spouses than do husbands (Thompson and Walker, 1991). Nevertheless, regardless of gender, people who are *happily* married are better off, as a group, than people who are unmarried (Ross, 1995; Gove, Hughes, and Style, 1983). Following the same logic, people who are happily "partnered" (either through cohabitation or a steady dating relationship) are better off, as a group, than those who lack a steady, intimate relationship (Ross, 1995).

The formation of satisfying, long-term relationships is also important because it provides the social and economic context for raising children. Although single individuals can rear children successfully, a household with two adults offers many advantages as a setting for children's socialization and development (Amato, 1995b). Furthermore, parents who are happily married exhibit more effective child-rearing skills. As the mediation model indicates, chronic, unresolved interparental discord places children at risk, largely because it disrupts parent-child relationships (Davies and Cummings, 1994; Emery, 1982, 1988; Grych and Fincham, 1990).

Because of recent historical changes, the process of establishing and maintaining intimate relationships is very different for the offspring in our sample than it was for their parents. The postponement of marriage, the increase in cohabitation (both premarital and postmarital), and the rise in divorce and remarriage have multiplied the number of people with whom adults form emotionally and sexually intimate relationships over a lifetime. One can interpret these changes either as declines in people's ability or willingness to form and maintain long-term intimate relationships, or as increases in people's freedom to try out new relationships, leave unsatisfying unions, and seek out better ones. Regardless of how one interprets these changes, it is not clear whether they have affected people's sense of well-being negatively or positively. It *is* clear, however, that the process through which people form intimate relationships has become more complex, and the outcomes of these relationships less certain, than in previous decades.

A life course perspective suggests that children carry forward into their adult lives a set of attitudes, social skills, and interpersonal orientations learned in the family of origin, and that these traits have implications for the formation and maintenance of intimate ties. However, although this assumption seems reasonable, little is known about how the family of origin influences young adults' intimate relationships. In this chapter, we investigate several aspects of dating experiences, including how frequent the dating is and whether offspring have a steady dating partner. We also examine the occurrence and timing of cohabitation and marriage. To see how these intimate bonds are faring, we consider the quality of dating, cohabiting, and marital relationships, as well as the dissolution of these unions. Finally, following the mediation model, we assess the extent to which parental support and control during adolescence account for associations between family-of-origin characteristics and offspring's relationship outcomes.

Measuring Intimate Relationships

DATING

In 1992, 275 offspring were neither married nor cohabiting. These individuals responded to a series of items dealing with dating. All items were worded so as not to exclude gay and lesbian relationships, although we did not specifically inquire about people's sexual orientation. About half of the unmarried, noncohabiting offspring were dating someone steadily, and the median length of these relationships was eleven months. Those with a steady dating partner responded to an additional seven questions dealing with relationship happiness. These items are similar to those on the parents' marital happiness scale described in Chapter 2. For example, people reported how happy they are with their friend as someone to do things with, with the love and affection received from their friend, and with their friend's faithfulness. When added together, these items form a scale of *dating happiness*. (See Table 4.1 in the Appendix for more details on all items and scales described in this chapter.)

Two questions dealt with the frequency of dating among the 144 offspring who did not have a steady dating partner. The first asked about the number of dates that people had had in the last month. The mean number of dates was about three, although 30% had no dates and 25% had five dates or more. The second question dealt with the number of people offspring dated in the previous year. Responses revealed considerable variability: the mean was about four people, but 11% had not dated anyone, and 10% had dated ten people or more. Because these two variables are positively skewed, we used log transformations to normalize the distributions.

Two additional questions dealt with people's evaluations of their dating situations. The first asked whether they would like to be dating more (or less) often. Of all nonmarried and noncohabiting offspring, 62% are satisfied, 33% want to date more often, and 5% want to date less often. Not surprisingly, offspring are more likely to be satisfied if they are dating someone steadily. Because so few young adults want to date less often, we simplified this variable into two categories: those who are satisfied versus those who are not. Of those with a steady dating partner, 83% are satisfied, compared with 41% of those without a steady dating partner. The other question dealt with whether offspring have difficulty dating people with whom they feel they could develop a serious relationship. Twenty-one percent of offspring report difficulty, including 11% of those currently in a steady relationship and 31% of those not in a relationship.

COHABITATION AND MARRIAGE

We used standard questions to determine offspring marital history. Additional questions dealt with cohabitation, including unions that may have ended either in marriage or dissolution. The questions about cohabitation were worded so as not to exclude relationships between lesbians or gays, but we are not able to identify which unions are nonheterosexual. All of these questions were part of the telephone interview in 1992 and were repeated in the 1995 follow-up survey.

In 1992, 32 offspring (7%) were cohabiting and another 119 (25%) had cohabited prior to the interview. By 1995, an additional 47 had entered a cohabiting relationship. After excluding 9 older offspring who had cohabited prior to 1980 (the year of our first parental interview), 189 people remained for whom we had data on the timing of cohabitation. In 1992, 164 (35%) of offspring were currently married, and another 27 (6%) were divorced or separated. By 1995, an additional 64 had married and 28 had divorced. After excluding 12 older offspring who had married prior to 1980, we had data on the timing of 243 marriages. Of those offspring who were ever-married, 55 had divorced by 1994. We excluded six cases of divorce that occurred prior to 1980; this left useable data on 49 cases. Similarly, of those offspring who cohabited after 1980, 59 ended their relationships without marrying by 1994. These data allow us to examine family factors that predict the formation as well as the dissolution of both marital and cohabiting relationships.

RELATIONSHIP QUALITY

We used five scales to measure offspring's relationship quality: *happiness, interaction, conflict, problems,* and *instability.* The happiness, interaction, and conflict scales are based on the ones we used to assess parents' marital quality (see Chapter 2). When interviewing married offspring, we referred to "your marriage" and "your spouse" in the questions for each scale. When interviewing cohabiting couples, we reworded the questions to refer to "your relationship" and "your partner." The relationship instability scale is the equivalent of the parents' divorce proneness scale. In applying this scale to offspring, we restricted scale content to items that are relevant to marital as well as cohabiting relationships. This situation also required a slight re-wording of items for cohabiting offspring. For example, we asked married offspring about "getting a divorce" and cohabiting offspring about "breaking up." The relationship problems scale involves offspring's reports of fourteen different problems in their relationship (someone gets angry easily, is jeal-ous, is moody, isn't home enough, and so on), and the sum of the "yes" responses serves as the measure of relationship problems.

Because these five scales have the same number of items, the same scoring conventions, the same ranges, and nearly identical wording, we are able to compare the scores of both married and cohabiting offspring. To facilitate interpretation, we pooled the scores of both groups and set the distributions to have means of 0 and standard deviations of 1.

Married and cohabiting offspring do not differ in relationship happiness, interaction, or conflict. However, relationship problems and instability are dramatically higher among cohabiting than married individuals. (See Table 4.2 in the Appendix.) These differences represent nearly two-thirds and over three-fourths of a standard deviation, respectively, which are large ef-fect sizes. Bumpass, Sweet, and Cherlin (1991) noted that 40% of cohab-iting unions break up within a year or two. They also found that cohabitors are twice as likely as married individuals to report that their relationships are in trouble. Similarly, Nock (1995) reported that cohabiting couples express less commitment and less happiness with their relationships than do comparable married couples. The relatively high levels of relationship problems and instability among cohabiting couples in our study, therefore, are consistent with previous research.

To assess the utility of the mediation model, we checked to see whether offspring's recollections of parental support and control during the teenage years are associated with our measures of offspring's intimate relationships. Both maternal support and paternal support are positively associated with dating happiness. Beyond this, however, few significant associations appear. Consequently, with the exception of dating happiness, it is unlikely that parental support and control mediate any of the associations between family-of-origin variables and aspects of offspring's intimate relationships. For this reason, we dispense with the mediation model for the remainder of this chapter.

Parents' Socioeconomic Resources and Offspring's Intimate Relationships

PREVIOUS STUDIES

Prior research suggests that parents' socioeconomic resources are related to the likelihood that offspring cohabit. Cohabitation has always been more common in lower than higher socioeconomic groups (Spanier, 1991). Although cohabitation became more popular among the college-educated in the United States during the 1970s, it increased among all social strata to about the same degree, so the inverse association between social class and cohabitation still persists (Bumpass, Sweet, and Cherlin, 1991). Part of the reason for this inverse association may be that high-resource parents discourage their children from cohabiting. Cohabitation—although more accepted now than in the past—is less respectable than marriage, and high-status parents have more to lose than low-status parents if their children engage in controversial (and disreputable) behavior. Consequently, high-resource parents not only may disapprove of cohabitation but also may pressure cohabitating offspring either to marry or to break up.

Early marriage is also less common when parents have high levels of education and income (Avery, Goldscheider, and Speare, 1992; Goldscheider and Goldscheider, 1993; Goldscheider and Waite, 1991; Keith and Finlay, 1988; Thornton, 1991). Well-educated parents tend to have less traditional attitudes about family life than do poorly educated parents. Consequently, instead of encouraging their children to marry early and form families of their own, high-resource parents are likely to encourage their children (daughters as well as sons) to obtain educations and plan for careers. And the role models provided by mothers in professional occupations may reduce daughters' desire for early marriage and increase their labor force attachment and preference for nontraditional family roles.

Few studies deal with the consequences of parents' socioeconomic resources for the *quality* of children's intimate relationships. One study shows that low parental education and parents' use of welfare increase the likelihood that daughters' marriages end in divorce (Bumpass, Martin, and Sweet, 1991). Similarly, a clinical study shows that individuals with marital problems are more likely than matched controls to report economic hardship in their families of origin (Overall, Henry, and Woodward, 1974). In contrast, Goldscheider and Waite (1991, chap. 5) found that high parental education increases the likelihood that children's marriages end in divorce. In spite of these contradictory findings, good reasons exist for assuming that parents' socioeconomic resources (including both education and income) *positively* affect the quality and stability of children's marital relationships.

First, parents' socioeconomic resources may improve children's marriages because they facilitate children's socioeconomic attainment. People with high levels of education and income report more marital happiness and less marital conflict than do people with low levels of education and income (Conger et al., 1990; Lewis and Spanier, 1979; Voydanoff, 1991). Similarly, parental income is negatively associated with the likelihood of divorce (Hernandez, 1993; White, 1991). Education promotes more effective communication among couples, thus helping them to resolve differences. In contrast, the stress generated by economic hardship increases disagreements over finances, makes spouses tense and irritable, and decreases expressions of emotional support. This reasoning suggests that parents' socioeconomic resources may improve the quality of children's marriages by increasing children's educational attainment and their ability to earn income. Consistent with this notion, Bumpass, Martin, and Sweet (1991) found that daughters' educational attainment mediates some of the impact of maternal education on daughters' likelihood of divorce.

A second, and related, explanation refers to age at marriage. Because people from economically disadvantaged families are unlikely to pursue higher education, they tend to marry at relatively young ages. Early marriage is one of the best predictors of marital problems and divorce (Bumpass, Martin, and Sweet, 1991; Keith and Finlay, 1988; Martin and Bumpass, 1989; South, 1995). People who marry at young ages have less time to search for an appropriate partner, are often unprepared to assume marital roles, have fewer economic resources to draw on, may experience disapproval from members of their social networks (Booth and Edwards, 1985), and exhibit more symptoms of psychological distress (Forthofer et al., 1996). Consistent with this interpretation, Bumpass, Martin, and Sweet (1991) found that daughters' age at marriage accounted for some of the impact of maternal education and family-of-origin welfare use on daughters' risk of divorce.

Third, parents' socioeconomic resources may affect children through their impact on the parents' marital relationship. High-resource parents tend to have more successful marriages than do low-resource parents. And, as we discuss next, evidence suggests that marital quality is often transmitted across generations.

Finally, as we show in Chapter 3, high-income parents are better able to assist their adult children than are low-income parents with gifts or loans of money. The assistance provided by relatively affluent parents may ease economic strain among offspring, especially in the early years of marriage, which might otherwise cause strains in the marital relationship.

HYPOTHESES

Consistent with a life course perspective, our literature review suggests several ways in which family-of-origin characteristics affect the relationship trajectories of offspring. For example, parents' socioeconomic resources appear to "slow down" children's formation of intimate relationships. For this reason, we hypothesize that parental education and income are negatively related to cohabitation and positively related to age at marriage. We also hypothesize that once children are married, parents' socioeconomic resources are positively related to offspring's marital quality. In addition, we assume that offspring's education and income, offsprings' age at marriage, parents' marital quality, and parental assistance to married children mediate these associations.

Gaps in the literature make it difficult to predict how parents' socioeconomic resources are associated with offspring's dating relationships; consequently, our examination of this issue is exploratory. It is also unclear how parental resources might affect relationship quality among cohabiting couples. High parental education and income might benefit offspring's cohabiting relationships for many of the same reasons that they benefit offspring's marital relationships. On the other hand, cohabiting individuals report being less close to their parents than do married individuals (Nock, 1995); and high status parents may disapprove of their children's cohabitation, thus depriving their children of psychological and economic support. These considerations suggest that parental resources are negatively associated with offspring's cohabitation quality. We test these contradictory predictions in our analyses.

RESULTS

Dating. Our data show little evidence that parental education affects young adults' dating experiences. Parental education is not related to having a steady partner, happiness with current dating partner, the number of dates in the last month, the number of dating partners in the previous year, satisfaction with the frequency of dating, or difficulty in meeting people with whom one could have a serious relationship. Similarly, neither fathers' nor mothers' incomes in 1980 are related to any aspect of dating among offspring in 1992.

Transitions to Cohabitation and Marriage. To estimate the impact of parental education (and other family-of-origin characteristics) on the likelihood of cohabiting or marrying, we relied on event history methods. We estimated our models by applying logistic regression analysis to person-year data files, using the same control variables as in other analysis. Contrary to our expectations, these analyses reveal that parental education in 1980 is unrelated to whether offspring enter cohabiting relationships between 1980 and 1995. However, as hypothesized, mothers' and fathers' educations in 1980 are negatively related to the odds of marrying between 1980 and 1995. Of the two parental education variables, only mothers' education is statistically significant when both are in the equation simultaneously. Our model indicates that each year of mothers' education decreases the odds of marrying by 9%, on average. The lack of a gender by parental education interaction indicates that the association between parental education and marriage among offspring is similar for both sons and daughters. (See Table 4.3 in the Appendix for details.)

When mothers have sixteen or more years of education, only 5% of their children are married by age 20, whereas when mothers have twelve or fewer years of education, 15% of their children are married by age twenty. The association between maternal education and marriage among offspring also persists when children are older. For the same two groups of mothers, 40% and 59% of their children are married by age 26, respectively. Figure 4.1 shows the implications of maternal education for offspring's marriages, based on simple percentages. As the figure reveals, although daughters are more likely than sons to marry at early ages, the association between mothers' age and marriage is similar for offspring of both genders.

Our literature review suggests that well-educated parents foster their children's educational and career plans, thus leading their children to delay marriage. We are able to test this idea by adding offspring's educational and occupational attainment to our models. Consistent with this notion, education and occupational status explain about one-fourth of the estimated impact of mothers' education on marriage among offspring, and the remaining coefficient is only marginally statistically significant.

In addition, fathers' income in 1980 is marginally related to offspring

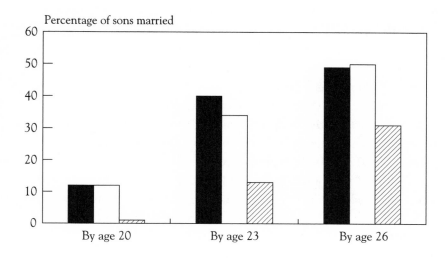

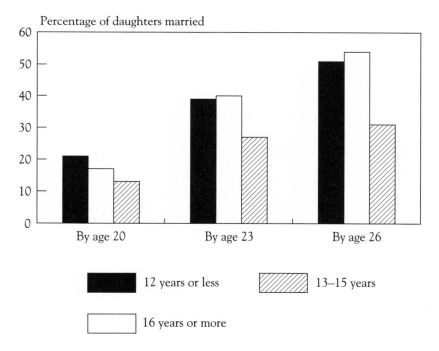

Figure 4.1 Percentage of sons and daughters married by age 20, age 23, and age 26 by mothers' years of education

marrying between 1980 and 1995, with each $1,000 of income decreasing the odds of marriage by 1%. This result is consistent with the finding, noted before, that parental education is associated with delayed marriage among offspring. Adding offspring's educational and occupational attainment to the models wipes out the estimated effect of paternal income on marriage among offspring, suggesting that offspring's attainment is a mediating factor.

Mothers' income yields a rather different finding. With parental education controlled, mothers' (but not fathers') income in 1980 is positively associated with the likelihood that children enter cohabiting relationships between 1980 and 1995. Each $1,000 increase in mothers' income raises the likelihood that offspring cohabit by 2%, a finding that is true for both sons and daughters. This runs contrary to our expectation that parents' socioeconomic status decreases the likelihood that children cohabit. The fact that fathers' income is not related to cohabitation, however, suggests the possibility that mothers' income is serving as a measure of gender non-traditionalism rather than socioeconomic status. As we argue later, nontraditional parents are more accepting of cohabitation among their children than are traditional parents. To assess this idea, we add three other variables reflecting parents' gender nontraditionalism to the model: the fathers' share of housework, the fathers' share of child care, and the parents' gender role attitudes. This process reduces the estimated effect of mothers' income by one-fourth, and the resulting coefficient is no longer statistically significant. It appears, therefore, that children of high-earning mothers are more likely than other children to cohabit at least partly because their parents are less traditional and, presumably, more accepting of cohabitation.

Marital and Cohabitation Quality.   Our data reveal that the consequences of parental education for relationship quality differ considerably for married and cohabiting offspring. This result is reflected in interactions between parental education and offspring's marriage/cohabitation for two relationship outcomes: relationship happiness and instability. For cohabitating offspring, as parents' education increases, offspring report *less* happiness with their relationships and greater instability. In contrast, for married offspring, as parents' education increases, offspring report *more* happiness with their relationships and less instability. Parents' education is also positively associated with interaction among married offspring but not among cohabiting offspring. The results are nearly identical if we use mothers' or fathers' education, and the results do not vary with offspring's gender. (See Table 4.4 in the Appendix for the full equations.)

Figure 4.2 shows the associations between parental education and offspring's relationship happiness and instability. Because the results for mothers' and fathers' educations are nearly identical, we combine them into a single measure of parental education by taking the mean of the two. In the figure, we define a high level of education as 13.5 years of education or more, which is approximately the median for the sample. For married offspring, the difference between those whose parents have high and low levels of education is slightly more than one-fourth of a standard deviation for happiness, indicating a moderate effect size. For cohabiting offspring, the difference between those whose parents have high and low levels of education is about four-tenths of a standard deviation for happiness, also indicating a moderate effect size—but in the opposite direction. Parental education also appears to lower the level of instability among married offspring. The difference is about one-fifth of a standard deviation, indicating

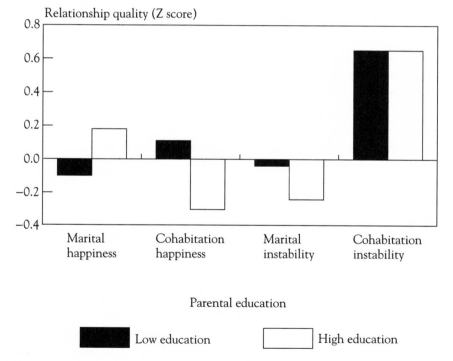

Figure 4.2   Quality of offspring's intimate relationships in 1992 by parental education

a weak but nontrivial effect size. However, parental education appears to have little impact on instability among cohabiting offspring.

The lower happiness of offspring with well-educated parents may reflect, as just suggested, parental disapproval of the relationship, given that cohabitation is less common (and presumably less socially acceptable) among high status groups. However, relationship instability is high for cohabiting couples, regardless of parental education. It appears that cohabiting relationships are so generally unstable that parental education makes little difference.

Although we have too few cases to attempt further analysis of relationship quality with the cohabiting group, it is possible to examine the married group in more detail. As we noted before, several explanations are possible for the link between parental education and offspring's marital quality. When we add offspring's educational attainment and household income (offspring's income plus spouses' income) to our equations, the associations between parental education and marital outcomes decline by about one-third for happiness and interaction and by about one-fourth for instability. The resulting coefficients for happiness and interaction are marginally significant, and the coefficient for instability is no longer significant. This finding suggests that parental education contributes positively to offspring's marital quality at least partly through its impact on offspring's socioeconomic attainment. Several other variables may mediate the association between parental education and offspring's marital quality, such as offspring's age at marriage, parents' marital quality in 1980, and parents' financial assistance to children. But adding these variables to our statistical models decreases the associations between parental education and offspring's outcomes by only trivial amounts.

In relation to financial resources, mothers' income in 1980 is not related to offspring's marital or cohabitation quality. However, fathers' income in 1980 interacts with children's marital status in predicting several relationship outcomes. With parental education controlled, as fathers' income increases, married offspring report more happiness, less conflict, and a smaller number of problems. In contrast, as fathers' income increases, cohabiting offspring report less happiness, more conflict, and a larger number of problems. These results are similar to those reported earlier for parental education.

We assume that the explanation for the link between fathers' income and offspring's marital quality is similar to the one advanced before for parental education. That is, fathers' income facilitates children's socioeconomic attainment, and high socioeconomic attainment contributes in a positive way to children's marital quality. Among married offspring, when we control for offspring's education and household income, the coefficients for happiness and conflict decline by about one-fifth, whereas the coefficient for marital problems declines by over one-third. The former two coefficients remain marginally significant, whereas the latter coefficient is no longer significant. Other variables (age at marriage, parents' marital quality, and parental assistance to children) mediate virtually none of the effect. So our conclusion, once again, is that parents' socioeconomic resources contribute in a positive way to children's marital quality partly through their impact on children's socioeconomic attainment.

Marital and Cohabitation Dissolution.   Among offspring who cohabited between 1980 and 1992, parental education does not predict which couples break up and which stay together or get married. However, paternal (but not maternal) education is negatively related to divorce among offspring who married after 1980, with each year of education decreasing the odds of divorce by 15%. This condition holds for both sons and daughters. (See Table 4.3 in the Appendix.) This finding is consistent with studies showing that marital problems and divorce rates are lower among children from high-resource families (Bumpass, Martin, and Sweet, 1991; Overall, Henry, and Woodward, 1974). It is also consistent with the finding that parental education is positively associated with offspring's marital quality. Parental income, however, is not related to the dissolution of marital or cohabiting relationships among offspring.

Economic Change between 1980 and 1988.   Because changes in parents' socioeconomic resources are highly correlated with parental divorce, we limit our analyses to families in which parents remained married between 1980 and 1988. We see no evidence that changes in parents' economic resources between 1980 and 1988 affect children's dating experiences in 1992. Furthermore, we find no evidence that shifts in parents' economic resources during this time affect children's tendency to cohabit or marry between 1988 and 1995.

   In contrast, shifts in parents' economic resources between 1980 and 1988 are related to several aspects of offspring's marital quality. We limit this analysis to ninety-four offspring who first married between 1988 and 1992;

because of the small number of cohabiting offspring, we do not consider them in this analysis. Increases in parents' household income between 1980 and 1988 are related positively to offspring's marital happiness in 1992. In addition, when parents report that their financial situation consistently improved between 1980 and 1988, offspring have less marital conflict and marginally fewer marital problems. Furthermore, a period of paternal unemployment between 1980 and 1988 is associated with less marital happiness and marginally more marital problems among offspring. Finally, when parents have a spell of welfare use between 1980 and 1988, offspring report more marital problems.

These results are consistent with our earlier finding that parental education and income are positively associated with offspring's marital quality. But in contrast to our earlier findings, offspring's education and earned income do not mediate the estimated effects of changes in parents' economic well-being between 1980 and 1988. Married children's receipt of assistance from parents—especially gifts and loans of money—accounts for about one-fifth of the association between parental income change and offspring's marital happiness, although the remaining coefficient is still significant.

SUMMARY

As the life course perspective suggests, family of origin resources have implications for offspring's relationship trajectories in young adulthood. Our study is consistent with prior literature in showing that children from high-resource families delay marriage relative to those in low-resource families (Avery, Goldscheider, and Speare, 1992; Goldscheider and Goldscheider, 1993; Thornton, 1991). However, unlike some previous studies (Keith and Finlay, 1988; Goldscheider and Waite, 1991), we see no evidence that parental education is more consequential for daughters than sons. Our data also suggest that offspring from high-resource families marry relatively late because they wait to complete their college educations and initiate their careers prior to marrying. Not only do children from high-resource families marry later, but also they have more satisfying marriages. This is the case not because they marry later but because they enter marriage with more education and higher income-earning potential. To round out the picture, married offspring are less likely to divorce if their fathers are well-educated, a finding that is consistent with Bumpass, Martin, and Sweet (1991) but which contradicts Goldscheider and Waite (1991). It stands to reason, though, that if parents' socioeconomic status increases the age at marriage and improves offspring's marital quality, parents' socioeconomic status should also decrease the probability that offspring's marriages end in divorce.

We also find that changes in parental resources over time—declines in income, paternal unemployment, and spells of welfare use—have implications for offspring's marriages. We are not able to account for most of this association, although it may be partly due to the fact that economic strain decreases parents' provision of financial assistance to their married offspring. Numerous studies have shown that declines into economic hardship are followed by decrements in parents' marital quality (e.g., Conger et al., 1990; Lewis and Spanier, 1979; Voydanoff, 1991). Our findings build on previous work by showing that declines in parents' economic fortunes also have consequences for the quality of their children's marriages. In this sense, the negative consequences of economic hardship persist into the next generation. Given that we are unable to determine the mechanism that underlies this association, further research on this topic is warranted.

Although parental education and income appear to improve the quality of children's marriages, they appear to have the opposite effect on the quality of children's cohabiting unions. Even though we are not able to assess this idea empirically, we suspect that parents who are highly educated and have high incomes disapprove of their children's cohabitation. This disapproval places pressure on the cohabiting couple, leading to tension in the relationship.

Finally, parents' socioeconomic resources do not appear to have implications for offspring's dating experiences. These findings suggest that the benefits of parental resources appear only later, when offspring are married. This outcome is what we would expect to find if parents' socioeconomic resources largely benefit children by facilitating their educational attainment, thus leading them to marry when they not only are more mature but also have more income-earning potential.

Parents' Gender Nontraditionalism and Offspring's Intimate Relationships

PREVIOUS STUDIES

We know of no studies that assess the long-term impact of parents' gender nontraditionalism on children's intimate relationships. However, as previously noted, children growing up with employed mothers have less stereotyped and more egalitarian beliefs about the roles of men and women than do children with nonemployed mothers (Hoffman, 1989; Kiecolt and Acock, 1988; Mischel and Fuhr, 1988; Richards and Duckett, 1991; Spitze, 1988). These same studies also suggest that maternal employment is associated with greater educational and occupational aspirations among daughters. Although we know little about the effects of growing up with fathers who are highly involved in family work or with parents who hold nontraditional attitudes, it seems likely that these experiences also make children's views about gender less traditional.

Career-oriented women are likely to postpone marriage until they have completed their educations (Goldscheider and Waite, 1991, chap. 5). For this reason, daughters who grow up in egalitarian, nontraditional families probably marry later than do those from traditional families. It is not clear, however, whether parents' nontraditionalism has an impact on the timing of sons' marriages. Parents with nontraditional gender arrangements and attitudes may be liberal about other issues, such as cohabitation. Axinn and Thornton (1993) demonstrated that when mothers hold liberal attitudes toward cohabitation, daughters are more likely to cohabit. It seems probable, therefore, that children with nontraditional parents adopt relatively unconventional attitudes, and for this reason, are more inclined to cohabit than are children with traditional parents.

Parents' gender nontraditionalism might have positive or negative implications for the quality and stability of offspring's relationships. These mixed predictions are based on three possible intervening mechanisms: offspring's age at marriage, offspring's gender attitudes, and offspring's educational and occupational attainment.

First, if parents' nontraditionalism increases children's (especially daughters') age at marriage, it is likely to improve the children's marital quality and chances of staying together. This is the case because early age at marriage predicts poor marital quality and divorce.

Second, daughters' liberal attitudes about gender (which may be at least partly acquired from parents) might have negative implications for their intimate relationships. Studies show that wives with nontraditional views tend to be less happy with their marriages than are wives with more traditional views (Amato and Booth, 1995; Greenstein, 1996; Lueptow, Guss, and Hyden, 1989; Vannoy-Hiller and Philliber, 1989). This situation happens because wives with egalitarian views expect more sharing of housework and child care than most husbands are willing to perform. On the other hand, husbands with nontraditional views, compared with husbands with traditional views, are more supportive of their wives' employment, do more housework and child care, and share decision-making more readily (Gerson, 1993; Vannoy-Hiller and Philliber, 1989). Husbands with egalitarian attitudes about gender relations also tend to be happier with their marriages (Amato and Booth, 1995). These considerations suggest that growing up with nontraditional parents might have negative implications for daughters' marital quality and positive implications for sons' marital quality. It is possible that similar processes apply in cohabiting relationships.

Third, daughters who are career-oriented may experience greater relationship instability than daughters who are content to play conventional family roles. This is the case because wives who are economically independent of husbands (or cohabiting partners) can more readily leave unsatisfying relationships. Although not all studies are in agreement, research shows that wives' full-time employment increases thoughts of divorce (Booth, Johnson, and White, 1984) and the likelihood of marital dissolution (Cherlin, 1992; White, 1991). This line of reasoning suggests that parents' gender nontraditionalism contributes to daughters' relationship instability by increasing their career attainment and financial independence.

HYPOTHESES

The general absence of previous work in this area makes it difficult to anticipate the life course consequences of parents' gender nontraditionalism. On the basis of a few prior studies, we hypothesize that growing up in nontraditional families increases age at marriage (especially for daughters) as well as the likelihood of entering cohabiting relationships. We also predict that parental nontraditionalism affects the marital quality and stability of sons and daughters, but these effects could be positive or negative. We have few guidelines as to how parents' gender nontraditionalism might affect offspring's dating relationships; consequently, our examination of the links between these two sets of variables is purely exploratory.

RESULTS

Dating. Maternal paid employment in 1980, paternal share of family work in 1980, and parents' gender role attitudes are not related in any systematic way to offspring's dating experiences in 1992. However, *changes* in parents' gender role traditionalism between 1980 and 1988 are related to several dimensions of dating. We see evidence for this finding in several indicators of nontraditionalism, although our summary index (which includes mothers' hours of employment, fathers' share of housework, and parents' gender role attitudes) best captures these results. Shifts in this index over time are related to children's reports of the number of people they dated during the previous year, difficulty in meeting people with whom they could have a serious relationship, and (marginally) being in a steady relationship at the time of the interview. (See Table 4.5 in the Appendix for the full equations.)

Figure 4.3 shows the associations between changes in parents' gender nontraditionalism and offspring's dating experiences. To construct the figure, we divided the change scores at natural cutting points to reflect parents who became less traditional, stayed about the same, or became more traditional between 1980 and 1988. These three groups correspond to 35%, 42%, and 24% of parents, respectively. The figure shows that offspring whose parents became more traditional between 1980 and 1988 are most likely to have dated four or more people during the previous year, are most

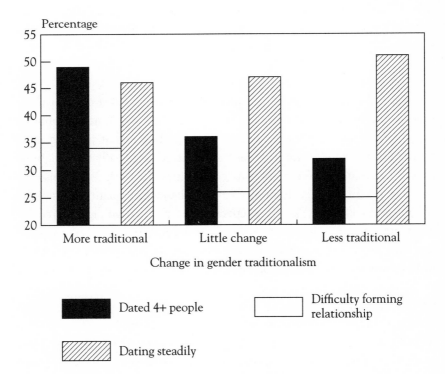

Figure 4.3   Offspring's dating relations in 1992 by changes in parents' gender
               nontraditionalism between 1980 and 1988

likely to claim that they have difficulty meeting people with whom they can form serious relationships, and are least likely to be in a steady relationship in 1992. In contrast, offspring whose parents became less traditional are least likely to have dated four or more people, are least likely to claim that they have difficulty meeting people with whom they can form serious relationships, and are most likely to be in a steady relationship in 1992. These results do not vary with offspring's gender or age.

The overall pattern for offspring whose parents became more traditional requires an explanation. Given that these young adults are more likely than others to report difficulty in finding people with whom they can form serious relationships, it makes sense that they would also report dating a large number of people in the last year and be less likely to have a steady partner at the time of the interview. The overall pattern suggests that offspring whose parents became more conventional in gender roles and beliefs during the 1980s are engaging in a comparatively more protracted, difficult search for intimate partners. In contrast, those whose parents became less conventional during the 1980s appear to be having an easier time finding intimate partners.

Offspring from traditional homes may have more problems establishing romantic relationships because young men and women, overall, are becoming less conventional about gender issues (Goldsheider and Waite, 1991; Thornton, 1989). Young adults from traditional families—assuming that they are influenced by their parents' behavior and attitudes—are probably attracted to partners who also hold traditional views. Consequently, these traditional young adults may have a difficult time finding compatible partners and may need to date a larger number of people before finding a suitable match. In contrast, offspring from nontraditional families may fare relatively well on the dating market because they encounter many like-minded others.

To assess this explanation, we employed a measure of offspring's attitudes toward gender roles in marriage, a scale identical to the one that parents completed. Offspring's nontraditional attitudes in 1992 are positively associated with scores on the parental nontraditionalism index in 1980, as well as shifts toward greater nontraditionalism between 1980 and 1988. This fact suggests that parents' behavior and attitudes do indeed influence children's attitudes. Furthermore, offspring with nontraditional attitudes are more likely to have steady dating partners and, if they have partners, are happier with these relationships than are offspring with traditional attitudes. Finally, adding offspring's attitudes to the equations in Table 4.5 accounts for, on average, about one-fifth of the association between changes in parental non-traditionalism and the dating outcomes (although the remaining coefficients are still significant). Overall, therefore, the evidence suggests that children's attitudes about gender explain at least part of the pattern depicted in Figure 4.3.

Transitions to Cohabitation and Marriage.   Mothers' employment in 1980 is not related to offspring's cohabitation between 1980 and 1995. However, fathers' share of child care (but not housework) in 1980 is positively related to offspring's cohabitation between 1980 and 1995, with each step on our 5-point scale increasing the odds by 23%. Combined with the finding reported earlier, that mothers' income is positively related to offspring's cohabitation, we see some evidence in support of our prediction that parents' gender nontraditionalism increases the chances that offspring cohabit either prior to, or as an alternative to, marriage. Contrary to our expectations, no aspect of parents' gender nontraditionalism in 1980 is associated with the probability of marriage between 1980 and 1995, either among sons or daughters.

Marital and Cohabitation Quality.   Our expectation that parents' gender nontraditionalism is related to the quality of children's intimate ties is not supported. Mothers' employment in 1980, fathers' share of family work in 1980, and parents' gender role attitudes in 1980 are not consistently related to dimensions of offspring's marital or cohabitation quality in 1992. Similarly, changes in these variables between 1980 and 1988 are not associated with the relationship quality.

Marital and Cohabitation Dissolution.   Although parents' gender nontraditionalism does not affect the quality of offspring's unions, we find some evidence that it affects the stability of offspring's unions. Offspring who initiated cohabiting relationships between 1980 and 1992 were more likely to end these relationships without marrying if parents were nontraditional in 1980. In particular, mothers' full-time employment increases the likelihood of relationship dissolution by 131% for both sons and daughters. Similarly, fathers' share of child care (among sons) and parents' nontraditional gender attitudes (among both sons and daughters) are positively associated with breaking up. Although we assumed that coming from a nontraditional family increases relationship instability primarily among daughters, the results suggest that this occurs among sons as well.

With regard to offspring's divorces, mothers' employment in 1980 is positively related to marital dissolution among daughters (but not among sons) who married between 1980 and 1995. When mothers were employed full-time (compared with those who were employed part-time or not in the labor force), the risk that daughters would see their own marriages end in divorce is 166% higher. This finding is consistent with the reasoning, outlined before, that daughters from nontraditional families have less stable marriages because (a) they have relatively high expectations for husbands, or (b) they are relatively well-educated and career-oriented, and hence, economically (and perhaps psychologically) independent of their husbands. In further analyses, we found no evidence that daughters' education or occupational attainment mediate this association, so the explanation based on attitudes and expectations appears to win by default. Unfortunately, the number of married daughters for whom we have data on gender attitudes (in 1992) prior to divorce (in 1995) is too small for meaningful analysis.

SUMMARY

Much of our investigation of parents' gender nontraditionalism and offspring's intimate relationships has been exploratory. As with any exploratory study, some of our findings were unanticipated. One example is our finding that shifts toward greater traditionalism among parents appear to complicate offspring's dating relationships. Although the larger trend has been for most Americans to become less traditional about gender issues during the last few decades, a significant number of people have become more traditional. Conservative religious and political movements during the 1980s encouraged a return to conventional gender roles more typical of the 1950s. Our data indicate that when parents become more traditional, children date a larger number of people and find it more difficult to meet people with whom they can have serious relationships. We interpret this finding to mean that these young adults are "out of step" with the attitudes and behaviors of most other young people. To find a compatible partner (that is, someone who shares conventional beliefs about gender relations), these youth need to sift through a relatively large number of potential partners. Once these young people eventually meet someone compatible, however, their relationships are as happy as those of youth from less traditional family backgrounds.

In referring to studies showing that daughters from nontraditional families tend to be relatively career-oriented (Hoffman, 1989; Kiecolt and Acock, 1988; Mischel and Fuhr, 1988; Richards and Duckett, 1991; Spitze, 1988), we expected that growing up in nontraditional families increases daughters' age at marriage. However, our data do not support this hypothesis. This lack of support is related to the fact that mothers' employment, as well as other indicators of nontraditionalism, do not predict daughters' educational or occupational attainment, once we take into account mothers' education (see Chapter 7). Nevertheless, parents' gender nontraditionalism—especially the fathers' involvement in child care—appears to increase the likelihood that offspring cohabit. This result is consistent with Axinn and Thornton (1993), who found that offspring are more likely to cohabit if parents hold nontraditional attitudes.

Contrary to our expectations, we find no evidence that parental nontraditionalism affects relationship quality among cohabiting or married offspring. Nevertheless, several aspects of parental nontraditionalism appear to increase the likelihood that cohabiting offspring will end their relationships without marrying. Similarly, daughters whose mothers were employed full-time are more likely to see their marriages end in divorce. Given that parental nontraditionalism is *not* related to offspring's relationship quality (happiness, interaction, conflict, or problems), it may be that parental nontraditionalism increases relationship instability by affecting offspring's commitment to their relationships. Those with nontraditional views, compared with offspring with traditional views, may enter relationships more casually, feel less constrained to marry their partners (if cohabiting), and leave these relationships more quickly when problems emerge. Although this is a provocative notion, we must take into account the large number of null findings in this section. Overall, our data suggest that parents' gender nontraditionalism has relatively few life course implications, either positive or negative, for offspring's intimate relationships

Parents' Marital Quality, Divorce, and Offspring's Intimate Relationships

PREVIOUS STUDIES

Parents' Marital Quality.   Although few studies have focused on the consequences of parents' marital conflict for adult offspring's intimate relationships, those that exist yield consistent findings. Most of these studies have relied on retrospective data on the parents' marriage. Booth, Brinkerhoff, and White (1984) found that college students from high-conflict intact families are more likely to consider breaking up their current relationships than are those from low-conflict intact families. In a study of married adults, Amato and Booth (1991a) and Booth and Edwards (1990) showed that those who report unhappiness in their parents' marriages tend to report less marital happiness, more conflict, and more problems in their own marriages. Similarly, Belsky and Isabela (1985) found that young parents who recall positive relationships between parents are less likely than other young parents to experience declines in marital quality following the birth of a baby. In a clinical study, Overall, Henry, and Woodward (1974) found that psychiatric outpatients with serious marital problems are more likely than other outpatients to report a family history of parental discord (but not necessarily divorce). These studies consistently show that people experiencing relationship problems tend to recall a relatively high level of interparental discord while growing up.

Furthermore, in a cross-sectional study of two generations, Rossi and Rossi (1990, p. 324) found a significant positive association between parents' and married offspring's ratings of marital happiness. In addition, using longitudinal data from the Berkeley Guidance Study, Caspi and Elder (1988) found that parents' ratings of marital conflict are positively associated with their offspring's reports of martial conflict. All of these studies are consistent with the life course notion that marital quality is transmitted across generations.

Parental Divorce.   In relation to parental divorce, Booth, Brinkerhoff, and White (1984) found that college students from divorced families, compared with those from continuously intact two-parent families, are more likely to have dated within the previous two weeks. This study also showed that among those from divorced backgrounds, recollections of interparental conflict during the marital dissolution period and afterward are associated both with a larger number of dating partners since the start of the school year and with a tendency to judge current dating relationships to be less than very happy. A consistent finding in this literature is that adolescents from divorced families (both sons and daughters) become sexually active at younger ages and have a greater number of partners than do other adolescents (Booth, Brinkerhoff, and White, 1984; Furstenberg and Teitler, 1994; Hetherington, 1972; Newcomer and Udry, 1987).

Although few in number, these studies suggest that parental divorce accelerates dating and sexual activity among offspring, especially if divorce is accompanied and followed by a high level of interparental conflict. Increased dating and sexual activity may reflect children's observation (and emulation) of parental dating and sexual behavior following divorce. Increased dating and sexual activity among adolescents from divorced families may also reflect a lower level of supervision by single parents (Booth, Brinkerhoff, and White, 1984; Thomson, McLanahan, and Curtin, 1992). And, as noted before, children from conflict-ridden families (regardless of divorce) may fail to learn interpersonal skills useful in conflict resolution, thus contributing to problems in their own intimate relationships. Alternatively, decreased satisfaction with relationships among children of high conflict families could reflect a more critical (but perhaps more realistic) attitude toward intimate relationships.

Parental divorce also appears to affect offspring's views about marriage and intimate relationships. Wallerstein and Kelly (1980) noted that because adolescents from divorced families witness the "failure" of their parents' marriage, they tend to worry about their own chances of success in maintaining long-term intimate relationships. Consequently, some adolescents express a desire never to marry, whereas others are determined to be more selective and wiser than their parents in choosing a marriage partner. In a follow-up study, Wallerstein and Blakeslee (1989) found that the persisting anxiety generated by parental divorce interferes with many young adults' ability to form satisfying romantic ties. For many, fears of betrayal or not finding genuine love make them unwilling to make long-term commitments. Young women may be particularly vulnerable because the absence of a close father-daughter relationship limits their experience in interacting with men.

A number of studies suggest that offspring from divorced families hold ambivalent views about intimate relationships and marriage. Dunlop and Burns (1988) found that although adolescents from divorced families are just as likely as those from intact families to want to marry one day, they also express more caution about entering marriage. Booth, Brinkerhoff, and White (1984) found that parental divorce is associated with fewer reservations about becoming involved with the opposite sex but with a decreased desire for engagement or marriage. Finally, Amato (1987b) found that young adults from divorced families generally view marriage in a positive light but are also more accepting of alternatives to marriages, such as cohabitation and single parenthood.

Given these ambivalent and cautious attitudes, one might expect children of divorce to marry later than children from continuously intact two-parent families. However, most studies have found that young people whose parents divorce marry *earlier* than do those whose parents remain married (Glenn and Kramer, 1987; Keith and Finlay, 1988; Kulka and Weingarten, 1979; McLanahan and Bumpass, 1988; McLeod, 1991). Both Thornton (1991) and Goldscheider and Goldscheider (1993) show that coming from a single-parent household increases the likelihood of early marriage for daughters, but only if their custodial parent remarried. In contrast, other studies suggest that parents' marital disruption leads young people to *delay* marriage, at least among white women (Goldscheider and Waite, 1991; Li and Wojtkiewicz, 1994). Taken together, these studies indicate that some children from divorced families marry relatively early, perhaps to escape from unhappy home environments. Yet, other children from divorced families marry relatively late, a pattern that is consistent with the notion that children of divorce adopt a more cautious attitude toward marriage.

Later age at marriage may be related to an increased likelihood that children of divorce cohabit prior to marriage (Booth, Brinkerhoff, and White, 1984; Bumpass, Sweet, and Cherlin, 1991; Furstenberg and Teitler, 1994; Thornton, 1991). In other words, adult children of divorce may not avoid entering into intimate relationships as much as they avoid (or at least postpone) entering into formal marriage.

A number of studies consistently show that parental divorce increases the risk that offspring will see their own marriages end in divorce (Amato, 1995a; Bumpass, Martin, and Sweet, 1991; Glenn and Kramer, 1987; Keith and Finlay, 1988; Kulka and Weingarten, 1979; Pope and Mueller, 1976). This association is present among African Americans as well as whites, although it is not as strong or as consistent in the former group (Heiss, 1972; McLanahan and Bumpass, 1988; Pope and Mueller, 1976). Parental divorce is also associated with lower marital quality among married offspring (Amato and Booth, 1991a; Glenn and Kramer, 1987; Kulka and Weingarten, 1979; McLeod, 1991).

Several explanations for what is sometimes called the "intergenerational transmission of marital quality and divorce" are possible. First, individuals who have seen their own parents divorce have more positive attitudes toward divorce than do individuals whose parents remained continuously married (Amato and Booth, 1991b). Consequently, they may enter marriage with less commitment to the idea of life-long marriage and may have fewer qualms about resorting to divorce as a solution to marital problems. Second, some children from chronic, high-conflict marriages or marriages that end in divorce may develop personal traits that predict poor relationship quality. For example, lack of exposure to models of successful dyadic behavior may leave offspring deficient in interpersonal skills (Amato, 1995a) or with maladaptive internalized "working models" of intimate relationships (Belsky and Pensky, 1988). In addition, persistent interparental conflict may interfere with parent-child relationships, thus leading to a state of emotional insecurity or other problematic personality traits among offspring (Caspi and Elder, 1988; Davies and Cummings, 1994; Wallerstein and Blakeslee, 1989). Third, some offspring from divorced families may marry early to escape from family conflict—particularly if they do not get along with their parents' new partners or stepparents. Finally, economic hardship following divorce, especially among the majority of offspring who reside with their mothers, may impede children's education and socioeconomic attainment; and low socioeconomic attainment, as noted earlier, increases the risk of poor marital quality and divorce. Consistent with this last idea, research generally supports the notion that early marriage and low educational attainment among offspring account for some of the effect of parents' marital dissolution on offspring's divorces (Bumpass, Martin, and Sweet, 1991; Glenn and Kramer, 1987; Mueller and Pope, 1977), although one study fails to bear this out (Keith and Finlay, 1988).

HYPOTHESES

Interparental discord and divorce appear to affect the life course relationship trajectories of offspring. On the basis of prior work and life course principles, we hypothesize that offspring from unhappy intact families or divorced families, compared with those from continuously intact families, (1) show an accelerated pattern of dating, (2) are more likely to cohabit, (3) marry either relatively early or relatively late, (4) have lower marital quality, and (5) are more likely to see the dissolution of intimate unions—cohabiting relationships as well as marriages. Unlike almost all previous studies on this topic, our study is able to use longitudinal data to explore the links between parents' marital quality as reported by parents and children's relationship outcomes as reported by offspring. Some studies may have found a link between marital happiness and retrospective reports of parents' marital conflict because of shared method variance (same-source bias). Furthermore, the availability of longitudinal data allows us to estimate the independent effects of marital quality and divorce on offspring's relationships. It may be, for example, that some of the observed "effects" of divorce are actually due to parental discord that precedes marital dissolution.

RESULTS

Dating. Neither parents' marital quality in 1980 nor parental divorce (prior to 1980 or after 1980) has consistent implications for children's dating relationships in 1992. In contrast, changes in parents' marital quality between 1980 and 1988 appear to have consistent consequences for offspring's dating experiences in 1992. Among families in which a divorce did *not* occur, increases in marital instability are associated with sons' and daughters' reports of fewer dating partners in the last month and with daughters' (but not sons') reports of dissatisfaction with dating frequency and difficulty in finding people with whom they can have serious relationships. Similarly, increases in parental conflict are associated with sons' and daughters' reports of difficulty in finding people with whom they can have a serious relationship. In addition, for offspring who were still living at home with parents in 1988 (but not for those who had already moved out), increases in parents' marital instability and conflict are related to less happiness with current dating partners among both sons and daughters. These results suggest that although early marital problems of parents (in 1980) do not affect offspring's dating experiences, more recent marital problems of parents (in 1988), when children are older and more likely to be dating, have a disruptive affect on offspring's relationships.

Transitions to Cohabitation and Marriage. Our review of previous studies suggests that poor marital quality and divorce might either increase or decrease the likelihood of marriage among offspring. However, we find no support for either hypothesis in our study: parents' marital quality in 1980 and divorce (either prior to or after 1980) neither increase nor decrease the likelihood of offspring's marrying between 1980 and 1995.

Although we find no significant results in relation to marriage among offspring, parents' divorce proneness in 1980 (in marriages that stay together) and divorce are both related to cohabitation. In relation to the divorce proneness scale, each increase of one point is associated with a 178% increase in the odds of cohabitation, although the estimated effect is somewhat smaller for younger than for older offspring. Similarly, offspring whose parents divorced between 1980 and 1992 are 80% more likely to cohabit than are those whose parents remained married. When we include parents' divorce proneness in 1980 and divorce between 1980 and 1992 in the same model, both variables make independent contributions to cohabitation.

These results are illustrated in Figure 4.4. This figure combines all parental divorces (including those that occurred prior to the beginning of the study) into a single category. The figure also divides parental marriages that remained intact throughout the study into those that were relatively stable (73%) and those that showed signs of instability (27%). Among offspring with continuously and stably married parents, 13% had cohabited by the age of 20, and 30% had cohabited by the age of 26. In contrast, among those whose parents had divorced, 30% had cohabited by the age of 20 and 48% had cohabited by the age of 26. Offspring from continuously married

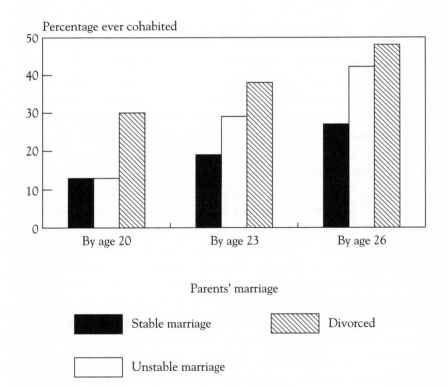

Figure 4.4   Percentage of offspring who cohabited by age 20, age 23, and age 26 by parents' marital instability and divorce

but unstable families fell in between the other two groups. Parents' marital instability was not associated with early cohabitation (by age 20), but appeared to increase the rate of cohabitation by ages 23 and 26.

These results suggest that divorce proneness and divorce among parents accelerate the process of union formation among offspring. However, this acceleration occurs primarily through cohabitation rather than marriage. Indeed, cohabitation may meet the needs of adult children of divorce (and those from intact but unstable families) especially well. On the one hand, some of these children may be emotionally needy or may seek out relationships as a way to escape from an unhappy home environment. On the other hand, young adults from divorced families, as noted before, are often wary of making life-long commitments. Cohabitation meets these conflicting needs by providing an emotionally supportive relationship, but one without the legal entanglements and life-long expectations of formal marriage.

Marriage and Cohabitation Quality. On the basis of previous literature, we hypothesized that parents' marital quality is positively related to offspring's relationship quality. Our preliminary analyses show that parents' marital quality in 1980 is related differently to the relationship quality of married and cohabiting offspring in 1992. In general, parents' marital quality is not related to the quality of children's cohabiting relationships, with most associations being close to zero. In contrast, parents' marital quality is consistently related to dimensions of offspring's marital quality. For example, parents' marital happiness is associated with greater marital happiness, less conflict, and fewer marital problems among offspring. Similarly, parents' divorce proneness is associated with less marital happiness, more conflict, more marital problems, and greater divorce proneness. (See Table 4.6 in the Appendix for more details.) Of the twenty associations (four dimensions of parents' marital quality by five dimensions of offspring's marital quality), eleven are significant at the .05 level, and nineteen are in the predicted direction, so the overall pattern is clear.

Figure 4.5 shows how dimensions of offspring's marital quality in 1992 are related to parents' divorce proneness in 1980. Although not shown in the figure, the results are similar for other dimensions of parents' marital quality. The sample in the figure is restricted to children living with both parents in 1980, but these patterns do not differ if we include offspring who were living with stepparents in 1980. The figure reveals that the more divorce-prone the parents' marriages are in 1980, the more problematic the

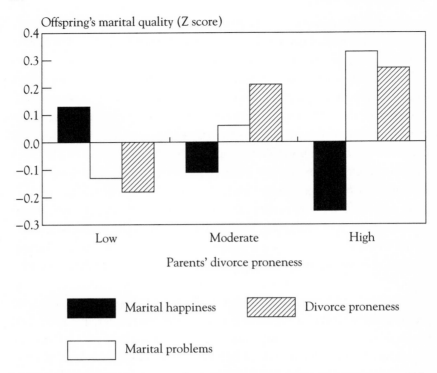

Figure 4.5   Offspring's marital quality in 1992 by parents' divorce proneness in 1980

children's marriages are in 1992. Furthermore, these estimated effects are moderately large. As we move from low to high for parents' divorce proneness, offspring's marital happiness declines by about one-third of a standard deviation, and offspring's marital problems and divorce proneness increase by between one-third and one-half of a standard deviation. Of the parental marriages represented in the figure, only a few divorced between 1980 and 1992. If we exclude these cases from the analysis, the pattern in Figure 4.5 (and the analysis in Table 4.6 in the Appendix) is virtually unchanged. This finding indicates that the estimated effects of parents' marital quality on offspring are *not* mediated by parental divorce.

We also considered changes in parents' marital quality between 1980 and 1988 for those marriages that did not end in divorce. In general, if parents' marriages improve during this period, children report more satisfying marital relationships in 1992, whereas if parents' marriage deteriorate, children report more problematic marital relationships. Interestingly, these patterns do not depend on whether offspring still lived at home with parents in 1988.

A finding of interest emerged from an analysis of the interaction between parents' marital quality in 1980 and parental divorce between 1980 and 1992. When marital conflict is high, offspring have *higher* marital quality when parents divorce than when they remain together. But when marital conflict is low, offspring have *lower* marital quality when parents divorce than when they remain together. This pattern holds for every measure of offspring's marital quality. These findings suggest that divorce is beneficial for offspring if it removes them from a highly conflicted household. Although the number of married offspring who experienced parental divorce between 1980 and 1992 was small, suggesting that we should regard the finding as tentative, we find similar interactions when using other dependent variables. (See Chapters 5, 7, and 8.)

Marital and Cohabitation Dissolution.   We find little consistent evidence that parents' marital quality affects the likelihood of divorce among offspring. Similarly, parental divorce is not related to any dimension of offspring's marital quality. However, parental divorce increases the risk of divorce among offspring by 76%. In terms of timing, parental divorces that occur when offspring are teenagers or young adults increase the likelihood of divorce more than do divorces that occur when offspring are 12 years or less. The estimated effects of parental divorce between 1980 and 1992 do not change if we control for predivorce marital quality. Parental divorce, however, does not appear to increase the risk that offspring's cohabiting unions will break up.

SUMMARY

Our results are consistent with the life course perspective, as well as with previous studies, in suggesting that parents' marital quality and divorce have broad implications for offspring's intimate relationships in later life. Among single offspring, if parents' marriages deteriorated during the 1980s, offspring report more difficulty in finding suitable partners as well as less happiness with their current dating partners. The life course perspective assumes that the timing of events is often crucial. Consistent with this assumption, declines in parents' marital quality are particularly problematic for offspring who were teenagers living at home during the 1980s—the period during which most offspring begin to date and form intimate relationships.

Our results also indicate that low marital quality and divorce among parents accelerate the process of union formation among offspring. However, whereas some previous studies have shown that this process occurs through marriage (Glenn and Kramer, 1987; Keith and Finlay, 1988; Kulka and Weingarten, 1979; McLeod, 1991; McLanahan and Bumpass, 1988), the present study indicates that this process occurs primarily through co-habitation. This difference in study results may be due to the recentness of the current sample of offspring and to the fact that cohabitation continues to be accepted by growing numbers of Americans as a legitimate alternative to marriage. Indeed, cohabitation may meet the emotional needs of adult children of divorced parents (and those from intact but unstable families) especially well by allowing emotionally supportive relationships without the commitment of formal marriage.

Consistent with the results for dating, poor marital quality among parents in 1980, as well as declines in marital quality between 1980 and 1988, predicts poor marital quality among offspring in 1992. These findings are consistent with a few earlier studies in demonstrating links between parents' and children's marital quality (Amato and Booth, 1991a; Belsky and Isabela, 1985; Booth and Edwards, 1990; Overall, Henry, and Woodward, 1974). However, previous studies have been unable to link parents' marital quality (as reported by parents) when children are still residing in the parental home to offspring's marital quality (as reported by children) when they reach adulthood. People who are generally unhappy may describe their own marriages, as well as their parents' marriages, negatively, regardless of the quality of these relationships. Because our study avoids this methodological problem, the present results provide the strongest evidence yet that marital quality is transmitted across generations. Furthermore, we are able to show that these estimated effects are largely independent of later parental divorces.

In contrast to the broad-ranging effects of parents' marital quality, we find few effects of parental divorce on the quality of offspring's relationships, a result that appears to clash with previous studies of dating (Booth, Brink-erhoff, and White, 1984; Wallerstein and Blakeslee, 1989) and marriage (Amato and Booth, 1991a; Glenn and Kramer, 1987; Kulka and Weingar-ten, 1979; McLeod, 1991). Some research suggests that the effects of divorce may be weaker for more recent cohorts of children than for earlier cohorts (Amato and Keith, 1991a). In other words, in the 1990s, a change in family structure may be less important for children than is the quality of interaction between parents.

Nevertheless, our results are consistent with prior studies in suggesting that divorce is transmitted across generations (Bumpass, Martin, and Sweet, 1991; Glenn and Kramer, 1987; Keith and Finlay, 1988; Kulka and Weingarten, 1979; Pope and Mueller, 1976). We also find that parental divorces that occur when offspring are teenagers or young adults increase the likelihood of divorce more than do divorces that occur when offspring are younger. This finding is consistent with two studies by McLanahan (1985, 1988), suggesting that more recent parental marital disruptions, when children are older, have the greatest effect on relationship outcomes for young adult offspring.

Conclusions

Our analysis shows that parents' education and income in 1980 are positively associated with the quality of their children's marriages in 1992. Similarly, changes in parental resources between 1980 and 1988 predict marital quality among offspring who married between 1988 and 1992. Although relatively little prior research has addressed this issue, our findings suggest that parents' socioeconomic resources increase the happiness and stability of children's marriages. Parental resources appear to benefit children's marriages partly because they improve children's socioeconomic attainment and partly because they affect parents' ability to provide economic support to their married children. Other reasons may also account for this link. For example, growing up with well-educated parents may affect children's ability to communicate effectively, children's sense of control, and other aspects of children's personalities that we are not able to measure in the present study.

The life course perspective leads us to reflect on the changing historical context of our findings. How have changes in the American economy during the last three decades affected young adults' intimate relationships in the 1990s? Our results suggest both positive and negative trends. On the positive side, the educational attainment of parents has increased steadily throughout this period. If parental education has indirect benefits for offspring's marriages, as our study suggests, then improvements in parental education have probably had a positive effect on recent marriages.

Economic trends, however, are not encouraging. Income for male workers has been largely stagnant since the 1970s, although the movement of wives into the paid labor force allowed many two-parent families to keep up with inflation and improve their financial situation somewhat. But income inequality has been increasing since the 1980s, with families at the top of the income distribution experiencing greater affluence and families at the bottom becoming more desperate. For families that are comfortable economically, additional increases in income are unlikely to improve marital relations or the general quality of family life. However, for families that are struggling to make ends meet, further declines in income may have serious consequences for marital quality. Our data suggest that the large declines in income experienced by some parents during the 1980s probably had negative consequences, not only for parents' marriages, but also for children's marriages. In this sense, the disruptive effects of family economic decline continue into the next generation.

In terms of gender relations, we see relatively little evidence that changes toward role-sharing and egalitarianism within marriage have a major long-term effect, either positive or negative, on children's intimate ties. However, parents' gender nontraditionalism appears to increase the risk of relationship dissolution among cohabiting offspring, as well as the risk of divorce among married daughters. Taken together, these findings suggest that growing up in a nontraditional household does not affect relationship quality but may weaken children's commitment to the norm of life-long relationships. Consequently, the shift toward less traditional gender relations in the United States may be contributing to a greater turnover in young adults' intimate ties.

Parental discord and divorce do not appear to affect the timing of children's marriages, although we find evidence that they increase the likelihood that their offspring will cohabit. This finding means that children from high-conflict intact families, as well as children from divorced families, form intimate partnerships earlier than do children from low-conflict intact families, but they do this through cohabitation rather than marriage. A combination of emotional neediness and cautiousness about marriage may make cohabitation the arrangement of choice for these young people. Our results suggest that the increase in cohabitation among young adults in recent decades has been at least partly propelled by the dramatic increase in divorce, as well as marital discord, in the parental generation. Given the continuing high divorce rate in the United States, we can expect to see frequent and early cohabitation among young adults in the foreseeable future. But because these relationships tend to be unstable, a high rate of cohabitation is accompanied by a high rate of relationship turnover. Indeed, some of the main factors that appear to increase the likelihood of cohabitation—parents' gender nontraditionalism and marital discord—also appear to increase the likelihood that these relationships will break up.

Most young people who cohabit eventually get married, if not to their cohabiting partner then to someone else. The present study, as well as many others, indicates that parental divorce raises the risk of marital dissolution among offspring. It appears, therefore, that increases in parental divorce during the last three decades have increased not only the level of cohabitation instability but also the level of marital instability in the next generation.

At the beginning of this chapter, we pointed out that the intimate relationships of adults have become less stable during the last few decades. Our study suggests that declines in parental income, shifts in gender relations, and the increase in divorce have exacerbated the instability of offspring's intimate ties. The long-term implications of entering and leaving multiple relationships for people's sense of well-being and mental health are mixed. High relationship turnover gives people increased opportunities to try out new partners and eventually settle down with a compatible mate. But ending relationships is also stressful for both parties, and singlehood (even if it is a temporary status between relationships) is associated with low levels of psychological and physical health. Consequently, a pattern in which people shift frequently from one relatively short-term intimate relationship to the next is unlikely to be one that maximizes the happiness of the next generation.

Finally, our study shows that marital discord among parents predicts marital discord among offspring. If marriages are as happy now as they were a generation or two ago, then there is little reason for concern. But if happy marriages have become more difficult to attain, and if, as our study strongly suggests, marital happiness is transmitted across generations, then we can expect the cohort of children currently reaching adulthood to face additional obstacles to achieving satisfying and stable intimate relationships.

Social

Integration

Social integration is a concept that researchers often apply to groups, but it can also describe the multiple roles of individuals. The distinction between structural and psychological integration is a useful one (Moen, Dempster-McClain, and Williams, 1989). Structural integration denotes the actual involvement of individuals with various groups, whereas psychological integration is the subjective experience of connectedness to others. In this chapter, we look at structural integration by examining offspring's church involvement and organizational membership. We look at psychological integration by examining the number of relatives and friends to whom offspring feel close and offspring's feelings of attachment to the community. These dimensions of social life are only modestly correlated; consequently, information on multiple dimensions is necessary to provide a comprehensive picture of people's social integration.

Both structural and psychological integration are essential for individuals to function well, both in personal life and in work-related activities (Kelly and Hansen, 1987). Research shows that a high level of social participation increases longevity, buffers individuals from the effects of stressful life events, and facilitates people's sense of well-being (Blazer, 1982; House, Umberson, and Landis, 1988; Moen, Dempster-McClain, and Williams, 1989; Umberson, 1987). Social networks also serve as control mechanisms that promote healthy lifestyles and discourage antisocial behavior (Umber-

This chapter was written with the assistance of Scott Myers.

son 1987). On a broader level, the unity of society is based on the ability of individuals to connect with one another and coordinate their activities. Therefore, social integration not only benefits individuals but also is necessary for the smooth functioning of social institutions.

In spite of the importance of social integration, we know little about why some individuals are more highly participatory than others. In this chapter, we examine the ways in which the family of origin affects young adults' ability to forge and maintain social relationships. Using the life course perspective, we assume that important social skills, such as communicating clearly, taking the viewpoints of others, feeling at ease around people, being assertive, and knowing how to negotiate and compromise, are learned during childhood. In adult life, these skills form the basis of social participation, for example, in obtaining job interviews, getting promotions, asking for dates, joining organizations, attaining leadership positions, maintaining kin ties, and establishing supportive networks of friends (Kelly and Hansen, 1987).

The timing of our study is propitious, as the median age of children in 1980—the first year of our study—was 11. Sullivan (1953) identified preadolescence (ages 8 to 11) as a critical period in the development of peer relationships. These years provide opportunities for children to generalize the social skills that were learned in the family to other social contexts. This is also a time when many children establish personal relationships with adults other than parents (Fullerton and Ursano, 1994). Our study allows us to examine family-of-origin characteristics during a key time in the development of children's social competence.

As in other chapters in this book, we concentrate on three sets of independent variables: parents' socioeconomic resources, parents' gender nontraditionalism, and the quality and stability of parents' marriages. Following the mediation model, we assume that these family-of-origin characteristics influence children's social orientations partly through their impact on parent-child interaction. Consistent with this assumption, some research indicates that the quality of parent-child relationships predicts children's later social competence and ability to marshal social support. For example, Sarason, Sarason, and Shearin (1986) found a positive association between the quality of parents' involvement with children and children's later sense of social embeddedness. Similarly, Parker and associates (Parker and Barrett, 1988; Parker, Barrett, and Hickie 1992) found that adults who have problems forming social bonds tend to recall more dysfunctional parenting during childhood. Furthermore, Lobdell and Perlman (1986) found that female college students' who reported being lonely also reported little involvement with and a lack of trust in their parents. Consequently, we assess the extent to which recollections of parental support and control during adolescence mediate any significant associations between family-of-origin characteristics and dimensions of offspring's social integration.

Measuring Social Integration

We used two measures of offspring's structural integration. Religious integration was based on the mean of two items that tap the frequency of attendance at church services and involvement in church social activities. Approximately the same number of offspring report weekly church attendance and never attending; 31% never attend, 22% attend several times a year, 19% attend monthly, and 28% attend weekly. However, involvement in church social activities is less common: 53% of offspring never participate in church social activities, 23% participate less than monthly, 13% participate monthly, and only 11% participate weekly. High scores on this scale indicate high levels of religious involvement. (Table 5.1 in the Appendix presents full details on all five measures of social integration.)

Two questions assessed organizational and club membership. The first determined if offspring are members of any clubs or organizations, and the second asked for a specific count of the number of memberships. The number of memberships ranged from 0 to 12. We logged the scale prior to analyses because a large majority of offspring have no (48%) or only one (24%) affiliation. Although we use logged values of this dependent variable (as well as several other dependent variables in this chapter), we take the antilogs of adjusted means to show results in graphic form.

The next two measures of social integration tapped into the social networks of relatives and friends. The first asked offspring whether there are relatives to whom they feel emotionally close; the second asked for a specific number. In answering this question, we instructed offspring to exclude relatives living in the same household, as well as parents, regardless of living arrangements. The median number of close relatives is three. However, 14% of young adults mention having no close relatives. We logged these scores prior to analysis to correct for right skewness. Similarly, we asked offspring to indicate whether there are any individuals whom they consider to be very close friends but who are not relatives; we also asked for a specific number. The median number of close friends is three, although 7% of young adults report none. We also logged this measure prior to analysis to correct for right skewness.

We measured perceived community attachment with a single item dealing with the extent to which people feel that they have strong roots in the community. Attachment scores range from a low of one to a high of four. More individuals feel no or little attachment (27%) than a high level of attachment (2%). This finding is not surprising, given that the United States has a high rate of residential mobility. Nevertheless, strong ties with one's community can foster psychological bonds in which the community becomes tied to the individual's conception of self (Feldman, 1990). For this reason, perceived community attachment is a strong indicator of psychological social integration.

As anticipated, the five measures of social integration are positively but modestly correlated. The coefficients range from .21 (church attendance and club membership) to .05 (church attendance and number of friends), with a mean of .13. This finding indicates that the five measures tap empirically distinct aspects of offspring's social integration.

Preliminary analyses reveal that women report more church involvement and more close kin than do men. This finding is consistent with research showing that women, compared with men, tend to be more religious (Batson and Ventis, 1982) and more closely integrated into kinship networks (Fischer et al., 1989; Rosenthal, 1985). Offspring age is positively associated with club and organizational membership—another finding consistent with previous studies (Tomeh, 1973). Age is also negatively associated with the number of close friends. This finding probably reflects people's stage in the life course. As youth grow into adulthood, time previously spent in friendship networks becomes increasingly devoted to careers, family, and formal organizations.

Consistent with the mediation model, offspring's recollections of parental support and control during adolescence are related to the outcomes of interest in this chapter. Support from mothers and fathers is positively associated with church involvement, community attachment, and the number of relatives and friends to whom offspring feel close. These findings are congruent with research showing that the quality of parent-child relationships has implications for children's later social functioning (Parker and Barrett, 1988; Parker, Barrett, and Hickie 1992; Sarason, Sarason, and Shearin, 1986). Parental control is positively related to church involvement. Parental control also yields two curvilinear trends, with a moderately high level of control being associated with the greatest number of friends and the highest level of community attachment. Because parental support and control are related to all aspects of offspring's social integration, we consider the mediating role of these variables in our analyses.

Parents' Socioeconomic Resources and Offspring's Social Integration

PREVIOUS STUDIES

Education and income are positively associated with organizational memberships, community attachment, and the size of friendship networks among adults (Boisjoly, Duncan, and Hofferth, 1995; Fischer, 1982; House, Umberson, and Landis, 1988; Tomeh, 1973). Similarly, studies show that parents' education and income are positively associated with measures of children's social competence and involvement (Amato, 1987a; Bolger et al., 1995; Gecas, 1979). It appears, therefore, that family socioeconomic resources are linked with aspects of social integration across generations.

The manner in which parents interact with and socialize their children is part of this process. Kohn (1963, 1977) argued that middle- and upper-class parents, because of the nature of their occupations, value autonomy and self-direction. Parents encourage these traits in their children by explaining the reasons behind rules. In contrast, working-class parents encourage conformity and obedience in children by using discipline. Through discussion and negotiation, high-resource parents provide their children with behavioral and cognitive skills that are useful in dealing with others. Paulsen (1991) argued that the educational system reinforces the association between family background and social competence through the tracking of students. Schools often place children from middle-class homes in leadership positions where they can develop a sense of efficacy that is actualized through social participation later in life.

With respect to political participation, Paulsen (1991) found a positive relationship between people's socioeconomic background and their involvement in collective action. Similarly, Sutherland (1981) and Leaky and Morgan (1978) found that political and social activists generally come from upper-middle-class family backgrounds. Because high-status parents often hold powerful positions in social institutions, their children have opportunities to interact with politically active or efficacious adults through family contact. Thus, the stratification system produces variations in the exposure of high- and low-status youth to politically active role models (Paulsen, 1991). Because high-resource parents often make political and social activity a central part of their adult lives, and because they integrate these activities with their families, their political and social values are often passed on to succeeding generations (Braungart and Braungart, 1986; Troll and Bengtson, 1979; Verba and Nie, 1972). For example, dedication to causes often persists as a family theme across generations.

Parents are also able to influence the social development of their offspring through residential location. Bryant (1985) suggested that the availability of neighborhood resources is an important correlate of children's social functioning. Children who have easy access (by walking or biking) to recreation centers, practice fields, and community-sponsored events and activities are more likely to utilize these resources. Parents with more economic resources often choose residential settings that facilitate such contact and avoid those that do not (Parke and Bhavnagri, 1989).

In addition, parents influence their offspring's social behavior by interfacing between offspring and institutional settings (Parke and Bhavnagri, 1989). Coser (1964) argued that through involvement in parent-teacher associations, Brownies, Cub Scouts, and the like, parents maintain community networks and integrate their children into them. O'Donnell and Stueve (1983) found that middle-class mothers are more likely than working-class mothers to sign their children up for specific community-based programs. In general, middle-class mothers have more purchasing power, are better able to use community resources, and are better prepared to introduce their offspring to a range of social activities (O'Donnell and Stueve, 1983).

These considerations suggest that family socioeconomic resources are positively associated with offspring's social integration. However, this conclusion requires two qualifications. First, there is little evidence that parents' socioeconomic resources increase children's church participation. For example, Francis and Brown (1991) and Hoge, Petrillo, and Smith (1982) found no links between parental education and income and offspring's religious involvement. Furthermore, Wilson and Sherkat (1994) cautioned that children of highly educated parents may have a comparatively low level of religious involvement. Well-educated parents, they argued, view conformity as being less important than individual development; consequently, they encourage their offspring to think independently. This outlook may lead offspring to question, and perhaps reject, religious authority and tradition.

Second, members of poor and working-class families appear to emphasize kin ties to a greater extent than do members of middle- or upper-class families. Indeed, some ethnographic studies find that poor African American families have more extensive ties and more frequent contact with relatives than do whites (Stack, 1974; Staples and Johnson, 1993). Recent research, controlling for socioeconomic status and family structure, challenges these racial difference (Hogan, Eggebeen, and Clogg, 1993). Nevertheless, highly educated young adults, especially if they are better educated than their parents, may turn away from kin and seek out companionship from similarly educated peers. Furthermore, the residential mobility of professional workers means that they often live great distances from their families. Consequently, high-status individuals may turn to friends rather than relatives for everyday assistance and emotional sustenance. Consistent with this idea, Campbell and Lee (1990) found that respondents with high socioeconomic status had relatively few kin living nearby. Furthermore, Amato (1993) found that education and income are positively associated with naming friends as sources of assistance and negatively associated with naming relatives as sources of assistance. In short, although the social networks of middle-class and lower-class families may be of similar size, their compositions may reflect different balances of friends and kin.

HYPOTHESES

Previous studies support the life course assumption that the roots of social integration in adulthood can be traced to the family of origin. Parents with a high level of socioeconomic resources, compared with parents with a low level of socioeconomic resources, socialize their children in ways that facilitate social competence, are more involved in formal organizations and political activities, live in neighborhoods with more community resources, and enroll their children in more organized social activities. The combination of these factors is likely to assist children in their efforts to form social bonds. Consequently, we hypothesize that parental education and income are *positively* related to several aspects of social participation in young adulthood, including membership in clubs and organizations, the number of close friends, and feelings of community attachment. At the same time, however, parental education and income may be *negatively* related to offspring's religious involvement and ties with kin.

Using the mediation model, we hypothesize that these associations are reduced substantially when we control for parental support and control during adolescence. In addition, we consider the role of offspring's socio-economic attainment in mediating associations between parents' socioeconomic resources and offspring's social integration.

RESULTS

Parental Education. Parents' education is associated with two measures of adult offspring's social integration. Adult offspring who were raised in households with higher parental education have more memberships in clubs and organizations and a larger number of friends to whom they feel close than do other offspring. Mothers' and fathers' educations appear to have similar consequences. These associations are not moderated by offspring's ages or whether offspring lived in a stepfamily in 1980. However, although parental education is positively associated with organizational membership among offspring of both genders, the association is somewhat stronger for daughters than for sons.

Figure 5.1 summarizes these results. Because mothers' and fathers' educations make unique contributions to offspring's social integration, the figure is based on the mean of both parents' educational levels. With all control variables in the model, offspring whose parents had sixteen or more years of education (on average) belonged to nearly one more club or organization (.7) than did offspring whose parents had less than twelve years of education, on average. Similarly, offspring with well-educated parents had about one-and-one-half more close friends than did offspring with poorly educated parents. These differences represent just under one-half and one-third of a standard deviation for organizations and friends, respectively, indicating moderate effect sizes. (See Table 5.2 in the Appendix for the full equations.)

Parental education is negatively, but not significantly, associated with the number of close relatives. We know from the results presented in Chapter 3 that parental education is positively associated with the distance that offspring live from parents. This information suggests that the absence of an association between parents' education and the size of offspring's kin networks may reflect geographical isolation from kin. In other words, dis-

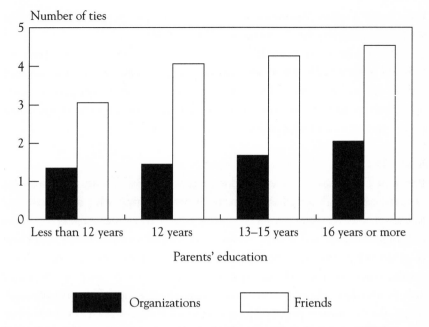

Figure 5.1 Offspring's organizational memberships and close friends in 1980 by parents' mean level of education

tance may be suppressing the association between parental education and the number of relatives considered to be close. However, when we add distance to our model, the results do not change.

To see if parental education is related to the overall size of offspring's support networks, we combined the number of friends and kin into a single variable. The correlation between parental education and total network size (friends plus kin) is virtually zero. However, parental education is negatively associated with the *percentage* of network members who are relatives. Therefore, offspring with well-educated and poorly educated parents have networks that are about the same size, but these networks are made up of different sources, that is, friends versus relatives.

We also investigated whether parental support and control can account for the associations between parents' education and offspring's social integration. A high level of parental investment may improve children's social competence and self-confidence, thus facilitating their entry into social networks beyond the family. Nevertheless, contrary to the mediation model, our analyses indicate that offspring's recollections of parental support and control during adolescence do *not* mediate any of the associations between parental education and offspring's number of organizational memberships or close friends.

Several other processes may be at work to create these differences. First, as just noted, middle-class parents provide more opportunities and encouragement for children to become involved in social activities not centered on the family (DeMartini, 1992; O'Donnell and Stueve, 1983). In contrast, working-class parents often lack the economic and cultural resources necessary to be familiar with and participate in social circles beyond the kin group (Sutherland, 1981). Second, outside the family, children from middle-class families are more likely to be involved in school systems and programs that encourage and teach community and political involvement than are children from working-class families (Paulsen, 1991). Consequently, the educational system may reinforce middle-class children's tendency to become involved in nonfamily networks and activities. Although these explanations are plausible, we are not able to test them with our data.

Another explanation entails offspring's education. Although many parents socialize daughters to be family-oriented, highly educated parents may encourage their daughters to postpone marriage and parenthood to pursue careers (Goldscheider and Waite, 1991; Stephan and Corder, 1985). Obtaining higher education and having a career are likely to facilitate women's entry into wider personal and organizational networks. Parental education may have a similar, albeit weaker, effect on sons. Indeed, we find support for this explanation in our data. When we add offspring's educational attainment to our model, the estimated effect of parental education on offspring's number of organizations and close friends declines by more than half and is no longer significant. Similarly, offspring's educational attainment accounts for about one-third of the association between parental education and the percentage of kin in offspring's social networks, and the remaining coefficient is no longer significant. This finding suggests that parental education facilitates children's educational achievement, and that educational achievement, in turn, increases children's involvement with organizations and friends.

Parental Income. With parental education controlled, parents' income in 1980 is not related to any dimension of adult offspring's social integration. Similarly, changes in parental income between 1980 and 1988 are not related to any of our outcomes. In addition, offspring's social integration is not associated with parents' judgments of changes in financial well-being, whether parents used public assistance, and whether fathers experienced unemployment during this period. The absence of any associations suggests that family influence on children's social participation has more to do with parental education than with levels of economic resources.

SUMMARY

Our general hypothesis that parents' socioeconomic resources are positively associated with offspring's social integration finds partial support. Parental education appears to have positive effects on organizational and club memberships and the number of friends to whom offspring feel close—results that are consistent with most of the studies reviewed previously, as well as with a life course perspective. We also hypothesized that parents' socioeconomic resources are negatively associated with offspring's involvement with church and kin. Our analysis indicates that although parental education is not related to the absolute number of relatives to whom offspring feel close, it is negatively associated with the *percentage* of relatives in offspring's support networks. In other words, relatives make up a comparatively large proportion of the networks of offspring with poorly educated parents, but a comparatively small proportion of the networks of offspring with well-educated parents. This finding is consistent with other research (Amato, 1993; Fischer, 1982) showing that the social networks of middle-class and lower-class families, although of similar size, contain different balances of friends and kin.

Contrary to the mediation model, parental support and control do not account for the links between parents' education and aspects of offspring's social integration. Instead, offspring's educational attainment appears to mediate these associations. This finding suggests that parents influence their children's level of social integration partly through the transmission of socioeconomic status across the generations.

Some previous research suggests that low parental income negatively affects children's peer relationships (Bolger et al., 1995). However, our data suggest that parents' economic resources contribute little to children's social participation, once we take into account parental education. Offspring's social integration appears to depend both on the values and skills offspring learn from parents through socialization and on offspring's own education, than on the commodities and experiences that affluent parents can afford to purchase for their children.

Parents' Gender Nontraditionalism and Offspring's Social Integration

Much research on maternal employment is based on the notion that secure attachments to caregivers early in life are necessary for the social development of children (Bowlby, 1977). Many observers have been concerned that the movement of mothers with young children into the paid labor force is increasing the risk that children are insecurely attached, with negative consequences for children's social development. Early research on maternal employment yields mixed results, with some studies suggesting negative effects on children's social adjustment and other studies suggesting no effects or even positive effects (Hoffman, 1989; Mischel and Fuhr, 1988; Richards and Duckett, 1991; Spitze, 1988). More recent studies continue to yield contradictory results. Belsky and Eggebeen (1991) and Baydar and Brooks-Gunn (1991) provide evidence that early maternal employment has negative effects on children's social behavior, whereas Greenstein (1995) and Parcel and Menaghan (1994) provide evidence that it does not.

Results of these studies are often difficult to interpret. For example, Ladd, Hart, Wadsworth, and Golter (1987) found that children with two employed parents, compared with other children, have larger peer networks and spend more time in peer interaction. One interpretation of this finding is that a high level of peer involvement reflects deficits in home-based interaction, which is due to the absence of both parents for long hours. An alternative interpretation is that mothers who work outside the home foster independence in their children and encourage nonfamily social involvement—outcomes that are benign or even beneficial as far as children's social integration is concerned. Indeed, many employed mothers place their children in daycare centers that involve group activities. Such settings have been observed to increase children's assertiveness and social skills (Clark-Stewart, 1992). These traits may facilitate social integration in adulthood.

In contrast to the mixed findings regarding mothers' employment, fathers' involvement in socialization generally appears to have beneficial consequences for children's social competence (Lamb, 1981; Radin and Russell, 1983; Snarey, 1993). For example, Cohn, Patterson, and Christopoulos (1991) found that children are more socially competent with peers when both parents are active in child rearing. Another study (Attili, 1989) found that fathers who are actively involved in joint child care activities with mothers have offspring who are more socially skilled with peers than do

fathers who are passively involved. In general, the physical presence, attention, and involvement of fathers increase the social capital of children
(Coleman, 1988), which may facilitate the development of socially skilled
behavior.

The link between parents' gender role attitudes and offspring's social
integration is not clear, and no research exists to guide our propositions. It
is possible that more traditional parents emphasize family and kin involvement, whereas less traditional parents stress political, organizational, and
community involvement. Stephan and Corder (1985) and Goldscheider
and Waite (1991) found that daughters from nontraditional families are
more likely than those from traditional families to desire to work outside
the home most of their lives. Although this finding does not directly address
social integration, it does suggest that daughters from less traditional families receive more encouragement to enter the labor force, which may lead
to other social activities and organizational involvement.

HYPOTHESES

Few studies have dealt with parents' gender nontraditionalism and offspring's social integration; consequently, our analysis of these life course
linkages is largely exploratory. In relation to maternal employment, research
suggests that it has relatively few harmful effects on children's social competence, except perhaps when it is extensive and occurs when children are
infants. Even under these circumstances, problems may appear only when
children are in poor quality day care. Although we do not have information
on maternal employment early in children's lives, we are able to examine
the role of mothers' employment during the preteen and teen years on
offspring's social bonds. We suspect that maternal employment increases
social integration among daughters, mainly because it encourages daughters
to join the paid labor force.

In relation to fathers, we hypothesize that paternal involvement in
housework and child care are positively associated with aspects of offspring's
social integration. In addition, we hypothesize that parents' nontraditional
attitudes about gender facilitate offspring's social integration, particularly
among daughters. Indeed, to the extent that any of these factors increases
daughters' social integration, we assume that these effects are at least partly
due to daughters' educational and occupational attainment.

Finally, because parental support and control are related to parents' gender nontraditionalism as well as to offspring's social integration, we assess

whether parental support and control mediate the estimated effects of parents' gender nontraditionalism on offspring's social integration.

RESULTS

Maternal Employment.   Our analyses suggest no general effect of mothers' work hours in 1980 on offspring's social integration in 1992. However, we find several interactions involving offspring's gender, with mothers' employment increasing daughters' (but not sons') social integration. Furthermore, the number of hours that mothers are employed is not as important as the fact that they are employed at all. The results of these analyses appear in Figure 5.2. Mothers' employment in 1980 is positively related to one of the structural integration measures (church involvement) and one of the psychological integration measures (feelings of community attachment). The differences between employed and nonemployed mothers reflect moderate effect sizes of between one-third and one-half of a standard deviation. (See Table 5.3 in the Appendix for more details.)

We also examined changes in mothers' hours of employment between

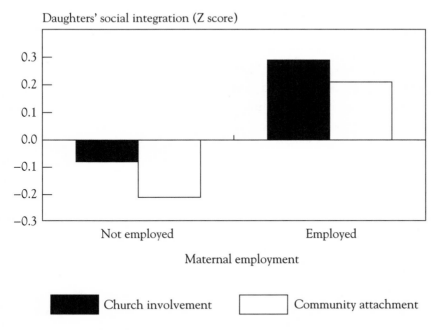

Figure 5.2   Daughters' church involvement and community attachment in 1992 by maternal employment in 1980

1980 and 1988 (among parents who remained married during this time). However, changes in hours of employment are not related to any aspect of social integration for daughters or sons.

We tried to explain the associations between mothers' employment and daughters' church involvement and community attachment by adding offspring's recollections of parental support and control to the model. However, these variables fail to explain these linkages. We then included daughters' education and workforce participation in our models, but these variables also contribute little to our understanding. It may be that mothers who work outside the home foster independence in their children and encourage nonfamily social involvement, and this may be especially true for daughters. However, we are unable to provide support for this explanation with our data.

Fathers' Share of Family Work. We use two measures of the presence of fathers in the daily household routine: involvement in housework in 1980 and involvement in child care in 1980. Fathers' share of housework is not related to any of the five measures of offspring's social integration in 1992. However, fathers' share of child care is positively associated with organizational membership and perceived community attachment among sons, and with the number of close kin among offspring of both genders. Furthermore, increases in fathers' share of housework between 1980 and 1988 are associated with more close friends and (marginally) more organizational memberships among both sons and daughters. These findings are consistent with our assumption that paternal involvement increases the social competence and involvement of children.

Figure 5.3 shows typical findings for sons. Compared with sons whose fathers did about half of the child care in 1980, those whose fathers did little or no child care have about one less person in their close kin network and score about one-third of a standard deviation lower in feelings of community attachment. It appears from the figure that the main difference is between sons whose fathers did little or no child care and sons whose fathers did more than this.

Offspring's recollections of support from parents during adolescence, especially fathers, mediate one-third of the association between fathers' involvement in child care and sons' community attachment. However, parental support and control mediate virtually none of the other associations. Contrary to our expectations, therefore, the links between paternal involve-

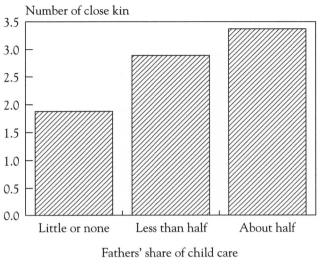

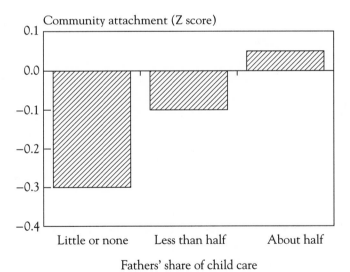

Figure 5.3   Sons' close kin and community attachment in 1992 by fathers' share of child care in 1980

ment during childhood and later social integration are largely independent of offspring's reports of parental behavior.

Gender Attitudes.   Our analyses reveal that parents' gender attitudes in 1980 have little apparent effect on offspring's social integration in 1992, with one exception: for daughters (but not for sons), parental traditionalism is associated with greater church involvement. Similarly, we find for daughters (but not for sons) that increases in parental traditionalism between 1980 and 1988 (among parents who remained married) are associated with greater church involvement. Further analyses of our data indicate that parents with traditional gender attitudes also tend to be religious. Consequently, it is likely that the association between parental traditionalism and offspring's church attendance is due to parents' and children's religiosity. Consistent with this explanation, when we control for parents' religiosity (church attendance and importance of religious beliefs), the association between parents' gender attitudes and offspring's church involvement declines to a nonsignificant level.

SUMMARY

Parents' gender nontraditionalism is linked in several ways with offspring's social integration. As we anticipated, daughters score higher on two indicators of social integration when their mothers are employed in 1980. Daughters may be more influenced by maternal behaviors than sons because daughters identify with their mothers and see them as appropriate role models. Indeed, daughters tend to identify with mothers throughout the life course, whereas sons increasingly shift their focus to their fathers during childhood and adolescence (Chodorow, 1978). The absence of any significant associations between maternal employment and aspects of sons' social integration supports previous research that maternal employment has few consequences for offspring's social competence. Parcel and Menaghan (1993) found that the structure of parents' jobs and forms of workplace control influence parenting styles at home. Therefore, it may not be maternal employment per se, but the conditions under which mothers work that affect children's social relationships.

Consistent with our hypothesis, fathers' involvement in family work appears to increase some aspects of offspring's social integration, especially for sons. This pattern of finding provides support for arguments by Snarey (1993) and Coleman (1988) that fathers' participation in household and family work increases the social skills and social capital of children. Our predictions regarding parents' gender attitudes, however, are not supported. Nontraditional attitudes do not appear to increase offspring's social integration. Indeed, nontraditional attitudes are associated with *less* church involvement among offspring.

In summary, we find some evidence that parents' gender relations, especially fathers' involvement in child care, predict social integration in young adulthood. Nevertheless, the general absence of significant findings in this section leads us to conclude, overall, that parents' gender nontraditionalism has relatively few life course consequences for offspring's social integration.

Parents' Marital Quality, Divorce, and Offspring's Social Integration

PREVIOUS STUDIES

Parents' Marital Quality. The life course perspective predicts a transmission of relationship quality across generations. This transmission occurs partly because children who are exposed to poor quality marriages are deprived of appropriate models of relationship functioning (Davies and Cummings, 1994; Doyle, Markiewicz, and Hardy, 1994). Children learn a variety of dyadic skills from observing parents, such as sharing, taking turns, discussing problems, compromising, and resolving differences amicably. Poor marital quality, therefore, negatively affects children's ability to form social bonds as a result of the transmission of inappropriate ways of relating to others (Skinner, Elder, and Conger, 1992). Consistent with this notion, Martin (1990) found a similarity of conflict styles between parents and their children, with children of conflictual parents adopting an avoidant or aggressive interactional style when dealing with peers.

In addition, the mediation model suggests that marital conflict affects children's social competence because it leads parents to be less affectionate, less responsive, and more punitive toward their children. These parental behaviors leave children from high-conflict families feeling emotionally insecure (Davies and Cummings, 1994). These children are also likely to perceive their social environments as unpredictable and uncontrollable (Amato, 1987a). These dispositions and beliefs may generalize and interfere with children's ability to form satisfying, stable social relationships outside the family. Consistent with this reasoning, several studies show that parents'

marital conflict is associated with lowered social competence, fewer friendships, and more loneliness among children and adolescents (Long et al.,
1987; Wolfe et al., 1986). If children carry these traits forward into adulthood, then we would expect relationship difficulties to persist, to some
degree, throughout the life course.

Parental Divorce.   Children of divorce tend to have lower scores on measures of social adjustment than do children with continuously married parents (Amato and Keith, 1991a). Parental divorce may be associated with
offspring's relationship problems because of the interparental conflict that
often precedes—and follows—divorce. However, marital disruption may
also affect offspring in ways that are independent of pre-divorce conflict.
For example, single parents are constrained in the amount of time and
attention that they can provide to children (Amato, 1995b; Thomson,
McLanahan, and Curtin, 1992). Consequently, single parents experience
more difficulty than do married parents in monitoring and controlling their
children. Cochran and Bø (1989) found that a low level of parental supervision was associated with antisocial behavior among children. In addition,
because parental divorce is followed by a decline in the standard of living,
single mothers and their children are often forced to search for affordable
accommodation in less affluent neighborhoods (McLanahan and Sandefur,
1994). Children growing up in poor neighborhoods without community
resources (such as recreation centers and sports facilities) have fewer opportunities to develop certain forms of social competence.

   Evidence for long-term effects of parental divorce on offspring's social
integration in adulthood is minimal. In a study based on a national sample
of adults, Amato and Booth (1991a) found no differences in social integration between individuals from divorced, unhappy intact, and happy intact
families. The absence of an association may be due to the fact that the
circumstances of marital dissolution vary considerably from case to case.
The life course perspective suggests that the effects of an event (such as
divorce) are moderated by people's ages at the time that the event occurs
and the circumstances that precede and follow the event. For example,
divorce may not have negative long-term consequences for children if it
signals a relief from a conflicted household (Furstenberg and Cherlin, 1991).
In other words, the effects of marital disruption may depend on the level
of interparental conflict prior to divorce, as well as circumstances that follow
the divorce, such as post-divorce conflict, moving, or parental remarriage.

HYPOTHESES

Our review of previous work suggests that poor marital quality among parents and parental divorce are linked with problems in children's social relationships across the life course. Consequently, we test the hypothesis that parents' marital discord and divorce are associated with low levels of structural and psychological social integration among offspring in early adulthood. Using the mediation model, we test the hypothesis that the associations between parents' marital quality, divorce, and offspring's social integration decline substantially when we control for parental support and control during adolescence. In addition, we explore the extent to which the consequences of marital dissolution vary with children's ages and a variety of postdivorce circumstances. Finally, we assess the possibility that divorce and predivorce marital conflict interact in predicting offspring's outcomes.

RESULTS

Parents' Marital Quality. In estimating the effects of parents' marital quality in 1980 on adult offspring's social integration in 1992, we concentrate on 429 offspring who did not experience a parental divorce after 1980. This number includes 45 offspring who lived in stepfamilies in 1980, as well as 384 whose parents were continuously married. The literature reviewed previously suggests that parents who argue frequently and create tension at home socialize their children in ways that interfere with children's ability to form long-term social relationships. Our results show a pattern of weak but consistent support for this notion. Parents' marital happiness is marginally associated with less religious involvement and fewer close relatives and friends. Similarly, parents' marital interaction is positively related to the number of close friends and to feelings of community attachment. Similarly, parents' marital conflict is associated with fewer relatives and with marginally lower religious involvement and community attachment. Finally, parents' divorce proneness is negatively related to church involvement and to the number of close relatives. These findings do not vary with offspring's gender, age in 1980, or stepfamily status in 1980. (See Table 5.4 in the Appendix for details.)

Figure 5.4 shows some typical findings. In this figure, marital conflict is split into roughly equal thirds, whereas divorce proneness is split at the fiftieth and eightieth percentiles, approximately. The figure indicates that as marital conflict and divorce proneness increase, church involvement and

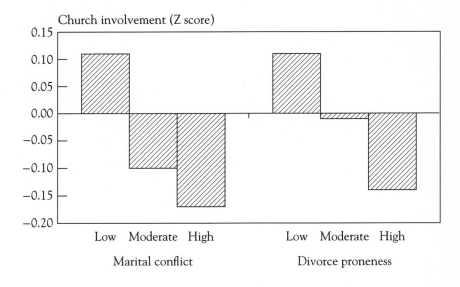

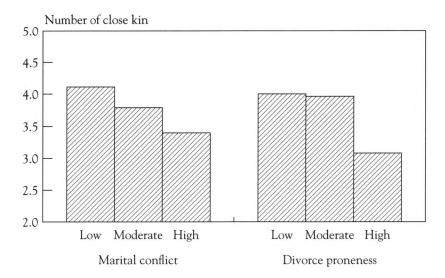

Figure 5.4   Offspring's social integration in 1992 by parents' marital conflict and divorce proneness in 1980

the number of close kin decline. For church involvement, the difference between the "low" and "high" groups represents about one-fourth of a standard deviation, regardless of which measure of parents' marital quality is used. For the number of close kin, offspring whose parents have a high level of divorce proneness report about one fewer close relative than do offspring whose parents have a low level of divorce proneness. The corresponding difference based on marital conflict is not as large.

Consistent with the mediation model, parental support appears to mediate many of the links between parents' marital quality and offspring's social integration. For example, adding our measures of maternal and paternal support to the equations reduces the estimated effect of parents' marital instability on church involvement and the number of close kin by about 40%. Similar reductions are apparent for most other significant associations. Unlike our measures of parental support, our measure of parental control does not appear to mediate any of these associations.

These results are shown in the path models in Figure 5.5. To simplify the figure, we combined maternal and paternal support by taking the mean. In addition, although all the control variables are in the analysis, we omit them from the figure. Note that with parental support in the model, parents' divorce proneness is no longer significantly related to church involvement

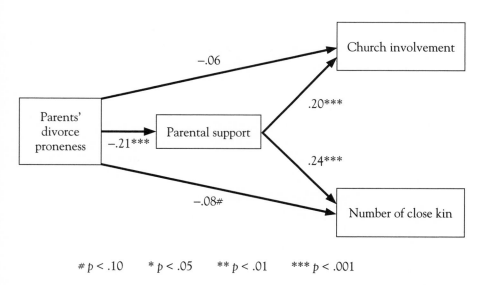

#p < .10   *p < .05   **p < .01   ***p < .001

Figure 5.5 Path model of parents' divorce proneness, parental support, and offspring's social integration

and is only marginally related to kinship ties. However, divorce proneness is negatively linked to parental support, whereas parental support is positively linked to church involvement and kinship ties. These results suggest that the effect of parental discord on children's later social relationships is due to disruptions in parent-child relationships during adolescence (and perhaps earlier).

Other explanations are also likely. For example, as most churches emphasize strong families, members of unstable families may tend to withdraw from such organizations, thus leading to less church involvement on the part of offspring in later life. Also, marital instability could disrupt the larger kin network if in-laws and other relatives take sides in marital disputes. Or, wanting to avoid conflict altogether, in-laws and relatives may reduce contact with parents, and hence, with offspring as well.

Changes in parents' marital quality between 1980 and 1988 are also associated with measures of offspring's social integration. Inspection of means reveals that improvements in marital quality have relatively few consequences; in contrast, declines in marital quality are problematic. In particular, declines in marital happiness are associated with fewer close friends, marginally less church involvement, and fewer organizational memberships. Similarly, decreases in martial interaction and increases in marital conflict are associated with fewer close friends. Finally, increases in parents' marital instability are associated with fewer organizational memberships and fewer friends. (See Table 5.5 in the Appendix for more details.) As in the analysis described before, our measures of maternal and paternal support during adolescence mediate substantial proportions (often up to one-half) of these associations.

Parental Divorce.   Divorce does not appear to affect any aspect of offspring's social integration. Nor are factors related to marital disruption, such as children's age at divorce, residential mobility, postdivorce conflict, or parental remarriage generally associated with social integration.

We suggested earlier that the effects of divorce may depend on the level of marital conflict prior to divorce. In a tension-filled marriage, children whose parents divorce may be better off in the long run than children whose parents remain married. But in a marriage that is relatively low in conflict, children whose parents divorce may experience considerable stress and, consequently, be worse off than those whose parents remain married. To test this idea, we created an interaction term between parents' marital conflict in 1980 and parents' marital dissolution after 1980 and then used it to predict offspring's social integration in 1992. This procedure reveals marginally significant interactions for two measures of social integration: the number of close relatives and the number of close friends. When we combine the two variables to form a summary measure of the size of offspring's support networks, the association is fully significant.

Figure 5.6 shows the nature of this interaction. When conflict in 1980 is high, offspring have more social support in 1992 if their parents divorce than if their parents remain married. But when conflict in 1980 is low, offspring have slightly more social support in 1992 if their parents remain married than if their parents divorce. In other words, children have the smallest number of close relatives and friends when they are exposed to a high degree of marital conflict that is not alleviated through parental divorce.

SUMMARY

Our results show that parents' marital quality in 1980 is positively associated with multiple aspects of adult offspring's social integration. Similarly, de-

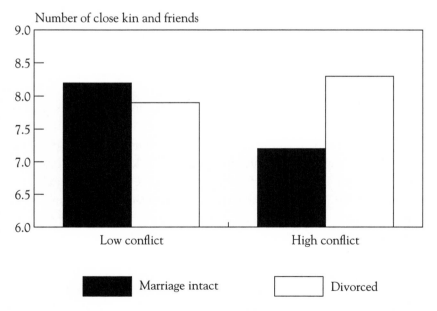

Figure 5.6   Offspring's close kin and friends in 1992 by parents' marital conflict in 1980 and divorce between 1980 and 1992

clines in marital quality between 1980 and 1988 are associated with lower social integration. These results are consistent with previous studies of children and adolescents (Long et al., 1987; Wolfe et al., 1986) and with a life course perspective emphasizing the intergenerational transmission of relationship problems. Through interparental discord, children observe and learn poor interpersonal skills, develop personality traits shaped by a sense of emotional insecurity, and internalize problematic working models of relationships (Davies and Cummings, 1994; Doyle, Markiewicz, and Hardy, 1994; Martin, 1990; Skinner, Elder, and Conger 1992). For these reasons, poor marital quality may negatively affect children's ability to form social bonds later in life through the transmission of inappropriate or negative ways of relating to others. Our results further suggest that some of the effects of poor marital quality among parents are due to disrupted relationships between parents and children—a finding consistent with the mediation model (Davies and Cummings, 1994; Grych and Fincham, 1990). Although these associations are not strong, they are consistent.

In contrast, parental divorce by itself is not associated with children's levels of social integration. However, children who experience high levels of marital conflict are better off if their parents divorce than if they remain married. Although many observers have suggested such a possibility (Furstenberg and Cherlin, 1992), our study is among the first to document it empirically.

Conclusions

In this chapter, we explored how parents' socioeconomic resources, gender nontraditionalism, and marital quality and stability affect children's social ties in young adulthood. Our results suggest that family characteristics measured when most children are preadolescents or adolescents have lingering consequences for the quality of offspring's social relationships, including aspects of both structural integration (church involvement and membership in clubs and organizations) and psychological integration (feeling close to others and attached to one's community). These results are consistent with arguments that preadolescence and adolescence are critical periods for the development of relationship skills necessary to form stable social bonds across the life course (Fullerton and Ursano, 1994; Sullivan, 1953).

In the opening paragraphs of this chapter, we argued that structural and psychological integration are necessary for individual well-being and for the smooth functioning of society. Given that we are living in a time of profound changes in the economy, gender relations, and marriage, it is useful to think about how these transformations might be affecting the interpersonal orientations of the next generation of young adults.

Parents' education appears to facilitate the social integration of offspring. At the same time, parental education decreases the proportion of relatives in offspring's social support networks. Because parents' educational levels have been rising, it is probable that young adults (especially daughters) are increasingly involved in networks based on friends rather than relatives. This association would confer some advantages, as well as some disadvantages. Friends are valuable sources of support, especially in the form of companionship and personal advice. However, most people prefer to turn to family members rather than friends for most forms of help, such as assistance with illness, child care, or money (Amato, 1993; Boisjoly, Duncan, and Hofferth, 1995; Litwak and Szelenyi, 1969). Nevertheless, our data suggest that the overall impact of socioeconomic changes at the societal level probably has been positive, or at least not harmful, for young people's social integration.

In relation to changes in gender roles, we see no evidence that maternal employment is problematic for children's social integration. Indeed, maternal employment increases some forms of social participation among daughters. Furthermore, fathers' involvement in child care and housework are positively associated with several aspects of social participation among sons and daughters. These results suggest that moves toward a more egalitarian division of labor in the family, with women sharing the provider role and men sharing the domestic role, may have increased children's social integration.

We also see little evidence that increases in the rate of divorce have had negative consequences for children's social integration. Offspring from divorced families have levels of social integration that are, on average, comparable to those of offspring from continuously intact families. However, parents' marital quality is weakly but consistently related to offsprings' social ties. When parents are unhappy with their marriages, fight frequently, and act as if they are going to divorce (even if they do not), children are less involved with the church and other organizations, report fewer close ties to friends and relatives, and report less attachment to the community. It appears, therefore, that it is not divorce but poor marital quality that is detrimental to the quality of children's social ties. Consistent with this conclusion, we find that children from high-conflict families have more social support in early adulthood if their parents divorce than if they remain married.

Although the increase in the proportion of children who have experienced divorce does not appear to be problematic for the social integration of the next generation, we cannot be so complacent about children's exposure to interparental discord. If marriage is becoming a more stressful, conflicted, and insecure arrangement, then offspring may be entering young adulthood with fewer social ties and weaker interpersonal orientations now than in the past. Some evidence suggests that social participation among Americans has been declining during the last few decades, as reflected in involvement with religious groups, labor unions, parent-teacher organizations, neighborhood associations, and civic groups (Putnam, 1995). It is possible that increasing levels of family discord have played a role in this decline.

CHAPTER SIX

Socioeconomic

Attainment

The educational and occupational attainment of children is a topic of great public and scholarly interest, partly because socioeconomic attainment is a primary marker of success in our society. But in addition to conferring status and income, a high level of education provides a range of other less tangible benefits. Well-educated individuals, compared with poorly educated individuals, report more stimulating and enjoyable experiences at home and at work (Campbell, 1981, 60–65). Education provides people with skills and information that help them cope with stressful circumstances (Ross and Huber, 1985), avoid depression (Kessler, 1982), and increase their sense of control (Ross and Wu, 1995). In addition, education is positively correlated with longevity and self-reported health (Ross and Wu, 1995). Income appears to have similar beneficial effects that are independent of education.

In addition to these individual benefits, a high level of educational attainment among the population is essential for a society to develop technologically and to compete in the global economy. Furthermore, it has long been assumed that a well-educated public is critical to the successful running of a democracy. Well-educated parents are also better able to provide for their children's financial needs and are motivated to seek out and assimilate information on effective child-rearing techniques, thus enhancing the well-being and competence of the next generation. For these reasons, educational advancement is not only a vehicle for promoting the success of particular individuals but also a necessary investment in the well-being of the community.

Given the centrality of educational and occupational attainment for well-being at both the individual and societal levels, it is appropriate that a chapter in this volume be devoted to an examination of the ways in which family-of-origin characteristics influence children's socioeconomic success. We define success broadly and include the number of years of education completed by offspring, their occupational status, and their earned income. Also, we examine indicators of economic adversity, including whether there have been times when offspring did not have enough money for necessities, used welfare, or perceived their financial situation as getting worse. Although researchers have studied the impact of parents' education and income on offspring's socioeconomic attainment, they have given little attention to the possible effects of parents' gender nontraditionalism and marital quality. Furthermore, even among studies of intergenerational mobility, few have considered whether parental support and control mediate the links between parents' and children's attainment. With regard to these latter topics, our study makes a unique contribution.

Measuring Attainment

To assess offspring's socioeconomic achievement, we relied mainly on data from the 1995 follow-up study. For the forty-one offspring who did not provide us with follow-up information in 1995 (9% of the original sample), we substituted the 1992 data when appropriate. Detailed information on the measures is shown in Table 6.1 in the Appendix. Educational achievement is reflected in the years of education completed. The status of offspring's current jobs is one indicator of occupational achievement. We classified offspring's occupations into eight broad census categories, then rank-ordered them by status (based on commonly used prestige scales), with higher numbers indicating higher status. Offspring's personal earned income is a second indicator of occupational achievement. Not all income is an indicator of achievement; for example, some people receive income from investments, gifts, or public assistance. Nevertheless, because we examine income only for individuals who are employed, the amount of bias is small. Similarly, we did not examine occupational status among offspring who were not in the workforce, thus excluding those who were keeping house full-time (6% of women) or going to school full-time (2% of men and 4% of women). Readers should note that the great majority of women in the sample are in the labor force; this is consistent with recent national trends for young women.

We also created a three-item index of economic adversity based on questions having to do with not having enough money for necessities (food, clothing, and medical care), whether offspring received public assistance in the last four years, and whether they thought their financial situation was getting worse. Responses to the three items were positively correlated, and a factor analysis indicated that all three items loaded on a single factor at .5 or greater. Therefore, we added the three items to form a single economic adversity index.

Unlike the data on education, occupational status, and income, data on economic adversity came from the 1992 offspring interview. Because of this limitation, some offspring experienced adversity while still living at home with parents in 1992. This factor could be problematic for some analyses; for example, using parental income to predict offspring's economic adversity when offspring are living in the same household with parents could be tautological. Therefore, we checked to see whether the associations between our independent variables and offspring's economic adversity (as well as other outcomes) depended on whether offspring lived at home with parents in 1992. We found no significant interactions, so we conclude that our findings are not distorted by this possibility.

As expected, our four indicators of socioeconomic attainment are intercorrelated, with the general pattern of associations being similar for both men and women. Offspring's occupational status, in particular, is a good predictor of income and (low) economic adversity. However, education is a weak predictor of income and is *not* associated with economic adversity. This finding probably reflects the young age of our sample. People in low-skill jobs do not usually experience much upward mobility during their years of employment. In contrast, the advantages of a good education tend to accrue gradually but continuously during people's careers. In an older population, education predicts income and economic adversity more strongly. Indeed, the correlation between education and income is higher for parents than for offspring in our sample.

Preliminary analyses of the offspring data show that women, compared with men, have an additional one-half year of education and higher occupational status scores. But in spite of their higher educations and occupational status, women earn about $7,000 less per year and have higher economic adversity scores than do men. Women's incomes represent about three-fourths of what men earn, and this gap does not change appreciably when we limit the comparison to men and women who are employed full-time. The gender differences in economic well-being in our sample are consistent with recent data on the U.S. population (U.S. Bureau of the Census, 1992, Table 713).

Before proceeding with our main analyses, we checked to see whether our main mediating variables—parental support and control—are associated with offspring's socioeconomic outcomes. Consistent with the mediation model, maternal and paternal support are positively associated with offspring's education, especially among daughters. Maternal support is also negatively associated with offspring's economic adversity, especially among daughters. Paternal support is positively associated with offspring's occupational status, especially among sons. Finally, parental control—particularly when it is very high—is negatively associated with offspring's education, negatively associated with offspring's income, and positively associated with offspring's economic adversity. This latter finding is consistent with Rossi and Rossi (1990), who found that a retrospective measure of parental "authority" when children were growing up (which included being strict and using frequent punishment) was negatively associated with adult offspring's educational attainment. Overall, these findings suggest that parental support tends to facilitate children's attainment, whereas excessive parental control tends to impede children's attainment. Consequently, we assess the potential mediating role of these variables in the analyses that follow.

Parents' Socioeconomic Resources and Offspring's Socioeconomic Attainment

PREVIOUS STUDIES

Parental Education.   Status attainment studies indicate that, aside from offspring's innate abilities, parental education is the best predictor of offspring's educational and occupational achievement (Blau and Duncan, 1967; Featherman and Hauser, 1978; Haveman and Wolfe, 1994; Sewell and Hauser, 1975). This well-replicated finding is entirely consistent with the life course assumption that achieved characteristics are transmitted across generations. Parents' and children's achievement are linked for several reasons. First, highly educated parents have verbal and quantitative skills to which offspring are exposed on a regular basis. Highly educated parents also tend to seek out educational experiences for their families in the form of television programs, newspapers, books, and visits to museums and libraries. Repeated exposure to a stimulating environment is likely to increase children's cognitive ability, thus benefiting their school performance (Parcel and Menaghan, 1994; Marjoribanks, 1979). Second, highly educated parents possess cultural capital (information about how the system works, correct forms of language, styles of dress) that they can pass on to their children, thus facilitating children's entry into elite social milieus (Bourdieu and Passeron, 1977). Third, highly educated parents tend to socialize their children to respond to internalized values rather than external controls (Kohn, 1969, 1977). Doing tasks and assignments in response to felt obligations rather than external pressure serves offspring well in school performance and later job success. Finally, highly educated parents tend to have high expectations for their children's education. Parents with high expectations help their children achieve these expectations through (1) a system of rewards and punishments tied to educational attainment, (2) helping young people with their homework, (3) becoming involved with children's schools, and (4) repeatedly encouraging their children to attend college (Conklin and Daily, 1981). All of these behaviors facilitate children's educational achievement (Christenson, 1992).

Although most studies have focused on fathers' status characteristics as predictors of children's attainment, several studies suggest that mothers' status characteristics are also relevant. For example, studies by Beck (1983), Haveman, Wolfe, and Spaulding (1991), Hill and Duncan (1987), Kalmijn (1994), and Murnane, Maynard, and Ohls (1981) all indicate that mothers' status characteristics (education and occupational status) have associations with offspring's attainment (both sons and daughters) that are independent of fathers' status characteristics. In addition, several studies suggest that maternal and paternal attainment affect daughters and sons differently. Marini (1978), Sewell, Hauser, and Wolf (1980), Rossi and Rossi (1990), and Teachman (1987) all found that fathers' education is a better predictor of sons' educational attainment, whereas mothers' education is a better predictor of daughters' educational attainment. These studies suggest a modeling effect, in which children are more similar in years of education to the same-sex than to the opposite-sex parent.

Parents' education has an indirect effect on offspring's occupational success (status and income) through its impact on offspring's educational attainment. But parental education may also have direct effects on offspring's occupational success that are independent of offspring's education, for many of the reasons noted before. For example, parents with more cultural capital are better able than other parents to help their children obtain good jobs. Highly educated parents have direct knowledge about how to find jobs, can help youth to fill out job applications and write application letters, may identify and persuade influential people to write letters of reference, and might help offspring to land a job in the parents' place of employment.

Parental Income.   Parental income is also related to offspring's educational and occupational success, even controlling for parental education (Blau and Duncan, 1967; Featherman and Hauser, 1978; Haveman and Wolfe, 1994; Kiker and Condon, 1981; Teachman, 1987). Indeed, some studies show that the effect of fathers' education on sons' earnings is largely mediated through fathers' income (Sewell and Hauser, 1975). This process occurs for a variety of reasons. For example, parents with high incomes can afford private lessons, educational toys, sports equipment, art supplies, home computers, and college expenses, all of which facilitate academic success. Parents with high incomes also tend to live in neighborhoods with high-quality schools. Well-financed schools, compared with poorly financed schools, have more competent teachers, better equipment, and fewer problems with disruptive students who divert instructors' energy and time away from teaching. Once children are educated, affluent parents can pay travel expenses so that offspring can seek interviews in areas where jobs are plentiful. For offspring who wish to go into business, affluent parents can help by paying start-up costs for equipment, licensing fees, and costs of incorporation. Finally, children growing up in affluent homes may gain a taste for a high standard of living, and hence, be especially motivated to aim for a lucrative career.

Family poverty adversely influences offspring's outcomes in additional ways. Economic hardship increases the likelihood of interparental conflict (Elder, 1974; Conger et al., 1990). Interparental conflict, in turn, tends to increase offspring's anxiety, depression, and antisocial behavior—all factors that interfere with school performance (Brody et al., 1994; Davies and Cummings, 1994; Emery, 1982, 1988; Grych and Fincham, 1990). Part of this pattern is due to the fact that economic hardship makes parents more punitive toward and less supportive of their children (Conger et al., 1992, 1993, 1994; Elder, van Nguyen, and Caspi, 1985). Poverty also increases the risk of parental divorce, which can disrupt children's educational attainment (Amato and Keith, 1991b; McLanahan and Sandefur, 1994). Furthermore, if youth are still living at home when they start full-time employment, the debilitating effects of parental conflict may interfere with effective performance on the job. These considerations suggest that some of the impact of parents' economic adversity on children's later attainment is mediated through interparental conflict and decreased parental support of children.

Parents' economic hardship may also affect parents' expectations for their offspring (McLoyd, 1989). Parents who experience poverty or economic decline are more pessimistic about the future (both for themselves and for their children) than are other parents. Parental pessimism, in turn, is related to depressed occupational expectations on the part of adolescent children (Galambos and Silbereisen, 1987). For example, adolescents growing up in poor homes think their chances of going to a four-year college are lower than do other adolescents (McLoyd, 1989). Some studies show that parents who are economically hard hit are more likely to lower educational plans for female than male offspring (Mott and Haurin, 1982); correspondingly, daughters' expectations appear to be affected more than sons' (McLoyd, 1989). If young people's self-expectation translate into lower performance, then we would anticipate lower occupational and educational achievement among youth from disadvantaged families.

HYPOTHESES

Consistent with the status attainment literature and with a life course perspective, we hypothesize that parental education and income are positively associated with offspring's socioeconomic attainment. Furthermore, the studies just reviewed suggest the utility of estimating the impact of mothers' and fathers' resources on daughters and sons separately. Although we cannot examine all of the mechanisms just discussed through which parental resources might influence offspring's attainment, we have information on several probable mediating variables: data from offspring on parental support and control (including the frequency with which parents helped them with homework), a measure of the strength of parents' desire to have their children attend college, and information on parents' marital quality and divorce. We assess the mediating role of these variables in the following analyses. Finally, we consider the extent to which offspring's education mediates the estimated impact of parental resources on offspring's occupational status, income, and economic adversity, and correspondingly, the extent to which parental resources have consequences for children that are independent of children's educational achievement.

RESULTS

Parental Education.   As previously noted, prior research suggests that the effects of mothers' and fathers' educations on children's attainment vary with children's gender. Consequently, we present results separately by gender of parent and gender of offspring.

Mothers' education is associated with three of the four dimensions of *daughters'* achievement; it is positively related to education, positively related to income, and negatively related to economic adversity. After taking the impact of fathers' education into account, mothers' education continues to be positively related to daughters' educational achievement and negatively related to economic adversity. Similarly, fathers' education is positively associated with daughters' education, positively associated with income (marginally), and negatively associated with economic adversity. However, with mothers' education in the equations, only the association between fathers' and daughters' education remains significant. These analyses indicate that although the education of both parents predict daughters' attainment, information on paternal education tends to be redundant once we have information on maternal education. (Table 6.2 in the Appendix contains detailed analyses.)

Figure 6.1 divides parents into three groups: those with twelve years or less of education, those with thirteen to fourteen years of education, and those with fifteen years or more of education. The figure shows that women whose mothers have more than two years of college obtain, on average, nearly one more year of education than do women whose mothers have a high school education (or less). In relation to fathers' education, the corresponding difference represents slightly more than one year. Because the education of the other parent is controlled in the statistical models on which Figure 6.1 is based, the effects of maternal and paternal education are additive. In other words, when both parents have more than two years of college, daughters have about two additional years of education, compared with families in which both parents have 12 years of education (or less).

Figure 6.1 also includes the results for economic adversity. To simplify interpretation, the figure shows standardized economic adversity scores. Women whose mothers have more than two years of college score, on average, more than a third of a standard deviation higher than do women whose mothers have a high school education (or less). This indicates a

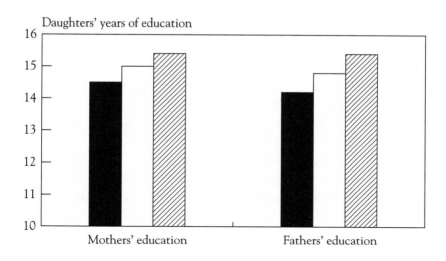

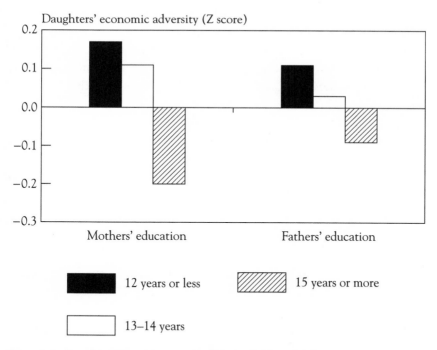

Figure 6.1   Daughters' attainment in 1995 by mothers' and fathers' years of education (controlling for the education of the other parent)

moderate effect size. With mothers' education in the model, the corresponding difference for fathers is much weaker, reflecting only about one-seventh of a standard deviation.

Although the results for daughters' income are not shown in Figure 6.1, the biggest difference is between mothers who have no college and mothers who have any college. When mothers have some college, daughters earn about $3,000 more annually than when mothers have a high school degree (or less). Fathers' education makes relatively little difference once mothers' education is taken into account.

We noted earlier that fathers' education predicts daughters' education. However, additional analysis reveals an interaction between fathers' education and 1980 family structure, with fathers' education increasing daughters' education in families with continuously married parents, but not in stepfamilies. To illustrate this interaction, women whose fathers have at least some college obtain about one-and-one-half more years of education than do women whose fathers have a high school education or less. In contrast, the gain to women associated with having a stepfather with at least some college is only about one-third of a year. These data suggest that daughters do not benefit (or suffer) when stepfathers are well (or poorly) educated. We return to this point later when considering parental income.

For *sons*, fathers' education is positively associated with educational achievement and occupational status. Mothers' education is related positively to education, but fathers' education completely accounts for the apparent effect of mothers' education. (See Table 6.3 in the Appendix for details.)

As Figure 6.2 shows, men whose fathers have more than two years of college obtain, on average, nearly two more years of education than do men whose fathers have a high school education (or less). With fathers' education in the model, the corresponding difference for mothers is trivial. Similar results are apparent for occupational status. Men whose fathers have more than two years of college score, on average, about one-half of a standard deviation higher than do men whose fathers have a high school education (or less). This finding represents a moderately large effect size. With fathers' education in the model, mothers' education makes little difference. None of the associations between parents' education and sons' outcomes vary with 1980 family structure.

We also explored the extent to which other variables mediate the influence of parental education. As we show next, below, although some of the

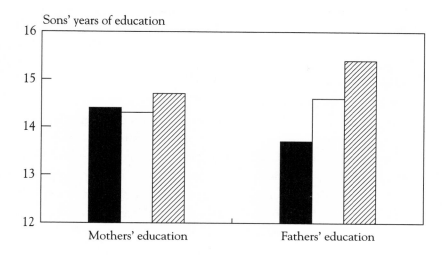

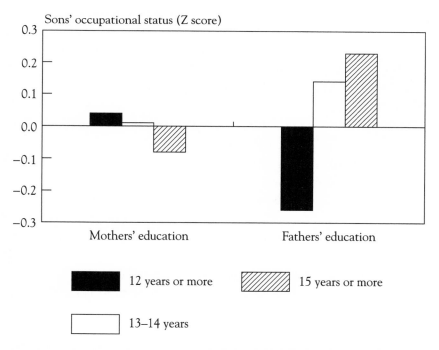

Figure 6.2   Sons' attainment in 1995 by mothers' and fathers' years of education
(controlling for the education of the other parent)

effects of parental education on offspring appear to work through parental income, the regression coefficients for parental education generally remain significant even with parental income in the models. Consequently, we look for other factors that might mediate these associations. Contrary to the mediation model, offspring's recollections of parental support and control during the teen years mediate little of these associations. In particular, the amount of help that parents provided with homework does not appear to be an important factor. In contrast, the extent to which parents felt it was important for their children to attend college accounts for between one-third and one-half of the estimated influence of parental education on daughters' and sons' education. It appears that highly educated parents think that college is an essential ingredient for their children's success and that these expectations positively influence children's later educational achievement. Parental expectations also account for many of the other associations just noted. For example, they account for about one-third of the association between mothers' education and daughters' economic adversity and about one-third of the association between fathers' education and sons' occupational status.

In further analyses, we checked to see how much the children's own educational achievement mediates the impact of parents' education on off-spring's income, occupational status, and economic adversity. After controlling for daughters' education, the estimated impact of parental education on income is reduced by one-third (but remains marginally significant). This finding suggests that parental education increases daughters' income largely through its impact on daughters' education. In contrast, daughters' education mediates virtually none of the estimated impact of parental education on daughters' economic adversity. This is the case because, as noted before, offspring's education and economic adversity are not correlated in our data. We also looked at several other potential mediators, including daughters' hours of employment, daughters' income, daughters' marital status, parents' income, and the amount of economic assistance parents give to children; but none of these variables accounts for the association. It may be that highly educated parents instill certain values or competencies in their daughters (such as money management skills) that allow them to avoid economic adversity, regardless of their educational levels. However, we are unable to test such an explanation.

In relation to sons' occupational status, when offspring's own educational achievement is taken into account, the estimated impact of fathers' education on sons' occupational status is reduced by more than half and is no longer statistically significant. This finding suggests that parental education facilitates sons' occupational status mainly through its impact on sons' education.

Parental Income. Fathers' and mothers' incomes in 1980 are related differently to their children's achievements. After adjusting for parental education, mothers' income is not related to any of the four dimensions of achievement for offspring of either gender. In contrast, after adjusting for mothers' income, fathers' income is positively associated with daughters' education and (marginally) with daughters' occupational status and income. Similarly, fathers' income is positively associated with sons' income and (marginally) with sons' education. These findings suggest that maternal income does *not* provide a critical increment to offspring's attainment once paternal income is take into account. (See Table 6.4 in the Appendix for details.)

A search for interactions reveals two exceptions to this pattern. First, mothers' income is positively associated with daughters' education, but only in stepfamilies. Second, fathers' income is associated with less economic adversity among daughters in continuously intact families, but not in stepfamilies. Combined with the finding (noted before) for stepfathers' education, it appears that daughters are not benefited by the education *or* income of stepfathers. In contrast, mothers' income appears to be especially important for daughters in stepfamilies. If stepfathers are reluctant to use their economic resources to benefit stepdaughters, mothers' income may compensate to a certain extent.

As noted above, we expected that the consequences of low parental income for children might be due to parental support and control, to interparental conflict, or to lowered parental expectations for children. We find no evidence that parental support and control account for any of the associations between fathers' income and dimensions of offspring's attainment. Similarly, parents' marital quality and divorce explain little of these associations. However, parents' educational expectations for children account for over one-half of the estimated impact of fathers' income on sons' education and about one-third of the estimated impact of fathers' income on daughters' education. Parental attitudes mediate relatively little of the association between paternal income and children's occupational status or earned income.

Economic Change between 1980 and 1988. In assessing the impact of changes in family economic well-being, we limit our analyses to families in which parents remained continuously married between 1980 and 1988; we do so because divorce is strongly correlated with changes in household income and standard of living. An increase in family income during these years is associated with lower economic adversity among daughters but appears to influence no other aspect of daughters' success. An increase in family income also has a positive impact on sons' occupational status and reduces the sons' chances of experiencing economic adversity. We find no evidence, however, that declines in income lead to interparental conflict, which, in turn, affects offspring's achievement, as some past research has been suggested.

Two significant interactions qualify the pattern for daughters (but not for sons). First, increases in stepfathers' income between 1980 and 1988 do not appear to benefit daughters. Increases in mothers' income, however, are associated with decreased economic adversity for daughters regardless of family structure. This finding is consistent with the trend, noted before, for stepfathers to contribute relatively little to daughters' attainment. Second, improvements in income primarily benefited daughters who were relatively young in 1980. Presumably, improvements in parental income occurred too late to benefit older adolescent daughters who had already finished high school and entered the labor force by 1988.

We also examined whether, between 1980 and 1988, parents (1) felt that things were getting worse financially, (2) used welfare, and (3) experienced unemployment. These features of the home economy are not associated with any outcomes for sons. However, paternal unemployment is associated with less education and greater economic adversity among daughters. In addition, parental welfare use is associated with marginally greater economic adversity among daughters. These findings suggest that deteriorations in economic conditions have greater consequences for daughters than for sons. It may be that parents who experience hardship concentrate their economic resources on sons at the expense of daughters, as some previous research has suggested.

SUMMARY

Consistent with the status attainment literature (Blau and Duncan, 1967; Featherman and Hauser, 1978; Haveman and Wolfe, 1994; White, 1982) and with the life course assumption of intergenerational continuity, we find that parental education and income generally predict offspring's socioeconomic success. For example, both fathers' and mothers' educations are significant predictors of daughters' educational achievement. This pattern is consistent with several studies showing that maternal education is an important predictor of children's success, regardless of paternal education (Beck, 1983; Hill and Duncan, 1987; Kalmijn, 1994). Our results are also consistent with studies showing that mothers' education is particularly important for daughters (Marini, 1978; Sewell, Hauser, and Wolf, 1980; Teachman, 1987). Correspondingly, fathers' education (but not mothers' education) predicts sons' educational achievement. This pattern of findings is consistent with a role-modeling interpretation, that is, that sons may be inclined to emulate the educational attainment of their fathers, whereas daughters may be inclined to emulate the educational attainment of their mothers. It is also likely that highly educated mothers take an active role in their daughters' educations. For example, highly educated mothers may make special efforts to encourage their daughters to do well academically and may encourage (or pressure) their husbands to invest economic resources in their daughters' education.

The fact that parental education makes contributions to offspring's attainment that are independent of parental income is noteworthy. This fact suggests that parental education benefits children in ways that go beyond the kinds of tangible resources that money can buy. Although we are not able to assess all possible mediators in our study, we find that parents' expectations for children's educational attainment account for a substantial proportion of the estimated effect of parental education on offspring's education.

The pattern for parental income is somewhat different, with fathers' income (but not mothers' income) predicting aspects of both sons' *and* daughters' attainment. The finding that parental income facilitates children's achievement independently of education is consistent with several previous studies (Blau and Duncan, 1967; Featherman and Hauser, 1978; Haveman and Wolfe, 1994; Teachman, 1987). As noted previously, high-income parents (regardless of their level of education) can afford consumer goods, private lessons, college expenses, and other resources that increase their children's chances of academic success. However, maternal income, unlike paternal income, does not translate into increases in children's education. Given that husbands tend to earn more money than do wives (both in the larger society and in our sample), fathers' earnings have a greater potential to affect children's attainment than do mothers' earnings. Indeed, many parents may use the fathers' earnings to pay for big budget items, such as children's college education, and may use the mothers' earnings to pay for day-to-day necessities.

We had anticipated that some of the estimated effects of parental income on children are mediated by parents' marital quality, parental support and control, and parents' expectations for children. We find no evidence suggesting that parental marital quality, divorce, or support and control mediate the effects of low income. However, consistent with some previous work (Galambos and Silbereisen, 1987; McLoyd, 1989) we find that parents' expectations mediate a substantial proportion of the estimated impact of fathers' income on offspring's education. This finding is consistent with the notion that parents who are struggling to get by are relatively pessimistic about their children's chances of educational success, whereas affluent parents are more optimistic. Some studies suggest that economically distressed parents lower educational plans more for daughters than for sons (Mott and Haurin, 1982). Our data are partly consistent with this notion. Although parental income in 1980, and changes in income between 1980 and 1988, appear to be as consequential for sons as for daughters, two indicators of severe hardship between 1980 and 1988—paternal unemployment and welfare use—predict poor outcomes for daughters but not for sons. This finding suggests that periods of economic distress are indeed more consequential for daughters than for sons.

Not surprisingly, children's education mediates much of the estimated impact of parental education on children's occupational attainment. However, even with children's education in the equations, our results suggest that parental education lowers daughters' economic adversity. We are not able to explain this effect with our data. One possibility is that highly educated parents socialize their daughters in ways that help them to avoid economic hardship in later life. Further research is needed to address this issue in more detail.

Finally, our research shows that the socioeconomic resources of stepfathers (including education, income, and changes in income) have few consequences for stepdaughters. This finding is consistent with research suggesting that young adult offspring receive less assistance from stepfamilies than from continuously intact families (White, 1992, 1994c). In particular, some stepfathers may be unwilling to invest economic or interpersonal resources in their stepdaughters because of the tension that frequently characterizes these relationships (Hetherington and Clingempeel, 1992). Other stepfathers may be unable to provide economic assistance to their step-daughters because they are financing their own biological children's education. However, we also find that among stepfamilies (but not among con-tinuously married parents), mothers' income predicts daughters' education. This finding suggests that remarried mothers may make a special effort to compensate for stepfathers' lack of support by investing their own earnings in their daughters' education.

Parents' Gender Nontraditionalism and Offspring's Socioeconomic Attainment

PREVIOUS STUDIES

Maternal Employment. Coleman (1988) warned that nonmaternal care lowers children's access to social capital within the family, with detrimental consequences for their achievement. However, other than studies of occu-pational status, which we noted earlier, little research examines how char-acteristics of maternal employment affect the socioeconomic outcomes of adult offspring. Although studies of young children are available, they yield mixed results. Some research suggests negative effects of maternal employ-ment on the cognitive development of boys (Hill and Duncan, 1987), es-pecially in middle-class families (Desai, Chase-Lansdale, and Michael, 1989; Hoffman, 1974; Zaslow, Rabinovich, and Suwalsky, 1991). These studies suggest that interaction with well-educated, middle-class mothers is bene-ficial to children, and that children may suffer when this time is reduced by mothers' employment. Why this situation should be true primarily for boys, however, is not clear. Other research suggests that full-time maternal employment in the first years of life can adversely affect children's social and cognitive development (Baydar and Brooks-Gunn, 1991; Belsky and Eggebeen, 1991). Although we have no studies that follow these children into adulthood, delayed cognitive development in early childhood could have long-term negative consequences for later educational and occupa-tional attainment.

Many other studies, however, have *not* found evidence of negative effects of maternal employment on children's cognitive ability or school perfor-mance (Armistead, Wierson, and Forehand, 1990; Blau and Grossberg, 1992; Gottfried, 1991; Vandell and Ramanan, 1992). Indeed, Haveman, Wolfe, and Spaulding (1991) find that maternal employment, especially during the teen years, is positively related to the likelihood that offspring complete high school. Other studies support the idea that maternal employment increases daughters' self-esteem by providing models of self-sufficiency and attainment (Hoffman, 1989; Mischel and Fuhr, 1988; Richards and Duckett, 1991; Spitze, 1988). Daughters' heightened self-esteem could spur them to greater educational attainment and lead them to take on more challenging jobs involving greater status and income.

Parcel and Menaghan (1994) suggest that the effects of maternal employment are complex and depend on factors such as mothers' hours of work and occupational complexity. Their research shows that mothers' part-time employment is positively related to children's cognitive development, whereas mothers' (and fathers') overtime employment (more than forty hours per week) is negatively related to children's mathematics scores. Other studies have also found that maternal employment is most beneficial to children's academic outcomes when it is part-time rather than full-time (Williams and Radin, 1993). This finding is similar to Muller's (1995) research in which mothers employed part-time were more likely than those employed full-time to engage in behaviors (such as discussing school with children, checking children's homework, and restricting children's television viewing) that facilitate achievement on mathematics tests. Both studies suggest that mothers who work part-time have more academically competent children, on average, than do mothers who work long hours or who are not in the labor force. Children may benefit most when mothers are employed a moderate number of hours because this employment not only increases family income but also provides mothers with a sense of self-efficacy derived from the employment. Long hours of employment, however, might increase work-family conflict, especially for mothers who (like most other mothers) continue to be responsible for the majority of household chores and child care.

Fathers' Share of Family Work.   Children's social competence and feelings of control have been shown to benefit from fathers' involvement in child care (Lamb, 1987; Radin and Russell, 1983). These benefits are likely to facilitate children's academic achievement. More directly, some studies show that paternal nurturance is positively associated with children's cognitive competence, especially for boys (Radin, 1981). In a longitudinal study, Snarey (1993) examined fathers' involvement in three aspects of children's development during their first decade of life and during adolescence: social-emotional (spending time with children), intellectual (consulting with children's teachers), and physical (teaching children to ride a bike). After controlling for fathers' education and other variables, Snarey found that fathers' contribution to social-emotional and physical development is positively associated with daughters' educational and occupational mobility in adulthood. Similarly, fathers' contribution to all three aspects of sons' development is positively related to educational and occupational mobility in adulthood. Taken together, these studies suggest that fathers' involvement with children has positive consequences for children's later socioeconomic attainment.

Nontraditional Gender Role Attitudes. Research has shown that offspring of parents with nontraditional attitudes are more likely to have nontraditional attitudes themselves (Axinn and Thornton, 1993). It is possible that daughters from nontraditional families are more career-oriented than daughters from traditional families. Conversely, it is possible that sons from nontraditional families are more family-oriented than sons from traditional families. Whether these orientations are reflected in different levels of socioeconomic achievement, however, is not clear.

HYPOTHESES

Overall, only a few studies have addressed the life course links between parents' gender relations and offspring's socioeconomic attainment. This deficiency limits our ability to formulate hypotheses about our own data. Although we cannot deal with the impact of maternal employment during early childhood, we can estimate the effects of mothers' hours of employment in 1980, when the children in our sample were 11 years old, on average. Although our analysis is largely exploratory, previous studies suggest the importance of looking at different levels of maternal employment (part-time, full-time, and over-time) as well as at differential effects on sons and daughters. In relation to paternal involvement, we hypothesize that it benefits children's attainment, although this expectation is based on only a small number of studies. Furthermore, we assume that paternal support and control during adolescence mediate the positive estimated effects of fathers' share of family work on offspring's attainment. Finally, our examination of parents' gender attitudes and children's attainment is purely exploratory.

RESULTS

Maternal Employment. Our preliminary analyses indicate that maternal employment interacts with children's gender in predicting offspring's attainment; consequently, we discuss the results separately for daughters and sons. The number of hours mothers worked in 1980 has no apparent impact on any aspect of *daughters'* socioeconomic achievement in 1995. In contrast, mothers' labor force participation in 1980 is related in a curvilinear fashion to *sons'* educational attainment and income. These results appear in Figure 6.3. In relation to education, sons with mothers who worked part-time or full-time in 1980 have about two-thirds of a year more education than do those with mothers who were not in the labor force. However, when mothers regularly worked forty-six hours or more per week in 1980 (over-time), sons have the lowest level of education. The difference between sons whose mothers worked full-time and those whose mothers worked over-time is one full year. The results for sons' income are similar. When mothers worked part-time, sons have the highest level of income, but when mothers worked over-time, sons have the lowest level of income. The difference between sons whose mothers worked part-time and those whose mothers worked over-time represents nearly $9,000 per year. Clearly, these are substantial differences. (See Table 6.5 in the Appendix for the full equations.)

These results are, to a certain extent, consistent with previous studies suggesting that the negative effects of maternal employment are mainly apparent when mothers work unusually long hours (Parcel and Menaghan, 1994). Because a few previous studies have found that detrimental effects of maternal employment are strongest when mothers are well educated (Desai, Chase-Lansdale, and Michael, 1989; Hoffman, 1974), we included interaction terms between mothers' education and hours of employment. These terms are significant for sons' education and income. Plotting the results (not shown) reveals that the curvilinear associations between mothers' hours of employment and sons' education and income (as represented in Figure 6.3) are especially pronounced when mothers have a high level of education. The same curvilinear pattern is present, but weaker, when mothers have a low level of education. Overall, these results suggest that maternal employment is, in general, not problematic for children. But when mothers regularly work very long hours, sons may be disadvantaged, particularly when their mothers are highly educated.

When highly educated mothers work long hours, their sons may benefit less from their mothers' human capital than when their mothers work fewer hours, and hence, spend more time in the home. But why aren't daughters similarly disadvantaged when mothers work long hours? The answer may be that although daughters, like sons, are deprived of access to their moth-

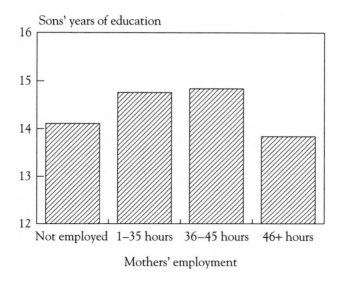

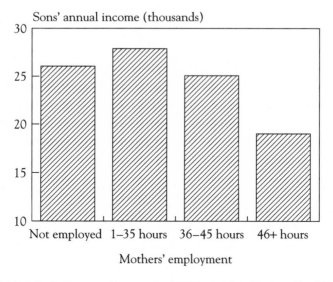

Figure 6.3   Sons' education and income in 1995 by mothers' hours of weekly paid employment in 1980

ers, daughters also benefit from being exposed to powerful models of female achievement. These two tendencies may balance one another, resulting in no net effect on daughters. Sons, in contrast, do not benefit from identification with a powerful female role model, and hence, have more to lose when highly educated mothers spend relatively little time at home.

Following this logic, we checked to see whether mothers' heavy involvement in the labor force is associated with sons' achievement because such involvement decreases the support that mothers give their sons during adolescence. Sons' recollections of maternal support, however, do not account for this pattern. Similarly, sons' recollections of the extent to which mothers and fathers controlled and supervised them as teenagers do not explain these associations. As we noted in Chapter 3, when mothers work especially long hours, fathers are more likely to exhibit certain problematic characteristics, including being unemployed within the last three years and having a high score on a behavior problem index. Controlling for these variables changes the original association but little. Nevertheless, it is possible that the comparatively low level of attainment seen among sons when mothers are employed long hours is related, in some fashion, to problematic characteristics of the father. Overall, sons have the highest level of attainment when their mothers are employed part-time and the lowest level of attainment when their mothers are employed over-time, but we are unable to demonstrate any explanatory mechanisms with our data.

In relation to changes between 1980 and 1988, we find that increases in maternal employment are associated with marginally greater occupational status among both sons and daughters. Other dimensions of offspring's achievement are not related to changes in mothers' hours of employment.

Fathers' Share of Family Work.   Following Snarey (1993), we hypothesized that fathers' involvement in family work is positively associated with children's achievement. In contrast to our expectations, however, fathers' involvement in housework in 1980 is *negatively* associated with offspring's educational achievement and income in 1995. This finding is true for both sons and daughters. As the data in Figure 6.4 indicate, when fathers did half of the housework, offspring have about one-half year less of education than when fathers did little or no housework. Similarly, when fathers did half of the housework, offspring earn about $5,000 less per year than when fathers did little or no housework. These differences are clearly large enough

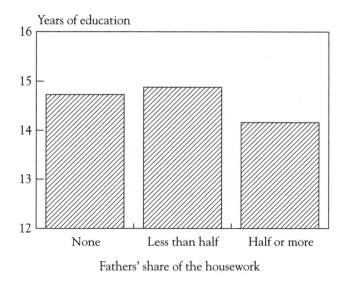

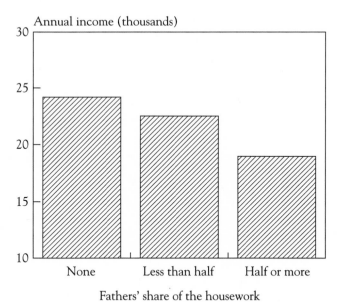

Figure 6.4   Offspring's education and income in 1995 by fathers' share of housework in 1980

to be nontrivial. However, paternal involvement in child care (as opposed to housework) is not related to offspring's socioeconomic attainment.

Our findings appear to contradict previous work suggesting that paternal involvement in family work benefits children. One possibility is that some highly involved fathers are pressured into this arrangement by their spouses, with the result that the coerced involvement serves as a source of tension in their marriages. Marital discord over the household division of labor might, in turn, negatively affect children's accomplishments. However, controlling for parents' marital quality in 1980, as well as divorce after 1980, does not affect the association between fathers' share of housework and offspring's attainment. We also checked to see whether fathers' involvement in housework interacts with parents' marital quality in predicting outcomes, but found no evidence for this either.

We also find that changes in fathers' involvement in housework between 1980 and 1988 (in families where parents remained continuously married) are associated with offspring's outcomes, although in a manner different from that described above. This finding is demonstrated in Figure 6.5 by

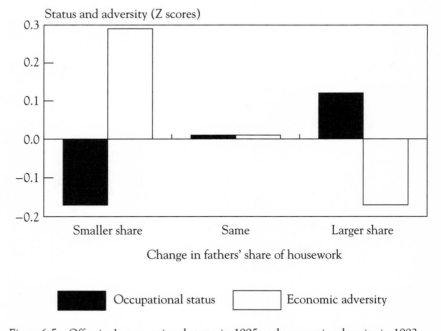

Figure 6.5 Offspring's occupational status in 1995 and economic adversity in 1992 by changes in fathers' share of housework between 1980 and 1988

looking at three groups of fathers: those who took on a smaller share of housework (20%), those who took on a larger share of housework (25%), and those who did not change (55%). When fathers decreased their share of housework (relative to fathers who did not change), offspring have lower occupational status and report more economic adversity. Correspondingly, when fathers increased their share of housework (relative to fathers who did not change), offspring have higher occupational status and report less economic adversity. The difference between fathers who took on a smaller share and those who took on a larger share represents over one-third of a standard deviation for offspring's occupational status and almost one-half of a standard deviation for offspring's economic adversity. Given that the median age of offspring increased from 11 in 1980 to 19 in 1988, this finding suggests that paternal involvement in family work is especially beneficial for offspring if it increases during their adolescent years. (See Table 6.6 in the Appendix for details.)

Gender Attitudes. Parents' gender attitudes in 1980 are not associated consistently with aspects of daughters' or sons' socioeconomic achievement.

SUMMARY

Our results appear to be contradictory. The data seem to suggest that nontraditional gender relations in 1980 depress offspring's attainment. That is, when mothers are highly involved in the paid labor force and when fathers are substantially involved in household work, children's attainment tends to be relatively low. And yet, our data also suggest that shifts toward less traditional gender relations between 1980 and 1988 improve children's socioeconomic chances. That is, sons' occupational status is marginally higher when mothers increase their labor force participation and children's occupational status is higher and economic adversity is lower when fathers increase their share of housework.

Why would offspring's socioeconomic attainment be positively associated with parental traditionalism in 1980 and with shifts toward less traditionalism between 1980 and 1988? One possibility—and one congruent with the life course perspective's emphasis on the timing of events—is that these trends reflect children's ages. In 1980, the average age of children in our sample was 11. When children are relatively young (of primary school age), they may benefit from a relatively traditional division of labor in the family. Under these conditions, mothers' part-time employment allows them to spend a good deal of time with their children, and fathers' involvement in the labor force (rather than in the home) ensures that children's standard of living is not jeopardized. Children (especially sons) may benefit most from this arrangement when their parents are highly educated, that is, when mothers are capable of creating stimulating home environments and fathers are capable of earning large incomes.

But by 1988, the average age of children in our sample was 19. During adolescence, it may be particularly beneficial to have a less traditional division of family labor. If fathers increase their hours in the home when children are teenagers, offspring may benefit from exposure to their fathers' cultural capital (for example, a father's knowledge of the workplace) and from the supervision and control that the father can exercise. Similarly, if mothers increase their participation in the paid labor force, adolescents (especially daughters) may benefit from seeing their mothers model a high level of occupational commitment, especially at a time when adolescents may be making their own career plans. This reasoning is consistent with Haveman, Wolfe, and Spaulding (1991), who found that maternal employment was positively associated with offspring's educational attainment, but only when it occurred during adolescence. This explanation, of course, is based on a post-hoc interpretation of unexpected findings, and therefore further research is needed to confirm such a pattern.

Parents' Marital Quality, Divorce, and Offspring's Socioeconomic Attainment

PREVIOUS STUDIES

Marital Quality.   Research examining the impact of parents' marital quality on offspring's educational and occupational success is scarce. A review of marital quality as an independent variable noted no studies that focus on the impact of marital quality on offspring's success (Glenn, 1990). Since then, two studies yield mixed results. One study found no associations between adult respondents' judgments of their parents' marital happiness and their education, achievement, occupational status, earned income, assets, or perceptions of economic well-being (Amato and Booth, 1991a). A second longitudinal study (Snarey, 1993) found that parents' marital commitment is positively associated with daughters' (but not sons') later educational and occupational attainment.

Although previous studies are ambiguous, parents' marital quality affects aspects of life that have the potential for disrupting success in school and on the job. As discussed in other chapters in this volume, unresolved interparental conflict is a source of stress for offspring because it threatens feelings of attachment to parents, often pulls children into the conflict with one or both parents, and generally decreases the quality of parent-child relations. In addition, parents who fight frequently, compared with less combative parents, tend to discipline their children more harshly, use discipline inconsistently, and supervise them less adequately. Outcomes for children include more antisocial behavior, anxiety and depression, and difficulty in concentrating—factors known to influence performance at school (Davies and Cummings, 1994; Emery, 1982, 1988; Grych and Fincham, 1990). These considerations suggest that the effects of interparental discord on children's attainment are mediated by parental support and control.

Parental Divorce. The literature on parental divorce, in contrast to the literature on parents' marital conflict, is replete with studies suggesting that divorce has an adverse effect on the educational and occupational attainment of offspring. A variety of studies show that adult children of divorce complete fewer years of education, on average, than do those from intact families (Amato and Keith, 1991c; Biblarz and Raftery, 1993; Furstenberg and Teitler, 1994; Keith and Finlay, 1988; Krein, 1986; Manski, Sandefur, McLanahan, and Powers, 1992; McLeod, 1991; Mueller and Cooper, 1986; Zill, Morrison, and Coiro, 1993). Furthermore, Amato and Keith's (1991a) meta-analysis of this literature suggested that the consequences of marital disruption for offspring's educational attainment are stronger for daughters than for sons.

Studies point to several factors that put children of divorce at an educational and occupational disadvantage. The primary reason appears to be the limited income associated with living with a single mother, but role overload and constraints in providing supervision may also contribute to children's school problems (Astone and McLanahan, 1991; Greenberg and Wolf, 1982; McLanahan, 1985, 1988; McLanahan and Sandefur, 1994; Mueller and Cooper, 1986). Another factor is living in a stepfamily; in these cases, the divided loyalties of the biological parent (to children and the new spouse) sometimes mean that fewer resources are allocated to offspring (Sandefur, McLanahan, and Wojtkiewicz, 1992; White, 1994c). However, remarriage following an early divorce (when children are of preschool age) can improve offspring's later life chances (Zill, Morrison, and Coiro, 1993).

Residential mobility following divorce is an additional factor. McLanahan and Sandefur (1994) show that children in single-parent families and step-families move more often than do children with continuously married parents. Residential mobility, in turn, predicts lowered school attendance and a greater likelihood of dropping out of school. McLanahan and Sandefur (1994) show that controlling for residential mobility eliminates much of the difference between children living in stepfamilies, single-parent families, and continuously intact two-parent families. Finally, as indicated in prior chapters, interparental conflict before (and following) marital dissolution can play a key role in the amount of distress experienced by offspring. Consequently, it is possible that some of the lowered attainment of children in divorced families is due to parents' marital conflict, rather than to a shift in family structure.

Amato and Booth (1991a) found no overall difference in socioeconomic achievement between adults who had experienced a parental divorce and those who had not. However, they did find that the type of divorce made a difference. Adult offspring who had been in father custody had more assets than did those who had been in mother custody. Offspring of mothers who remarried had lower educational achievement (by nearly one year) than did those whose mothers did not remarry. In contrast, the remarriage of the noncustodial father appeared to benefit offspring; in these cases, adult offspring reported more assets and less economic hardship, although the source of this advantage was not clear. A decline in the quality of mother-offspring relations following marital disruption was associated with greater economic strain, whereas a decline in the quality of father-offspring relations was associated with fewer assets. The Amato and Booth (1991a) study suggested that the effects of divorce are not uniform and depend on a variety of circumstances that follow parental separation. This conclusion is consistent with the life course perspective's emphasis on the importance of understanding the impact of an event within the context of other events and circumstances that precede and follow it.

HYPOTHESES

Although we have few studies to serve as a guide, it seems likely that parents' marital quality (among parents who remain continuously married) is related to children's school performance, and later in life, to their educational and occupational attainment. Consequently, we hypothesize that low marital quality among parents is associated with lowered attainment among young adult offspring. Prior research consistently indicates that children from divorced families have lower levels of attainment than do children from continuously intact families, and we hypothesize that a similar pattern exists in our own data. Furthermore, we anticipate that parental support and control mediate some of the impact of parents' marital quality and divorce on offspring's attainment. Our longitudinal data also allow us to see whether predivorce marital conflict accounts for any of the association between marital disruption and children's socioeconomic attainment. Finally, we expect to find differences among adult children of divorce depending on factors such as what their age was at the time of marital disruption, which parent had custody, whether parents remarried, how much conflict there was between parents following separation, and how many times children moved following parental separation.

RESULTS

Parents' Marital Quality. To estimate the impact of parents' marital quality, we focused only on those offspring whose biological parents remained married throughout the course of the study. Of our four indicators of parents' marital quality, only divorce proneness is related to any outcome: the greater the level of divorce proneness in 1980, the lower the education of offspring in 1995. Consistent with this finding, increases in divorce proneness between 1980 and 1988 are associated with further declines in offspring's educational achievement. Our measures of parental support account for one-eighth and one-sixth of these associations, respectively, although the remaining coefficients are still significant. This finding suggests that divorce proneness may affect children's education at least partly by lowering the amount of support that they experience as teenagers. Overall, however, the general absence of findings indicates that parents' marital quality (in continuously married families) has relatively few consequences for children's attainment.

Parental Divorce. Unlike parents' marital quality, parental divorce appears to lower educational achievement, lower occupational status, and increase economic adversity. These results appear in Figure 6.6. As the figure indicates, offspring who experience parental divorce, compared with those whose parents remained continuously married, attain slightly less than one-half-year of education. In addition, young adult children of divorce score about one-fifth of a standard deviation lower in occupational status and

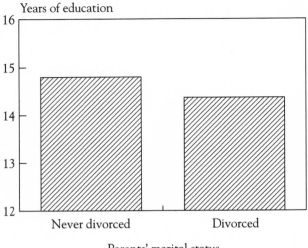

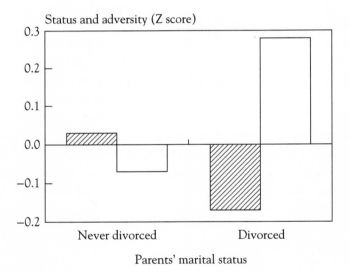

Figure 6.6   Offspring's socioeconomic attainment in 1995 by parental divorce

about one-third of a standard deviation higher in economic adversity. These findings represent weak and moderate effect sizes, respectively.

Several qualifications to these group differences are necessary, however. Divorce prior to 1980 has a stronger association with education than does divorce after that year; this finding suggests that the effects of divorce on educational attainment are more pronounced when children are younger. Early marital dissolutions are marginally related to lower occupational status among both sons and daughters. Divorces between 1980 and 1988, however, are associated with lower occupational status only among sons. In contrast to these variations, the estimated effects of marital disruption on offspring's economic adversity hold regardless of time period or offspring's gender. (See Table 6.7 in the appendix for details.)

Two sets of variables explain the associations between parental divorce and offspring's socioeconomic attainment: parental support while offspring were teenagers and parents' expectations for children's educational attainment. Parental divorce is negatively associated with offspring's recollections of parental support during adolescence and with parents' expectations that their children would attend college. Adding parental support to the model reduces the associations between early divorce and offspring years of education by one-fifth, and between early divorce and offspring's occupational status by one-third. Adding parents' expectations to the model results in additional declines of one-third and one-tenth in the associations for education and occupational status, respectively. In other words, the two sets of variables jointly account for about half of the original associations. These results suggest that the effects of early divorce on offspring's attainment are due to disrupted relations between parents and children during their teen years (and perhaps earlier), as well as parents' lowered expectations for their children.

However, these mediating variables account for little of the estimated effect of late divorce (after 1980) on daughters' occupational status, or for little of the estimated effect of early or late divorces on offspring's economic adversity. We also tested to see whether parents' marital quality in 1980 explains any of the estimated effect of marital dissolution after 1980 on daughters' occupational status or on offspring's economic adversity. However, controlling for predivorce marital quality does not change the size or significance of the coefficients. Consequently, although we see that marital disruption is associated with these problematic outcomes, we are not able to explain the associations with our data.

We examined offspring whose parents divorced to see whether aspects of divorce that are shown in other studies to have an adverse influence on offspring's outcomes are also important to later achievements. Consistent with the finding just noted (that is, that early rather than late divorces are associated with lowered education), children's age at marital disruption is positively associated with education and income. This finding suggests that the impact of divorce is more problematic when children are younger rather than older. Overall, however, we find little evidence that postdivorce circumstances modify children's socioeconomic outcomes. The lack of findings may be due to our small sample size and, hence, the weak statistical power of our tests to detect effects.

SUMMARY

Consistent with our hypothesis that interparental discord lowers offspring's socioeconomic outcomes, we find that both parents' divorce proneness and increases in divorce proneness over time are associated with lowered educational attainment. Overall, however, our data provide limited support for this hypothesis. In contrast, our hypothesis that parental divorce is associated with lower outcomes is strongly supported. Parents' marital dissolution is associated with three out of four measures of offspring's attainment—a finding that is consistent with a large number of previous studies (Amato, 1988; Amato and Keith, 1991c; Biblarz and Raftery, 1993; Furstenberg and Teitler, 1994; Keith and Finlay, 1988; Krein, 1986; McLanahan and Sandefur, 1994; McLeod, 1991; Mueller and Cooper, 1986; Zill, Morrison, and Coiro, 1993). Furthermore, we find no evidence that interparental conflict prior to divorce accounts for any of the estimated effects of divorce. This finding suggests that the apparent effects of marital disruption are not spurious, that is, they cannot be accounted for by predivorce marital quality.

Consistent with a few studies, we find some evidence that parental divorce is more consequential for daughters than for sons (in relation to occupational status), but most of the estimated effects in our data are similar for both sons and daughters. Congruent with the mediation model, divorce appears to lower achievement partly by reducing the amount of support parents give to children during the teen years and partly by lowering parents' expectations for children's education. Also, because we find that the effects of divorce do not depend on whether custodial mothers remarried, our results do not support an economic interpretation of divorce effects. However, consistent with a life course perspective, the timing of divorce appears to be important, with marital disruptions being particularly detrimental when children are young.

Conclusions

Socioeconomic attainment (as reflected in education, occupational status, income, and economic security) is a critical component of most people's definition of success. Besides being valued in its own right, socioeconomic status predicts marital quality, subjective well-being, mental and physical health, and longevity. Consequently, socioeconomic attainment is a key factor in understanding the well-being of the current generation of young adults.

The life course perspective leads us to speculate about the impact of recent historical changes in family life on the socioeconomic outcomes of youth. Consistent with status attainment models and with the notion of continuity across generations, our analysis indicates that parental education is central to offspring's achievement. As we pointed out in Chapter 1, the educational levels of men and women in the United States have been increasing for decades. Because educational attainment is, to a certain extent, transmitted from parents to children, improvements in education in one generation are likely to increase the likelihood that a high level of education is maintained in the next generation. Furthermore, although studies of children's achievement often omit mothers' characteristics, our data show that maternal education has a unique impact on daughters' socioeconomic attainment. Consequently, the rising educational status of women in recent decades suggests additional beneficial effects for daughters as they enter adulthood. And although we do not have enough nonwhites in our sample to draw conclusions about particular minority populations, the marked increase in educational levels among African Americans in recent years is likely to have positive implications for future generations as well.

Our data are also consistent with status attainment models in showing that fathers' income increases the socioeconomic success of both sons and daughters. But in contrast to our optimistic interpretation of educational trends in the larger society, our views about changes in family income during the last few decades are pessimistic. Because of structural changes in the economy, married men's wages have been stagnant (or declined) since the 1970s. In spite of this fact, family incomes have risen slightly during the last two decades because of the greater labor force participation of married women and of modest increases in women's wages. But our data reveal that mothers' incomes—unlike fathers' incomes—do not predict offspring's attainment, perhaps because women's incomes are not large enough (relative to men's) to make substantial contributions to their children's education. Although modest improvements in mothers' wages during the last few decades may have improved (or at least helped to maintain) children's everyday standard of living, they appear to have few implications for offspring's long-term economic well-being after they leave the parental home.

We also find evidence that paternal unemployment and periods of welfare use are related to poorer outcomes, especially for daughters. As pointed out in Chapter 1, unemployment increased during the 1970s and remained high during the 1980s. Although the unemployment rate has declined in recent years, workers in some industries have experienced job loss as companies downsize to remain competitive. Uncertainty about economic trends in the United States makes it difficult to predict future trends in employment. But taken together, our results suggest that declines in fathers' wages and increases in unemployment may have negated some of the benefits derived from higher levels of parental education.

In relation to changes in gender relations during the last several decades, our study suggests mixed effects. We expected mothers' involvement in the labor force to have positive consequences for daughters' attainment; however, we do not see any evidence of beneficial effects. Instead, our results indicate a curvilinear association between mothers' hours of employment and sons' education and income. Sons appear to benefit when mothers work part-time but to be disadvantaged if mothers work especially long hours. In addition, fathers' share of housework in 1980 is related to lower attainment among both sons and daughters. Yet, we also find that shifts toward less traditional gender arrangements in families between 1980 and 1988 are associated with enhanced attainment among offspring.

Our results are difficult to interpret, but as we have suggested, they may reflect offspring's ages, with traditional family arrangements benefiting younger children and nontraditional family arrangements benefiting older children. If this possibility is true, then it is difficult to make straightforward statements about the consequences of more egalitarian family relations for children. Increases in mothers' labor force participation and fathers' share of family work have the potential to benefit older children, but they may disadvantage younger children. Therefore, we cannot say that changes in gender arrangements have either increased or decreased children's chances of socioeconomic success overall. If anything, our results indicate that more research is needed to understand how emerging egalitarian family relations might affect children's attainment.

The results for parental divorce are more straightforward. Divorce appears to suppress most dimensions of socioeconomic attainment, and it appears to do so by lowering parental support of children (helping children with homework, discussing children's personal problems, and so on) and parents' expectations for children's education. It is interesting, that the one dimension of parents' marital quality (in continuously married families) that predicts offspring's outcomes is parents' divorce proneness. It appears that both the increasing divorce rate and the increasing instability of intact marriages are lowering the potential of future generations to succeed economically.

Overall, our data suggest that changes in the last three decades in parental education, income, gender relations, marital stability, and divorce have had mixed consequences. Improvements in parental education have probably been beneficial. And yet, at the same time that parental education has been increasing, the proportion of parents who end their marriages in divorce has also been rising, a trend that has probably been detrimental. Given these contrary influences, it is probable that changes in family life in recent history have had relatively little net impact on children's socioeconomic success. However, depending on the specific changes to which they are exposed, some children are presumably benefited, whereas others suffer. Children who grow up in harmonious, stable families with well-educated parents will enter adulthood with many advantages. In contrast, children who experience economic hardship and parental divorce will have a more difficult time achieving financial success as adults.

Psychological
Well-Being

The life course perspective assumes that the roots of well-being in adulthood can be traced to experiences in the family of origin. In earlier chapters, we have seen that family-of-origin characteristics predict a variety of forms of well-being in early adulthood, including the quality of ties with parents, intimate partners, and members of extended social networks. We also observed links between the family of origin and young adults' socioeconomic success. In this chapter, we focus on what is perhaps the most central of all outcomes: psychological well-being. A sense of subjective well-being is of fundamental importance to individuals, of course. But troubled youth are also unlikely to meet their role expectations and contribute in a positive way to their families and to the larger community. In this sense, psychological well-being has implications that extend far beyond the individual.

The term *psychological well-being* embodies many dimensions. We examine four related but unique aspects of human psychological experience: psychological distress, self-esteem, happiness, and life satisfaction. Distress reflects feelings of nervousness and depression, as well as somatic symptoms such as frequent headaches. Self-esteem refers to the value that one attaches to one's self. Self-esteem is a central component of psychological adjustment, with high self-esteem being associated with low anxiety, good social relationships, and general emotional stability (Burns, 1979). Happiness reflects a general emotional state that the individual feels on a day-to-day basis. Life satisfaction reflects the amount of satisfaction people derive from specific aspects of their environments, such as home, neighborhood, job, relatives, friends, and leisure pursuits. Satisfaction is different from happiness in that it implies a judgment of a situation against a standard of comparison, such as the experiences of friends or one's personal aspirations (Campbell, Converse, and Rogers, 1976, 31). Consequently, it is possible for a person with low expectations to be satisfied with a given outcome but not happy in general. Conversely, a person with high expectations might be dissatisfied with a particular outcome but happy in general. By using measures of four different dimensions of psychological functioning, we are able to cast a broad net in assessing offspring's well-being.

As in previous chapters, we focus on the potential impact of parents' socioeconomic resources, gender relations, and marital quality and stability on offspring. And, as in previous chapters, we turn to the mediation model to help account for any observed associations. Parenting practices and the quality of the parent-child relationship have been shown to have consequences for children's personalities, behavior problems, and psychological adjustment, both in childhood (Maccoby and Martin, 1983; Rollins and Thomas, 1979) and in adulthood (Belsky and Pensky, 1988; Caspi and Elder, 1988). Consequently, it is likely that many family-of-origin characteristics affect adult offspring's psychological well-being, at least partly through their impact on parental support and control.

Measuring Psychological Well-Being

The first measure, *psychological distress*, is based on eight items from the Langner (1962) scale of symptoms. Offspring were asked about the frequency of both physical and mental indicators during the previous year. The former includes acid stomach, headaches, and cold sweats, whereas the latter includes nervousness, isolation, and the feeling that things are not worthwhile. The higher the score on this scale, the more distress people feel. Most people (56%) report having experienced one to three symptoms at least occasionally during the previous year. Few people report no symptoms during the previous year, and a substantial minority (19%) report experiencing three or more symptoms often. (See Table 7.1 in the Appendix for more details on this and the other measures of offspring's psychological well-being.)

Self-esteem is based on the Rosenberg (1965) scale and consists of six items with which people can agree strongly, agree, disagree, and disagree strongly. The statements tap the extent to which individuals believe they have good qualities, are proud of things they have done, are satisfied with themselves, and feel useful. Higher scores indicate greater self-esteem.

We assess *happiness* with a measure widely used in survey research: "Taking all things together, how would you say you are these days? Would you say you are very happy, pretty happy, or not too happy?" Thirty-five percent of offspring are very happy, whereas only four percent are not too happy. A higher score on this item means greater happiness.

Life satisfaction assesses the amount of satisfaction people receive from a number of aspects of everyday life. They are asked to indicate whether they "get a great deal of satisfaction, quite a bit of satisfaction, some, a little bit, or no satisfaction" from nine areas: neighborhood, job or career, house or apartment, friends, hobbies or leisure activities, marriage, children, other family relations, and their financial situation. Scale scores were based only on relevant items. For example, the item dealing with marriage was not asked of unmarried respondents. Higher scores indicate greater satisfaction. Ninety-two percent report a great deal of satisfaction from at least one aspect of their lives. However, nearly half (45%) receive little or no satisfaction from one or two aspects of their lives.

As anticipated, the four outcomes are intercorrelated at moderate but significant levels. This finding suggests that these variables reflect a general domain of psychological well-being; yet each captures a somewhat different dimension. Some research suggests that women experience more "internalizing" problems (such as depression) than do men. However, in our sample, women report more happiness and marginally higher self-esteem than do men. Age is positively related to self-esteem and life satisfaction, suggesting that some aspects of well-being increase as people move through the early years of adulthood.

We also find consistent evidence that recollections of maternal and paternal support are associated with the four measures of psychological well-being, with higher levels of support predicting more positive outcomes. Moreover, maternal and paternal support have associations that are independent of one another, in most cases. That is, when both variables are entered jointly into regression equations, each makes a significant contribution to well-being. In addition, recollections of parental control are related in a curvilinear fashion to all four outcomes, with moderate levels of control being associated with the highest level of well-being. Correspondingly, when parental control is very low or very high, offspring report relatively poor outcomes. These results suggest the utility of examining the role of parental support and control in mediating the impact of parents' socio-economic resources, gender nontraditionalism, and marital quality on off-spring's psychological well-being.

Parents' Socioeconomic Resources and Offspring's Psychological Well-Being

PREVIOUS STUDIES

Parental Education. Prior research suggests that the educational attain-ment of parents has a positive impact on children's psychological well-being. Children with well-educated parents, compared with children with poorly educated parents, have higher self-esteem (Rosenberg, 1965); exhibit fewer behavior problems (Harnish, Dodge, and Valente, 1995; Parcel and Menaghan, 1994); are more popular with peers (Hess, 1970); show fewer signs of maladjustment (Felner et al., 1995); and have a larger repertoire of life skills (Amato, 1987a). These differences appear to persist into adulthood. Using data from the General Social Survey, Acock and Kiecolt (1989) show that maternal education at the time the child is 16 is a consistent predictor of five measures of adult offspring's well-being. Other research shows that mothers' education is associated with high self-esteem, less depression, and higher self-reported health among adult offspring (Acock and Demo, 1994).

Although these findings are consistent, the process by which this comes about is unclear. One explanation refers to the positive impact of education on parents' sense of well-being. Educational achievement is related to peo-ple's reports of being happy and having stimulating, pleasant, and rewarding experiences at work and at home (Campbell, 1981, 60–65). Education also decreases the risk of depression (Kessler, 1982) and increases people's sense of control (Ross and Wu, 1995). These findings are generally independent of income, because education provides people with skills and information that help them cope with economic strain (Ross and Huber, 1985). Con-sequently, the sense of well-being experienced by highly educated parents may translate into a secure and supportive home environment, which, in turn, contributes directly to children's sense of well-being.

Parental education may also affect children through parents' specific child-rearing practices (Harnish, Dodge, and Valente, 1995). As suggested in Chapter 3, well-educated parents, by relying on reasoning rather than harsh discipline, may socialize their children in ways that facilitate emo-tional closeness between parents and offspring. This conduct allows the formation of secure attachments that bode well for children's long-term psychological adjustment (Belsky, 1991).

In addition, parental education may have an indirect effect on children's well-being through its impact on parents' marital quality. As noted in Chapter 4, parental education is positively correlated with marital quality. Parents' marital quality, in turn, is positively correlated with children's psychological and behavioral functioning (see the discussion that follows). We also know that offspring of well-educated parents attain more education than do offspring of poorly educated parents (see Chapter 6). Offspring therefore may enjoy higher levels of psychological well-being as a result of their own educational achievements, which, in turn, reflect their parents' educational achievements.

Parental Income.   Scholars have given a great deal of attention to the impact of parents' income and income loss on children. This research is particularly rich with respect to the impact of economic circumstances on children and adolescents, but less so with respect to long-term effects on young adults. Extensive literature reviews by McLoyd (1989) and McLoyd and Wilson (1991) find that parental job and income loss are related to children's depression, low self-esteem, loneliness, feelings of incompetence, and deviant behavior. More recent research continues to support this pattern. For example, in a study using longitudinal data from the Infant Health and Development Program, Duncan, Brooks-Gunn, and Klebanov (1994) find that persistent poverty is related to higher levels of internalizing (anxiety, depression) and externalizing (aggression, temper tantrums) problems among children at age 5. Similarly, Bolger, Patterson, and Thompson (1995) find that both persistent and intermittent economic hardship are associated with a broad variety of child problems, including difficulties in peer relations, conduct problems at school, and low self-esteem.

Consistent with the mediation model, the effects of economic hardship appear to be mediated though parental punitiveness, inconsistency, and rejection (McLoyd, 1989; McLoyd and Wilson, 1991). For example, Elder, Nguyen, and Caspi (1985) found, in a study of children of the Great Depression, that economic hardship adversely affects the psychological functioning of daughters by increasing the rejecting behavior of fathers. Similarly, a study of economic stress in rural families (Conger et al., 1992, 1993, 1994) indicates that economic pressure increases parent-child conflict, which, in turn, raises anxiety, depression, and antisocial behavior in adolescents. Another study found that economic hardship lowers early adoles-cents' self-esteem indirectly by decreasing parental support and involvement (Whitbeck et al., 1991). Using data from a classic large-scale study of de-linquency in Boston, Sampson and Laub (1994) note that family poverty is related to parents' meting out harsher discipline, providing less supervi-sion, and having weaker attachment to their children; this conduct, in turn, leads to higher rates of delinquency and antisocial behavior as an adult. Delinquency is also associated with higher rates of depression and other mental health problems (Elliott, Huizinga, and Mennard, 1989). Thus, we have abundant evidence that poverty influences offspring's well-being by the way in which it affects parenting processes.

In addition, the effects of poverty on children may be bound up with parents' marital quality in two ways. First, McLoyd's (1989) review suggests that the effects of poverty are magnified if the parents' marriage is weak. This finding assumes that economic hardship and parents' marital quality interact in affecting children's well-being. In other words, marital discord may *moderate* the effects of poverty. Second, parents' marital quality may *mediate* some of the impact of economic hardship on children. Consistent with this notion, a recent study of rural African American intact families (Brody et al., 1994) reveals that limited income is related to parental con-flict over child rearing which, in turn, is related to preadolescent depression, anxiety, and antisocial behavior.

McLoyd (1989) also notes that very few studies address the long-term consequences of economic problems; consequently, there is little evidence that parental income and job loss during childhood adversely affect psy-chological well-being in adulthood. Acock and Kiecolt (1989) show that adults' assessment of family income when they were 16 years of age is pos-itively related to several measures of psychological well-being. However, people's retrospective knowledge of family-of-origin income is bound to be inexact. Moreover, the current psychological state influences people's per-ceptions of parental income. A longitudinal study by Amato (1991) shows that increases in depression are associated with more negative recollections of economic hardship in the family-of-origin. Consequently, it is not clear whether the effects of childhood poverty (or affluence) persist into adult-hood.

HYPOTHESES

Our review of the literature indicates that parental education and income are positively related to the psychological well-being of children. However, relatively little is known about the life course consequences of parents' socioeconomic resources for adult offspring. Because the life course perspective assumes a degree of continuity between childhood and adulthood, we hypothesize that parental education and income are positively related to aspects of offspring's psychological well-being in early adulthood. On the basis of the mediation model, we hypothesize that these associations decline substantially, perhaps to nonsignificant levels, if we control for parental support and control during adolescence. We also expect that several other factors may mediate these associations, including parents' psychological well-being, parents' marital quality, and offspring's educational attainment. In addition, we assess the possibility that the effects of low parental income are moderated by parental education and marital quality, that is, that the impact of economic hardship on children is especially pronounced when parents are poorly educated or have a poor-quality marriage.

RESULTS

Parental Education.   Parental education while children are growing up is associated with every aspect of adult offspring's psychological well-being. Figure 7.1 shows the associations between parental education and our four outcomes. (The full regression equations can be viewed in Table 7.2 in the appendix). Because the results are similar for mothers' and fathers' educations, we use the mean of the two. To facilitate interpretation, the figure shows standardized outcomes (with means of 0 and standard deviations of 1). The figure reveals that offspring whose parents had three or more years of post-high-school education (on average) are approximately one-third of a standard deviation lower in psychological distress than are offspring whose parents had 12 years of education or less. Differences of a similar magnitude apply to the other three measures of well-being. Daughters are affected no differently than sons. Furthermore, these associations are not moderated by whether the children grew up with a stepparent, are living with their parents, are married, have children, or are working or going to school. Therefore, the link between parental education and offspring's psychological well-being is a general one that holds under a variety of circumstances.

We attempted to sort out the way in which parental education influences offspring in several ways. First, we assessed the extent to which parental support and control mediate the estimated impact of parental education. However, entering offspring's reports of parental support and control during adolescence into the equations reduces the links between parental educa-

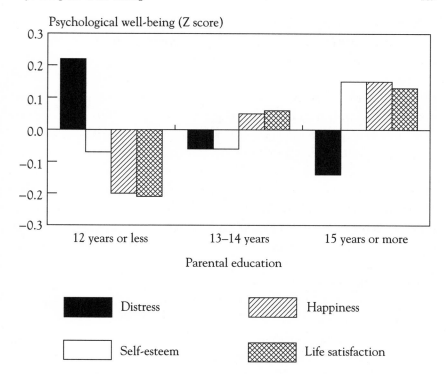

Figure 7.1   Offspring's psychological well-being in 1992 by parents' years of education

tion and offspring's psychological well-being only slightly. Another possibility is that parental education improves parental well-being; and parental well-being, in turn, affects children's well-being. We have information on parental happiness in 1980 and parents' psychological distress in 1983. However, these factors do not explain the associations between parental education and offspring's outcomes. Because parents' marital quality and divorce are related to parental education, it is also possible that these variables mediate the impact of parental education on offspring, but our analyses suggest that they do not. Also, as described later, we find no evidence that parental income mediates the association between parental education and offspring's outcomes.

We also considered the possibility that children's own educational achievements affect their psychological well-being. In fact, entering offspring education into the equations reduces the associations between parental education and well-being by about one-third, on average, although the associations continue to be significant. Therefore, we conclude that the link between parental education and offspring's psychological well-being is due, in part, to the way in which parental education enhances offspring's educational attainment.

Parental Income.   Paternal, maternal, and total family income in 1980 are not associated with any of the four offspring outcomes in 1992. The absence of associations holds for daughters as well as for sons, for those still living at home in 1992 as well as for those living elsewhere, and for those in stepfamilies in 1980 as well as for those in two-parent families. Our literature review suggested the possibility that parental education moderates the effect of income. That is, low income may have a greater adverse effect on off-spring with poorly educated parents than on offspring with highly educated parents. However, our analysis does not support such an interpretation. Another possibility (also suggested by the literature review) is that marital quality moderates the effect of low income on offspring. That is, low income may have a greater adverse effect on offspring when parents' marital quality is low than when parents' marital quality is high. But we find no support for this idea with our data either.

We also estimated the impact of changes in parental income between 1980 and 1988, but no effects are apparent. Consistent with these null results, periods of parental unemployment and welfare use between 1980 and 1992 are not associated with offspring's psychological well-being. Factors that have the potential for moderating these associations (whether or not offspring were living with parents, residing in a stepfamily in 1980, and the gender of the offspring) do not do so.

In addition to changes in objective circumstances, parents' subjective evaluations of financial circumstances may affect offspring. Parents' judgment that things "got better" between 1980 and 1988 has no apparent impact on offspring's well-being. However, parents' judgment that things "got worse" is associated with higher levels of psychological distress and lower levels of happiness, but only among daughters still living at home in 1992. Parental perceptions of financial decline over the eight-year period do not appear to affect other offspring. Furthermore, this finding holds even when we control for family income. These results are consistent with studies showing that perceptions of economic hardship predict problems for daughters (Conger et al., 1993; Elder, 1974; Elder, Nguyen, and Caspi, 1985). However, this finding is contrary to research showing that family income affects the adjustment of adolescent boys (Flanagan, 1990; Conger et al.,

1992). Consistent with the mediation model, when we add maternal (but not paternal) support to the model, the association between parents' perceptions of economic decline and daughters' happiness declines by about one-third and is no longer significant. However, the association involving psychological distress declines only by one-tenth and remains significant.

SUMMARY

Consistent both with a life course perspective and with several studies of adult offspring (Acock and Kiecolt, 1989; Acock and Demo, 1994), our results suggest that parental education has a broad positive effect on offspring's psychological outcomes. These findings stem partly from the way in which parents' education gets translated into offspring's educational achievements. However, we find no support for the mediation model: When we control for parental support and control during adolescence, the links between parents' education and offsprings' psychological well-being change little.

In contrast to parental education, parental income has little apparent influence on offspring's outcomes. Similarly, changes in income and periods of parental unemployment and welfare use are unrelated to offspring's well-being. These findings clash with previous research showing negative effects of economic hardship on offspring (McLoyd, 1989; McLoyd and Wilson, 1991). There are two explanations for this discrepancy, one methodological and the other substantive. First, in many studies, samples are selected so that poor families are overrepresented. Perhaps our subsample of families experiencing severe hardship is not large enough to allow us to detect negative effects. Second, family economic resources may have only short-term effects on offspring. Once children reach adulthood and leave home, effects may be minimal because offspring focus on their own financial circumstances rather than on those of their parents. Indeed, our data reveal that offspring's *own* education and income are both consistent predictors of (low) psychological distress, self-esteem, happiness, and life satisfaction. The notion that parents' economic resources have few long-term negative consequences (once offspring are grown and leave home) is also consistent with our failure in Chapter 3 to find any associations between parental income and the quality of parent-child relationships in early adulthood.

There is one exception to the general absence of findings: daughters who reside at home in 1992 and whose parents believe that their financial circumstances deteriorated during the 1980s report more psychological distress and less happiness than do other daughters. This exception suggests that continuing to live as a young adult in a household that parents' perceive as strained is problematic for daughters. It is also of interest that the one association that attains significance deals with parents' perceptions of economic hardship rather than actual events (income decline, unemployment, and welfare use). This finding is consistent with the life course perspective's emphasis on actors' subjective interpretations of events. If parents perceive their financial situations to be problematic, then offspring may experience the consequences of economic stress, regardless of the actual level of parental income. Recollections of support from mothers appear to mediate part of this association. When parents experienced economic strain, daughters report having been less close to their mothers during the teen years; low support from mothers, in turn, is linked to lower happiness among daughters in adulthood. Therefore, we find some limited support for the mediation model under these particular circumstances.

Parents' Gender Nontraditionalism and Offspring's Psychological Well-Being

PREVIOUS STUDIES

Maternal Employment.   As the reviews of research in previous chapters indicate, few studies show maternal employment to have either positive or negative effects on offspring's relations with parents, intimate relationships, social integration, or socioeconomic attainment. The same may be said for the research on psychological outcomes (for example, see Armistead, Wierson, and Forehand, 1990). There is a suggestion in the literature that maternal employment has positive consequences for daughters' self-esteem (Hoffman, 1989; Mischel and Fuhr, 1988; Richards and Duckett, 1991; Spitze, 1988). There is also a hint that maternal employment is associated with decrements in boys' cognitive development (Desai, Chase-Lansdale, and Michael, 1989), which could result in depression or anxiety in adulthood if it leads to poor educational or occupational attainment. A few studies suggest that mother absence due to employment during the first six months of life increases the risk of insecure attachment to parents, and that this can have negative repercussions for children's adjustment and behavior (Baydar and Brooks-Gunn, 1991; Belsky, 1991; Chase-Lansdale and Owen, 1987), but other studies contradict this finding (Parcel and Menaghan,

1994). Although this point is hotly debated, we cannot address it in our data because we do not have information on maternal employment while our youth were infants.

Fathers' Share of Family Work. Father involvement in child rearing has been shown to have positive effects on children's social competence and feelings of efficacy (Lamb, 1987; Radin and Russell, 1983; Snarey, 1993). These effects may carry over to adulthood and be reflected in less depression and higher self-esteem. On the other hand, it is sometimes argued that intense and nurturant father involvement may result in uncertainty about gender role identification, especially among sons. Available research does not generally support this line of reasoning (Pleck, 1981). However, if true, it could increase depression and lower self-esteem among boys. All of this may be moot if father-child relations are controlled by the mother, such that intense father involvement in child rearing occurs only when the marriage is of high quality. If positive parents' marital quality increases fathers' involvement with children and also improves children's outcomes, then the association between paternal involvement and children's well-being may be spurious. Whether this is the case is something that we will explore.

Nontraditional Gender Role Attitudes. We know of no studies that have examined the links between parents' gender role attitudes and offspring's outcomes. However, a shift toward less traditional gender role attitudes among wives is related to a deterioration in wives' reported marital quality (Amato and Booth, 1995). This may be because wives with nontraditional views are more likely to challenge the division of household labor, thus leading to marital strain (Barnett and Baruch, 1987). Amato and Booth (1995) also found that a shift toward less traditional gender role attitudes among husbands is related to improvements in husbands' reported marital quality. As reviewed below, research consistently shows that marital conflict is associated with low psychological well-being among children. These findings suggest that nontraditional attitudes on the part of mothers may lower well-being among children, whereas nontraditional attitudes on the part of fathers may increase well-being among children. However, we would only expect that mothers' and fathers' nontraditional attitudes to have effects on offspring to the extent that they are bound up with parents' marital happiness and conflict.

HYPOTHESES

On the basis of previous research, we expect to find few effects of maternal employment on offspring, with the exception that it may improve the self-esteem of daughters. We hypothesize that fathers' involvement in house-work and child care is positively related to most outcomes. Furthermore, we assume that parental support and control mediate these relationships. We also assume that mothers' nontraditional attitudes, to the extent that they are bound up with low marital quality, are associated with poorer out-comes among offspring. Fathers' nontraditional attitudes, in contrast, may be related to better outcomes among offspring.

RESULTS

For the most part, mothers' participation in the labor force in 1980 has no apparent effect on offspring's psychological well-being in 1992. Further-more, the number of hours worked, shift work, job satisfaction, and working overtime are not related to any dimension of well-being. However, mothers' reasons for employment in 1980 are associated with several outcomes. When mothers worked "to get away from the family or children," offspring have lower self-esteem and life satisfaction. Similarly, when mothers worked because they "don't like staying at home," offspring have lower self-esteem and happiness. Finally, when mothers worked "to be more financially in-dependent," offspring have lower scores on all four measures of well-being. These mothers may be in the workforce because they do not get along with their spouses or because they have relatively little interest in family roles. However, these associations are not accounted for by poor marital quality or offspring's recollections of maternal or paternal support. Although these motives for mothers' employment suggest problems in the home environ-ment, we cannot identify these problems more precisely.

   The amount of housework and child care done by the father in 1980, as well as mothers' and fathers' gender role attitudes in 1980, are unrelated to the psychological well-being of sons or daughters in 1992. Similarly, changes in these variables between 1980 and 1988 are not related to offspring's outcomes. Moreover, offspring's gender, living in a stepfamily, living with parents in 1988, and living at home in 1992 do not moderate the generally weak and nonsignificant associations between gender nontraditionalism and offspring's outcomes. We also checked to see whether marital conflict mod-erates the effect of nontraditional gender role attitudes, and it does not. In short, with the exception for mothers' reasons for working, gender role orientations in the family of origin appear to have no long-term consequences for offspring's well-being. This pattern of null findings is consistent with the general tenor of prior research.

Parents' Marital Quality, Divorce, and Offspring's Psychological Well-Being

PREVIOUS STUDIES

Parents' Marital Quality.   A variety of studies show significant negative associations between the level of conflict between married parents and children's functioning and well-being (see Davies and Cummings, 1994; Emery, 1982, 1988; and Grych and Fincham, 1990, for reviews). The effects of family conflict may be long-lasting. Clinical research shows that adults suffering from depression and other psychological disorders report more childhood family conflict than do matched controls (Adams, Bouckoms, and Streiner, 1982; Overall, Henry, and Woodward, 1974). Similarly, Booth and Edwards (1990) and Amato and Booth (1991a), using a representative national sample of married couples, found that respondents who recalled their parents' marriage as being unhappy reported more psychological and marital problems than did other adults.

Several mechanisms exist through which marital conflict might have both short- and long-term negative consequences for children's psychological adjustment. First, overt conflict between parents is a direct stressor. Observational studies show that children react to conflict between parents with fear, anger, or the inhibition of normal behavior (Cummings, 1987; Cummings, Zahn-Waxler, and Radke-Yarrow, 1981). And preschool children—who tend to be egocentric—may attribute blame for marital conflict to themselves (Grych and Fincham, 1990), resulting in feelings of guilt and lowered self-esteem.

The mediation model, however, assumes that interparental discord affects children through its impact on parent-child relationships. Children are often drawn into conflict between parents, resulting in deteriorations in parent-child relationships and general family cohesiveness (Amato, 1986; Johnston, Kline, and Tschann, 1989). Physical violence between parents, in particular, appears to increase problems among children by increasing the risk of parent-to-child aggression (Hughes, 1988; Jouriles, Barling, and O'Leary, 1987). Children exposed to persistent conflict become insecure about the continued emotional and physical availability of parents; emotional insecurity, in turn, decreases children's ability to regulate their emotions and behavior, effectiveness in coping with stress, and sense of control (Davies and Cummings, 1994). Consistent with this argument, some studies show that the quality of parent-child relationships mediates the psychological effects of marital conflict on children (Caspi and Elder, 1988; Fauber et al., 1990).

Parental Divorce.   Parental divorce is also associated with a number of difficulties among children, including low self-esteem, behavior problems, and psychological distress (Amato and Keith, 1991a). For some children, problems associated with marital disruption improve over time, as children and their parents adjust to their new circumstances (Hetherington, Cox, and Cox, 1982). But for others, the effects of parental divorce appear to last far into adulthood. A meta-analysis of thirty-seven studies involving over eighty thousand individuals (Amato and Keith, 1991b) indicates that adults who experienced parental divorce as children, compared with adults from continuously intact two-parent families, score slightly higher on measures of psychological and behavioral problems.

Divorce may be associated with child problems because of the interparental conflict that often precedes and sometimes follows marital disruption. Consistent with a conflict interpretation, a number of prospective studies show that child problems are present many years prior to divorce (Block, Block, and Gjerde, 1986; Cherlin et al., 1991; Doherty and Needle, 1991). The Cherlin et al. (1991) study also shows that predivorce conflict accounts for part of the association between parents' marital dissolution and behavior problems among boys, but not girls. In addition, Furstenberg and Teitler (1994) found that predivorce risk factors such as maternal education, age at marriage, and age at first birth account for a significant portion of the association between parental divorce and psychological problems among young adult offspring. These studies demonstrate the need for a more thorough comparison of the influence of the predivorce context and the dissolution itself on offspring's psychological well-being.

Although parents' marital conflict and other predivorce factors may account for some of the apparent effects of divorce, marital disruption introduces new stressors that may affect children negatively. For example, divorce often results in residential moves (Astone and McLanahan, 1994); conflict between parents over custody and visitation (Johnston, 1994); loss of contact with noncustodial fathers (Furstenberg and Nord, 1985); and changing schools, parental remarriage, and other life events that many children find to be stressful (Wolchik et al., 1985). Furthermore, divorce is frequently followed by a decrease in children's standard of living (Duncan and Hoffman, 1985; McLanahan and Booth, 1989). The economic deprivation associated with divorce may reduce the chances of attending college and acquiring a high-paying job (McLanahan and Sandefur, 1994). The resulting low socioeconomic status and thwarted opportunities may be an additional source of psychological stress for young adults.

These considerations suggest that marital dissolution is more stressful for some children than others, depending on the particular circumstances that follow parental separation. This reasoning is consistent with the life course notion that the effects of an event (such as divorce) depend on the conditions that follow the event. The life course perspective also sensitizes us to the importance of conditions that exist *prior* to the event, as well as to people's appraisals of the event. Children for whom divorce is an opportunity to escape from a highly conflictual, hostile, and abusive home may be better off in a well-functioning single-parent household. In contrast, other children have parents with quiescent but less than satisfactory marriages. These parents may divorce for reasons of personal fulfillment or because of the presence of a more attractive partner. These latter cases are likely to represent an unexpected and unwanted change that is particularly disturbing to children (Wallerstein and Kelly, 1980). In general, the mental health consequences of life transitions depend on the stress of the situation prior to the transition (Wheaton, 1990). Transitions are nonproblematic when the situation that is about to change is characterized by a high level of stress. But when the pre-transition situation is not stressful, change is likely to be detrimental to psychological well-being.

Marital disruption may also lead to some positive outcomes among children, such as greater independence and (for women) attachment to the labor force (Barber and Eccles, 1992). These considerations help to explain why the average differences between children from divorced and continuously intact families tend to be small rather than large. Although divorce harms many children, its long-term psychological effects are less serious for other children and may benefit some. Consequently, a diversity of outcomes for children of divorce is likely, depending on a variety of pre- and post-divorce contingencies.

HYPOTHESES

Previous research is clear in suggesting that interparental conflict is problematic for children's development. Studies also indicate that distressed adults tend to recall a high level of family discord as children. However, few longitudinal studies have been able to trace the effects of parents' marital quality during childhood and adolescence on well-being in adulthood. Because of the consistency of prior research, we hypothesize that parents' marital quality in 1980 is positively related to offspring's psychological well-being in 1992. Furthermore, using the mediation model, we expect that levels of parental support and control explain at least some of the estimated effects of parents' marital conflict on children.

Previous studies lead us to hypothesize that adult offspring who experienced parental divorce have lower psychological well-being, on average, than do those whose parents remained continuously married. However, the relative importance of interparental discord and parental divorce is not well understood. On the one hand, if parents in an unhappy marriage do not divorce, then they are better able to maintain a high standard of living that benefits their children. On the other hand, if they dissolve the marriage, then their children are no longer subject to damaging interparental discord. With our longitudinal data, we will address the often-posed question of whether it is better for the children if parents preserve or if they dissolve a poor quality marriage.

In addition, previous work suggests a number of divorce circumstances that are stressful for children, including declines in standard of living, moving, loss of contact with noncustodial parents, postdivorce conflict between parents, and parental remarriage. Following a life course perspective, we consider the role of these contextual factors, as well as the age of children at the time of divorce, as predictors of adjustment among adult children of divorce.

RESULTS

Parents' Marital Quality.   Our analysis of parents' marital quality is limited to those offspring whose parents remained continuously married between 1980 and 1992. For these families, the quality of the parents' marriage in 1980 is consistently associated with the psychological well-being of offspring in 1992. When parents' marital quality is high, offspring report less psychological distress and greater self-esteem, happiness, and life satisfaction. Our four measures of parents' marital quality—marital happiness, interaction, conflict, and divorce proneness—all have similar associations with offspring's outcomes. For marital happiness and interaction, three out of four associations are statistically significant, whereas for marital conflict and divorce proneness, all four associations are statistically significant. The size of these associations is similar for all dimensions of parents' marital quality; consequently, we use marital conflict to illustrate our findings, as conflict is the focus of most previous research. Figure 7.2 shows the associations between conflict and the four measures of offspring's psychological well-being. The difference between little or no marital conflict and a relatively high level of conflict is approximately one-third of a standard deviation—a moderate effect size. (The full regression equations may be viewed in Table 7.3 in the Appendix.)

The pattern of results is similar for both sons and daughters, with a few exceptions. The estimated effects of parents' conflict on psychological distress and self-esteem are stronger for sons than daughters (as reflected in significant interaction terms). Similarly, the estimated effects of parents' marital instability on psychological distress and self-esteem are marginally stronger for sons than daughters. Early research suggested that parents' marital conflict and instability are more problematic for boys than girls (Block, Block, and Gjerde, 1986; Hetherington, Cox, and Cox, 1982; Wallerstein and Kelly, 1980). However, later studies have failed to consistently support this notion. Nevertheless, we see some evidence in our data that sons are affected more than daughters when parents' marriages are marked by conflict and instability.

We expected that recollections of parental support and control mediate some of the associations between parents' marital quality and offspring's psychological well-being. This situation is true in a few cases. For example, parental support and control mediate about 30% of the associations between parents' marital instability and offspring's happiness and life satisfaction. In most cases, however, parental support and control mediate little or none of the association. This finding suggests that parents' marital quality affects children's psychological well-being through some mechanism other than parent-child relationships during adolescence. Interestingly, our findings suggest that a decline in paternal involvement with children cannot account for the greater impact of parental conflict on sons, as noted before.

Changes in marital quality between 1980 and 1988 have little discernable effect. This conclusion is based on comparisons of marriages that im-

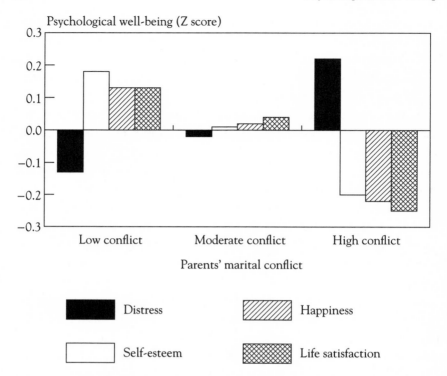

Figure 7.2   Offspring's psychological well-being in 1992 by parents' marital conflict in 1980

proved in quality, declined in quality, remained of poor quality, and remained of high quality during this eight-year interval. There is no difference between those whose parents' marriages improved and those whose parents' marriages declined. It appears that a poor quality marriage at any time has a detrimental impact on offspring's well-being. We find some evidence that marriages that changed (in either direction) have greater adverse effects than marriages that remained stable for the duration, but this is only true for parents' marital happiness. Therefore, we conclude that if parents' marital quality is high and stable, youth benefit; if it is of consistently low quality or unstable in quality, youth are adversely affected.

Parental Divorce.   As has been noted in prior work, divorce by itself has relatively small effects on children, on average. Our findings are consistent with prior research on the topic. Indeed, we found no effects of parental divorces that occurred since 1980, when the study began. However, divorces that occurred prior to 1980 were associated with two of the four measures of well-being: happiness and life satisfaction. The difference is one-third of a standard deviation in each case. Readers should recall that all of these cases were ones in which children were living in stepfamilies in 1980. This finding suggests that divorces that occur at a young age and are followed by parental remarriage are more problematic than those that occur when children are older and not followed by remarriage prior to children's departure from the parental home.

The factor that seems to account best for the association between divorces prior to 1980 and offspring's happiness and life satisfaction is the level of parental support during adolescence. When the two parental support variables are added to the equations, the estimated effects of early divorce (followed by remarriage) completely disappear. Changes in family structure may interfere with the ability of parents to provide social and emotional support; this, in turn, may negatively affect children's adjustment.

To consider the joint effects of predivorce marital quality and divorce, we exclude those offspring whose parents ended their marriages prior to the beginning of the study and turn to those offspring who experienced divorce after 1980. When the quality of the parents' marriage in 1980 (prior to divorce) is taken into account, it is clear that some offspring suffer more than others. (This finding is reflected in significant interactions between 1980 marital conflict and divorce between 1980 and 1992.) Those offspring who live in homes where parental conflict is high and a divorce ensues do as well as individuals who grow up in happily married, intact homes. However, children who live in homes in which parents seldom fight, but then divorce, show relatively high levels of psychological distress and unhappiness. It seems likely that the dissolution of a home that they thought was stable is an unwelcome and disturbing event in the lives of these offspring. By way of illustration, the results for happiness appear in Figure 7.3. Note that it is offspring from low conflict marriages that end in divorce who are particularly unhappy as adults.

Dimensions of Divorce. We also examined the impact of a variety of postdivorce variables for those 87 offspring who experienced parental divorce. Consistent with the preceding analysis, having a mother who remarries following divorce is negatively associated with two aspects of well-being: happiness and life satisfaction. The differences are about one-third of a

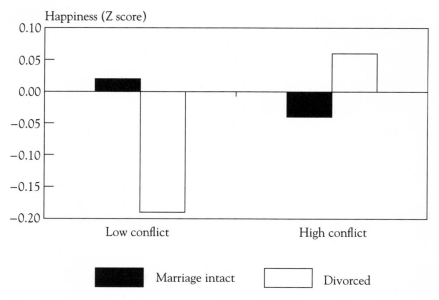

Figure 7.3   Offspring's happiness in 1992 by parents' marital conflict in 1980 and
divorce between 1980 and 1992

standard deviation in each case. These results are congruent with other
step-family literature that shows that child-stepparent relations are sometimes problematic, leading to conflicting loyalties between parents, spouses,
and children (Hetherington and Clingempeel, 1992; White, 1994c; White
and Booth, 1985).

Postdivorce conflict between parents is another source of stress that appear to affect offspring later in life. As can be seen in Figure 7.4, the estimated effect of postdivorce conflict on self-esteem follows a predictable
pattern and is quite large. Our measure includes four areas of disagreement:
support payments, visitation, child rearing practices, and custody. The difference between offspring whose parents fought over three or more issues,
compared with those who fought over none, is about two-thirds of a standard deviation—a large effect size. This is not surprising, given that support,
visitation, child rearing, and custody all involve the child. Under these
circumstances, children are likely to feel caught in the middle—a situation
that is especially aversive for children (Buchanan, Maccoby, and Dornbusch, 1991).

Changing residences following marital disruption is also associated with

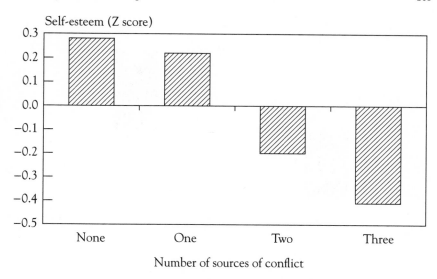

Figure 7.4 Offspring's self-esteem and parents' postdivorce conflict

psychological distress and unhappiness. Figure 7.5 shows that the effect of moving is more than .4 of a standard deviation in both cases. Other studies have documented the stress associated with residential change for parents (Booth and Amato, 1993) and young children (Astone and McLanahan, 1994; McLanahan and Sandefur, 1994). No study, to our knowledge, has shown comparable findings for adult offspring.

Finally, offspring's reports of having less contact with one (or both) parents following divorce and objective assessments of income decline in children's households following divorce are not associated with any measures of psychological well-being. Similarly, children's ages at the time of marital disruption are not related to any outcome.

SUMMARY

Consistent with several studies of adults (Adams, Bouckoms, and Streiner, 1982; Amato and Booth, 1991a; Booth and Edwards, 1990; Caspi and Elder, 1988; Overall, Henry, and Woodward, 1974), parents' marital conflict when children are growing up is associated with multiple dimensions of psychological well-being in adulthood. This finding is consistent with the life course perspective's assumption of continuity across generations. However, because most previous studies were cross-sectional, researchers have had to

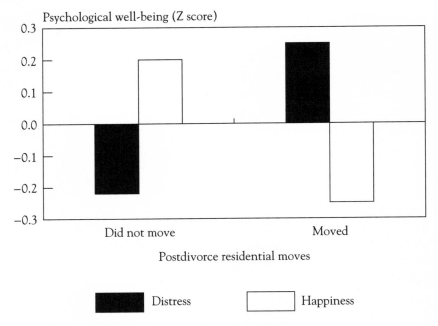

Figure 7.5   Offspring's psychological well-being and postdivorce residential moves

rely on retrospective data derived from a single source. In contrast, our study uses national longitudinal data, with parents reporting on their marital quality and offspring reporting on their psychological well-being. Consequently, our study provides strong evidence that interparental conflict has long-term negative consequences for children's psychological well-being. Furthermore, our study suggests that a stable, high-quality parental marriage maximizes offspring's mental health. Vacillations in parents' marital quality have effects similar to living with parents who have consistently poor marital quality.

With respect to divorce, our study documents that the consequences of marital dissolution are linked to predivorce marital quality. For offspring residing with parents in poor quality marriages, divorce does not appear to have negative long-term consequences for well-being. In contrast, offspring whose parents' marriages are not highly conflicted appear to suffer when the marriage ends. It is precisely under these conditions that children are most likely to view marital disruption as an unexpected and unwelcome event. This finding has rarely appeared in the literature on children and divorce, perhaps because of the small number of investigations that have included data on marital quality measured prior to divorce. However, a recent study by Jekielek (1996) using the National Longitudinal Survey of Youth yields results similar to our own. In this study, children in high-conflict environments exhibit lower levels of anxiety and depression if their parents divorce than if their parents remain together. Consistent with a framework proposed by Wheaton (1990), transitions out of a stressful role are likely to be beneficial, whereas transitions out of a pleasant role are likely to be stressful. This principle would appear to apply to children of divorce.

Our findings, in one sense, seem to be incongruent. On the one hand, offspring appear to benefit from divorce when there are high levels of parental conflict. On the other hand, they do not appear to benefit when two married parents reduce their level of conflict. We think the answer lies in the stability of the pattern. A detailed analysis of change in marital quality among married couples using data from this study (between 1980 and 1992) shows that an improvement in marital quality is as likely to be followed by a decline as it is to remain stable. Consequently, because many improvements in marital quality are not permanent, continued instability in the parents' marriage is likely to disturb children and undermine their sense of emotional security (Davies and Cummings, 1994). Divorce, in contrast, represents a permanent change. Unless the custodial parent reestablishes a high-conflict pattern in a second marriage, or a pattern of sustained conflict with the ex-spouse (which is rare, as postdivorce conflict between ex-spouses tends to decline over time), the situation represents an improvement for offspring.

Conclusions

As in previous chapters, we conclude by considering the possible implications of social change during the last three decades for the current generation of youths' transition to adulthood—an interest that grows out of the life course perspective's emphasis on historical context. Our analysis of the impact of parents' socioeconomic resources, nontraditional gender behavior and beliefs, and marital quality and stability on offspring's psychological well-being yields a tableau of mixed results. In relation to parents' socioeconomic resources, we see evidence for cautious optimism. Parental education appears to have consistently positive long-term effects on the psychological well-being of offspring. This circumstance appears to be due, in part, to the impact of parental education on offspring's educational attainment.

These findings suggest that changes during the last few decades in education have been, if anything, beneficial to young adults. Improvements in education benefit people in many positive ways. Education enhances the ability to earn income, raises the likelihood of finding interesting and rewarding jobs, strengthens perceptions of self-competence and internal control, and increases satisfaction with life in general. Well-educated parents may convey their positive outlooks to their children, resulting in a transmission of well-being across generations. In addition, well-educated parents may socialize their children in ways that facilitate close parent-child relationships (for example, through the use of induction rather than coercive punishment). And because well-educated parents tend to have high aspirations for their children (as well as the financial resources to realize these aspirations), their children tend to attain relatively high levels of education. For these reasons, the rise in educational levels may well have had a positive impact on the psychological well-being of the generation currently reaching adulthood.

In contrast, economic hardship among families has been increasing in the last two decades, with those in the working and lower middle classes slipping further down the economic ladder. Economic strain makes life difficult in many ways for children, and previous studies have amply documented the toll that poverty takes on children's psychological and behavioral adjustment. Nevertheless, research dealing with the consequences of economic hardship once offspring have grown and left the parental home is sparse. Our data show no negative consequences of low parental income, declines in income, parental unemployment, or parental welfare use during the 1980s on the psychological well-being of young adult offspring in the 1990s. Although the disadvantages experienced by children in poor families should not be underestimated, we are cautiously optimistic that children are not "scarred for life" by economic hardship in their families of origin; indeed, most enter adulthood as well-functioning, reasonably happy individuals.

In relation to changes in gender relations, we find little evidence that nontraditionalism in the family of origin has any consequences (positive or negative) for offspring's psychological well-being. The only aspect of gender roles that is related to offspring's well-being is the reason that mothers give for being in the paid labor force. Offspring appear to be adversely affected when the reasons reflect little commitment to or interest in family roles. However, we suspect that these findings have less to do with changing gender relations than with family tension or with problems that a small number of mothers (or fathers) have enacting family roles. Overall, our data suggest that shifts toward greater gender egalitarianism do not have consequences for offspring's psychological adjustment one way or the other.

In contrast, low marital quality among parents while offspring are growing up appears to have adverse consequences for the psychological well-being of offspring long after they reach adulthood. These results are remarkably consistent, with virtually every dimension of parents' marital quality significantly predicting every dimension of offspring's well-being. As in previous chapters, these findings lead us to the question of whether marital quality in the United States is declining. If marriage is becoming a more difficult and stressful arrangement for parents, then the prognosis for young adults is not good. At best, the decline in marital quality has probably offset any good that may have accrued to children through increasing levels of parental education.

Although there is debate about whether marital quality has changed, everyone agrees that divorce has increased since the 1960s. We see some evidence that early parental divorce followed by remarriage is associated with lower psychological well-being among young adults. Given that most divorces occur when children are young, and given that remarriage often follows divorce, this finding is troubling. But the picture is more complex. Our longitudinal analysis indicates that divorce is beneficial for children when it removes them from a high-conflict marriage. In contrast, divorce is problematic for children when it removes them from a low-conflict marriage. These results suggest that divorce can have positive or negative effects on children, depending on the family dynamics that precede it.

Combined with our findings on the effects of parents' marital quality, we are led to the following conclusions. On the one hand, divorce appears to be a necessary "safety valve" for children (and parents) in high-conflict households. On the other hand, as divorce becomes increasingly normative, people may be leaving marriages that are only moderately unhappy. If the threshold for unhappiness at which parents abandon marriage is declining, then divorce is removing a growing number of children from two-parent homes that still provide many benefits. Although children in these latter situations gain little, they are likely to be exposed to many of the stressors that frequently follow divorce, such as moving, changing schools, conflict between parents over postdivorce arrangements, and declines in household income. According to this latter scenario, most divorces in the past (when marital dissolution was uncommon and occurred only under the most troubling circumstances) freed children from home environments that were especially aversive. In contrast, many divorces today (when marital dissolution is common) subject children to a range of stressful experiences with few compensating advantages.

Conclusions,

Implications, and

Policy Recommendations

Controversy continues to rage over whether the American family is declining or becoming more diverse. This debate has been ubiquitous in the 1990s, appearing in one form or another in scholarly journals, the popular press, and political discourse. Given the dramatic changes that have occurred during the last three decades—in the economy, in the roles of men and women in the family and the workplace, in the nature of marriage, and in family structure—the intensity of this debate is not surprising.

At the heart of this controversy is a concern over whether changes in family life have harmed or benefited children. People are right to be concerned, as young children are highly dependent on the adults who care for them. If family life is becoming more stressful and less supportive, then children will suffer. But an even more important issue refers to the consequences of family change for offspring as they make the transition to adulthood. It is possible that most children eventually recover from family stress and manage to overcome early obstacles to success. As offspring take on adult roles, they may be increasingly affected by their current situations and relationships; correspondingly, the impact of the family of origin may gradually fade until its influence is nil. Indeed, most offspring may enter adulthood with few noticeable ill effects, regardless of the number of stressors to which they were exposed during childhood.

However, if children are not as resilient as this optimistic scenario suggests, then increasing numbers of people may be entering adulthood with serious personal and social deficits, including fragile ties to parents, diffi-

culties in maintaining intimate relationships, weak community attachments, a limited ability to support themselves and their dependents, and a
general sense of malaise. This latter possibility suggests that young adults
in the 1990s are less prepared than young adults of previous generations,
not only to lead satisfying lives but also to carry out their responsibilities as
members of society. According to this pessimistic view, the unraveling of
the American family is a precursor to the unraveling of the larger social
bond.

A large number of studies have addressed the implications for children
of particular family changes, such as periods of economic hardship, the
movement of mothers into the paid labor force, and parental divorce. However, no previous study has been able to provide a comprehensive picture
of how these factors are related to multiple outcomes among young adult
offspring. In the present study, we used longitudinal data from two generations to accomplish this task. We began by examining associations between
parents' reports of family characteristics in 1980 and offspring's reports of
well-being in 1992–1995. This process allowed us to establish whether differences *between* families are related to offspring outcomes. We then examined associations between parents' reports of changes in family
characteristics during the 1980s and offspring's reports of well-being in
1992–1995, thus allowing us to establish whether changes *within* families
are related to offspring outcomes. These procedures generated a great deal
of information about the connections between the family of origin and
offspring well-being in early adulthood.

In this chapter, we integrate the findings from the entire study. The life
course perspective suggests that data not only need to be interpreted with
a historical context, but also can illuminate the dynamics of a particular
period of history. Consequently, we begin by using the results of our study
to draw tentative conclusions about the impact of recent shifts in family
life for the well-being of the current generation of young adults. After this,
we discuss some of the connections between our results and the life course
perspective. We then address the implications of our research for the mediation model based on parental support and control. Next, we focus on
the roles of mothers versus fathers in predicting offspring well-being and on
the differential consequences of family-of-origin characteristics for sons and
daughters. We conclude with a consideration of policy issues.

Family Change and Offspring Well-Being

PARENTS' SOCIOECONOMIC RESOURCES

Educational levels of Americans have increased substantially throughout much of this century. For children born in the 1950s, 56% of fathers and 58% of mothers were high school graduates; correspondingly, 14% of fathers and 7% of mothers were college graduates. In comparison, for children born in the 1980s, 85% of fathers and 81% of mothers were high school graduates; correspondingly, 28% of fathers and 19% of mothers were college graduates (Hernandez, 1993, Chap. 6). Similar increases occurred among most racial and ethnic groups, including whites, African Americans, and Hispanics.

Our study consistently highlights the benefits of parental education for offspring. For example, parental education is positively associated with children's socioeconomic attainment. Parental education is also positively associated with aspects of social integration, including the size of offspring's friendship networks and the number of clubs and organizations to which they belong. In addition, high parental education predicts multiple dimensions of offspring psychological well-being, including a low level of distress and high levels of self-esteem, happiness, and life satisfaction. Moreover, parental education is associated with later age at marriage. And among married offspring, parental education is positively related to offspring marital quality and negatively related to the probability of divorce. The link between parental education and offspring education is of central importance, as offspring education accounts for substantial proportions of the associations between parental education and offspring social integration, psychological well-being, marital quality, and marital stability. To the extent that it increases children's educational attainment, parental education provides multiple benefits to offspring in early adulthood.

Only one finding from our study suggests that a high level of parental education is a disadvantage: Parental education is negatively associated with relationship quality among cohabiting offspring. We assume that this situation is due to parental disapproval of cohabiting relationships, although we cannot test this idea with our data. Given that cohabitation is increasingly common among young adults, including those with well-educated parents, we should not minimize the gravity of this finding. Nevertheless, cohabiting relationships tend to be short-lived, with most breaking up or ending in marriage within two year (Bumpass, Sweet, and Cherlin, 1991). Consequently, this negative consequence of high parental education is not a long-lasting one for most offspring who are affected.

Overall, our results indicate that young adult offspring with well-educated parents experience a higher level of general well-being than do those with poorly educated parents. Combining this finding with recent historical trends leads to a straightforward conclusion: if parental education improves a variety of long-term outcomes for offspring, then the rising educational level of parents in the United States during this century has probably benefited succeeding generations of young adults, including the current one. But it is also possible that the apparent effects of parents' educational attainment on offspring are due to an unmeasured variable, with innate cognitive ability being a likely contender. According to this view, offspring of well-educated parents are advantaged because they inherit a high level of cognitive ability (and perhaps other desirable traits as well) from their parents genetically. If this view is true, then the associations between parental education and children's outcomes are spurious, and increases in parental education are unlikely to provide real benefits to children.

However, even if some portion of the association is spurious, it is difficult to conclude that a high level of parental education has no favorable consequences for children. Indeed, some indirect evidence suggests that we are seeing some benefits of increasing levels of educational attainment in the United States. For example, mathematics and science scores on the National Assessment of Educational Progress have been increasing for the last twenty years (U.S. Bureau of the Census, 1992, Table 251). And scores on intelligence tests have been rising in the United States for the last fifty years (Begley, 1996). These improvements in cognitive ability may have come about because well-educated parents tend to adopt child-rearing practices (such as using explanations and reasoning, encouraging autonomy and creativity, and conveying high aspirations) that facilitate children's cognitive growth. Indeed, studies show consistent declines during this century in the proportion of parents who value strict obedience, encourage conformity, or use corporal punishment with their children (Bronfenbrenner, 1958; Gecas, 1979). Alwin (1984) found that increases in education account for much —but not all—of these shifts in parents' socialization values. These are precisely the society-wide changes in parental behavior that we would expect to see if improvements in parental education have direct and beneficial consequences for children.

One study found evidence that seems to contradict this view. Alwin (1991) showed that the trend toward more education has not resulted in corresponding improvements in vocabulary, as reflected in a word knowledge test administered as part of the annual General Social Survey between 1974 and 1990. Indeed, when Alwin adjusted for education, vocabulary scores declined during this period. In a more detailed analysis of this issue, Glenn (1994) demonstrated that a likely cause of this education-adjusted decline in vocabulary is a decrease in time spent reading as a result of greater television viewing. Regardless of the explanation, though, Alwin's (1991) analysis suggests that higher levels of education have offset this decline, resulting in no net change in vocabulary scores. If educational levels had not increased, then vocabulary scores, rather than remaining constant, would have decreased during this period.

Overall, the evidence suggests that increases in parental education have benefited children. This does not mean that parental education has increased children's well-being in an absolute sense, only that children would be worse off if parental education had not increased. Much of the discussion about family decline—and its presumed detrimental impact on children— has failed to acknowledge this important trend, focusing instead on more controversial changes such as the increase in divorce and the growing number of young children in nonparental care. However, our study suggests that a more balanced view of family change must recognize the broad benefits for children of continuing improvements in parental education during recent decades.

When we turn to trends in family income, the picture is less rosy. Starting with World War II and continuing through the 1960s, earned income grew as the U.S. economy expanded. However, this favorable situation changed with the recessions of the 1970s and 1980s; during these two decades, the median income of male workers fell, unemployment rose, family poverty increased, and welfare use expanded. Currently, income inequality is increasing, with many families becoming poorer at the same time that other families are becoming richer. The increase in the number of mother-only households has exacerbated this trend. In spite of the gains of many middle-class two-parent families, the proportion of families and children experiencing economic hardship has continued to rise in recent decades.

What are the consequences of these economic changes for children's lives? Prior research clearly shows the toll that financial distress takes on young children's psychological adjustment, behavior, and academic achievement. However, we know relatively little about the long-term consequences of parental economic resources for offspring as they enter adulthood. Our study yields some evidence of enduring long-term effects. For example, fathers' (but not mothers') income is related to the amount of education that children obtain, as well as other aspects of offspring achievement, even with parental education controlled. Also, spells of paternal unemployment and parental welfare use are associated with lower education and greater economic adversity among daughters. Furthermore, declines in parental income and periods of paternal unemployment predict less parental assistance to children, especially with money and transportation. And among daughters still living at home, parents' perceptions of economic decline are associated with greater unhappiness and psychological distress. Finally, among married offspring, low paternal income, declines in parental income over time, and periods of paternal unemployment and welfare use are linked with low marital quality. These latter associations can be accounted for partly by the effects of parents' economic resources on offspring's education and partly by the inability of poor parents to provide economic assistance to their married children.

These results support the notion that financial stress has long-term consequences for children's socioeconomic attainment and marital quality. Therefore, it appears that a declining standard of living for many parents has made it more difficult for their children to succeed occupationally and to obtain the material rewards associated with success. In addition, economic decline in the family of origin has indirectly weakened the marriages of young adults, placing greater stress on an already beleaguered institution. In this sense, the ill effects of parental economic hardship extend well into the next generation.

In contrast to these findings, parental economic resources are not related to aspects of offspring social integration or psychological well-being (with the exception of daughters still living at home). The absence of associations between parental income (and other indicators of parental financial hardship) and these outcomes appears to clash with the results of prior research dealing with young children and adolescents. Taken together, these findings suggest that offspring may recover from some of the social and psychological consequences of economic hardship as they grow older and leave the parental home. Of course, it may only be in cases of severe hardship that long-term negative consequences persist, and we may not have enough cases like this in our sample to detect any effects. Nevertheless, our results suggest that in the broad majority of families, economic factors have relatively little to do with the social integration and psychological well-being of offspring when they reach adulthood.

Before concluding this discussion of parental socioeconomic resources, it is useful to consider another change in family life. In the 1950s, the typical adolescent (aged 12 to 17) had three or four siblings; by the 1980s, this figure had decreased to two (Hernandez, 1993, Chap. 2). This decline in family size has implications for our understanding of how parental educational and economic resources affect children. First, decreases in family size have accentuated any positive effects of parental education. Siblings compete with one another for parental time and attention, with the result that a declining number of siblings are sharing the benefits of improvements in parental education (Blake, 1989). Second, the decline in family size has helped to ease some of the economic strain associated with declining wages and employment opportunities. Indeed, it is likely that some parents decreased their desired family size as a way of dealing with a declining standard of living (Hernandez, 1993, Chap. 2).

In summary, educational levels of parents have risen, which is probably good for children. Furthermore, these benefits are being divided among a smaller number of siblings within households, which is better yet. But at the same time, many parents, regardless of education, hold jobs for which they are overqualified, are forced to work part-time, or face unemployment as corporations across the country "downsize." The financial stress created by the lack of well-paying jobs for parents is probably bad for children, although decreases in family size have improved the situation somewhat. Overall, our study suggests that the beneficial effects of parental education are more pervasive than the detrimental effects of economic hardship. However, if economic well-being continues to decline for many families (and there is no sign that this trend will abate), the long-term negative consequences for children may become stronger. In short, the decline in economic opportunities in the United States during the last few decades may have undermined some of the benefits that might otherwise have accrued to children because of the rise in parental education, and this trend may become more pronounced in the foreseeable future.

PARENTS' GENDER NONTRADITIONALISM

The roles of men and women in the family and in the workplace have shifted dramatically in the last few decades. In contrast to the 1950s, a majority of married mothers are now in the labor force. This change was accompanied by a shift in people's attitudes, with most Americans now agreeing that husbands and wives should share employment as well as domestic responsibilities. But although married men have increased the amount of time they spend in household chores and child care, married women (even if employed full-time) still do the majority of family work. Although strict father-breadwinner, mother-homemaker arrangements now characterize only a small minority of American households, most families are far from egalitarian in their division of labor.

How have changes in gender roles within the family affected long-term outcomes for children? Our study reveals mixed findings. In relation to maternal employment, some of the results are positive. For example, mothers' employment is associated with greater church involvement and community attachment among daughters. Also, increases in mothers' employment over time are associated with higher perceived assistance from parents, more actual help received from parents, and slightly higher occupational status among both sons and daughters. On the negative side, mothers' employment increases the probability of relationship dissolution among offspring; in particular, it increases the probability that cohabiting sons and daughters end their relationships without marrying and that married daughters get divorced. The number of hours that mothers work appears to be critical for some outcomes. Compared with mothers who are not employed, mothers' part-time employment is associated with more affection for fathers, more consensus with fathers, more frequent contact with fathers, and (among sons) higher socioeconomic attainment. However, when mothers regularly work long overtime hours, children have less affection for fathers, less consensus with fathers, less contact with fathers, and (among sons) lower socioeconomic attainment.

Perhaps a mixed set of results is to be expected. Previous research suggests that the impact of maternal employment depends on mothers' reasons for employment, the types of jobs that mothers hold, mothers' job satisfaction, and the amount of support that mothers get from their spouses (Hoffman, 1989; Mischel and Fuhr, 1988; Parcel and Menaghan, 1994; Spitze, 1988; Zaslow, Rabinovich, and Suwalsky, 1991). We were not able to explore all of these moderating factors in our study. Nevertheless, our results suggest that as long as mothers do not work excessively long hours, the long-term consequences for children tend to be positive—or at least neutral. The one exception involves offspring relationship dissolution. However, the fact that daughters of employed mothers are at increased risk of divorce may reflect enhanced feelings of independence. That is, daughters of employed mothers may be especially likely to feel that they are capable of supporting themselves, and hence, be inclined to leave unsatisfying relationships. We caution readers, however, that the estimated effects of mothers' employment that we find in this study cannot be generalized to mothers' employment during children's first year of life, as none of our offspring were that young when the initial data were collected.

In relation to fathers' involvement in family work, the picture is mainly positive, with some exceptions. Fathers' share of child care is positively associated with later father-child affection, but negatively associated with later father-child coresidence. Fathers' share of child care is positively associated with aspects of social integration, including the number of kin to whom offspring feel close, the number of organizations and clubs to which offspring belong, and offspring's feelings of community attachment. Similarly, increases in fathers' share of housework over time are associated with a greater number of friends and organizational memberships. The generally positive impact of paternal involvement is consistent with previous work done with children. However, fathers' share of housework is negatively related to several aspects of children's socioeconomic attainment—at least in 1980 when most children were relatively young. But if fathers increased their share of housework during the 1980s, then offspring tend to have a high level of socioeconomic attainment. Fathers' share of child care also increases the probability of offspring cohabitation, as well as the likelihood that sons end cohabiting relationships without marrying.

As for parents' gender attitudes, relatively few significant findings emerged from our study. And the results that emerged were not consistently negative or positive.

It is difficult to generalize across this mixed set of findings. However, one theme is apparent: when parents have nontraditional gender relations, offspring appear to be more unconventional. For example, when fathers are highly involved in child care and when parents hold nontraditional gender attitudes, unmarried offspring are less likely to coreside with parents. Furthermore, maternal income and paternal involvement in child care appear to increase the likelihood that offspring will cohabit. Similarly, maternal employment, paternal involvement in child care, and nontraditional gender attitudes increase the likelihood that cohabiting offspring end their relationships without marrying. The fact that nontraditional parents have nontraditional children is not surprising, as offspring are likely to learn individualistic or unconventional attitudes from observing their parents. In addition, parents with unconventional views are probably tolerant of such behavior in their children, thus making it easier for children to make unconventional choices.

In summary, we conclude that changes in gender relations within families have had relatively few negative consequences, overall, for offspring. In particular, they appear to have no impact on such vital aspects of offspring well-being as marital relations, educational attainment, psychological distress, self-esteem, happiness, or life satisfaction. Such a conclusion makes sense when we consider the fact that families, across time and cultures, have found a variety of ways of organizing the division of labor. Indeed, our findings suggest that shifts toward gender egalitarianism have benefited offspring in some ways. Those on the religious and political right assume that egalitarian gender relations are problematic for children; consequently, they call for a return to the father-breadwinner, mother-homemaker model of family life (Davidson, 1989; Falwell, 1981; Gilder, 1986; Schafly, 1977). Our findings contradict this view. From a child's perspective, a basic sense of emotional security and economic stability are more important than how breadwinning and domestic responsibilities are divided between parents.

PARENTS' MARITAL QUALITY AND STABILITY

After remaining stable throughout the 1950s, the divorce rate in the United States increased in the 1960s, doubled between 1966 and 1976, then leveled off during the 1980s at a historically high level. This rise was at least partly due to the fact that barriers to marital dissolution became weaker, as reflected in growing community tolerance of divorce, the introduction of no-fault divorce laws, and the rising economic independence of women. However, it is also likely that a decline in marital quality contributed to the upward trend in divorce. Increases in marital tension during this period are probable, given (a) the eroding financial security of many families; (b) the conflicting gender-role expectations held by many husbands and wives; (c) an increase in standards for what constitutes a successful marriage, thus making satisfactory marriages more difficult to attain; and (d) a weakening commitment to the norm of lifelong marriage that may have lessened some people's willingness to put time and effort into making their marriages work. According to Glenn (1996), prior to marriage, people evaluate potential partners under the best of circumstances. But after marriage (or remarriage), continuous contact reveals deficiencies in the new partner, resulting in dissatisfaction followed by divorce. Thus, high expectations for marriage, and relaxed restrictions on divorce, work together to erode marital satisfaction and elevate divorce to record highs that are unlikely to subside in the future.

Our data show that the long-term consequences of interparental discord for children are pervasive and consistently detrimental. Poor marital quality, as well as declines in marital quality over time, are associated with problematic relationships with mothers and fathers (less affection, less consensus, less perceived support, and less help exchanged); more difficulties in dating among single offspring (fewer dates, more difficulty finding dating partners, and less happiness with current dating partner); lower marital quality among married offspring (less happiness, less interaction, more conflict, more problems, and more divorce proneness); a greater probability of offspring relationship dissolution (cohabiting relationships as well as marriages); lower social integration (less church involvement, smaller networks of close kin and friends, and less community attachment); less education; and poorer psychological well-being (greater psychological distress, lower self-esteem, less happiness, and lower life satisfaction). These results suggest that parents' marital unhappiness and discord have a broad negative impact on virtually every dimension of offspring well-being. Although many of the effect sizes generated by our analyses are not large, even modest declines in well-being, spread across large numbers of offspring, reflect a serious social deficit. If marital quality is indeed declining in the United States, then prospects for the future are not encouraging.

Parental divorce also appears to have negative consequences for offspring, although these are not as pervasive as the effects of parents' marital quality. Parental divorce is associated with more problematic parent-child relationships (less affection, less consensus, less contact, and less perceived support); an increased probability of divorce among married offspring; and lower socioeconomic attainment (lower education, lower occupational status, and greater economic adversity). Furthermore, these associations are independent of predivorce conflict between parents. In other words, for these outcomes, low parental marital quality lowers offspring well-being, and parental divorce lowers it even further.

However, our longitudinal analyses suggest that some of the consequences of divorce depend on the level of marital conflict that precedes it. When marital conflict is low in 1980, parental divorce between 1980 and 1992 is associated with lower social integration (fewer friends and kin), lower marital quality among married offspring, and lower psychological well-being (greater psychological distress and lower happiness). But when marital conflict is high in 1980, parental divorce between 1980 and 1992 is associated with *positive* outcomes. It appears that parental divorce benefits children in certain ways if it removes them from a discordant parental household. Our faith in this finding is supported by a recent longitudinal study, based on the National Longitudinal Survey of Youth, showing essentially the same result among children aged 6–14 (Jekielek, 1996).

This finding raises an interesting question: What proportion of divorces are preceded by a long period of overt interparental conflict, and hence, are beneficial to children? From our own data we estimate that less than a third of parental divorces involve highly conflicted marriages. Only 28% of parents who divorced during the study reported any sort of spousal physical abuse prior to divorce, 30% reported more than two serious quarrels in the last month, and 23% reported that they disagreed "often" or "very often" with their spouses. Thus, it would appear that only a minority of divorces between 1980 and 1992 involve high-conflict marriages.

If divorce were limited only to high-conflict marriages, then divorce would generally be in children's best interest. But the fact that one-half of all marriages today end in divorce suggests that this is not the case. Instead, with marital dissolution becoming increasingly socially acceptable, it is likely that people are leaving marriages at lower thresholds of unhappiness now than in the past. Unfortunately, these are the very divorces that are most likely to be stressful for children. Consequently, we conclude that the rise in marital disruption, although beneficial to some children, has, in balance, been detrimental to children. Furthermore, if the threshold of marital unhappiness required to trigger a divorce continues to decline, then outcomes for children of divorced parents may become more problematic in the future.

SUMMARY

Our study leads to both positive and negative conclusions. The increase in parental education has probably benefited children in multiple (often unacknowledged) ways. Furthermore, the trend toward greater gender egalitarianism within marriage has not harmed children, overall. Indeed, it has benefited them in certain respects. However, increases in financial hardship and the growing popularity of divorce have negatively affected children. But parental marital quality is the key variable, for it is bound up with virtually every dimension of offspring well-being. If marital quality is no lower now than it was thirty years ago, then the positive and negative trends of the last three decades may well have balanced one another, leaving children no worse off, but no better. Yet larger social trends, as well as a handful of studies (Glenn, 1991, 1996; Rogers and Amato, in press), suggest that marital quality is declining. If this is true, then the balance for offspring making the transition to adulthood has tilted in a negative direction. Unless marriage becomes a more satisfying and secure arrangement in the future, the outlook for future generations of youth may be even more pessimistic.

The Life Course Perspective

One of the fundamental assumptions of the life course perspective is that parents' and children's lives are intertwined over time. Many offspring, as they leave home and become independent of parents, may think that their families had little impact on them. Indeed, some youth may actively reject various aspects of their parents' beliefs and lifestyles. Similarly, many parents with teenage or young adult children may shake their heads in disbelief and wonder how their children came to be the way they are. Given the variety of influences on children, including the media, peers, and schools, these feelings are not only to be expected but also contain a measure of truth. The family of origin is not a monolithic institution that irrevocably shapes children's personalities and lives for all time.

Nevertheless, it would be a mistake to conclude that the family of origin has little long-term influence on children. Our study documents numerous examples of the ways in which family-of-origin characteristics affect offspring as they make the transition to adulthood. Most of these associations—measured over a twelve- to fifteen-year period—are not strong, as reflected in the modest effect sizes reported in Chapters 3 through 7. Of course, measurement error in both our independent and dependent variables attenuates the magnitude of associations; this circumstance means that most of the coefficients reported in our study are *underestimates* of the true association between variables. Furthermore, even modest differences between groups can have substantively important implications for individuals.

For example, parental divorce is associated with about one-half-year less of education among offspring. One-half-year may not sound like much, but each year of education raises annual income by nearly $4,000 (Kominski, 1990). So the annual gap in income associated with one-half-year of education, multiplied by the number of years that a person is in the workforce, amounts to a substantial lifetime difference in earnings.

In addition, some of the effect sizes in our study are substantial. For example, when we look at offspring's affection for fathers, the difference between those whose fathers were highly involved in child care and those whose fathers were not represents three-fourths of a standard deviation. Similarly, parental divorce during adolescence lowers daughters' affection for fathers by nearly an entire standard deviation. In addition, full-time maternal employment increases the probability that married daughters will divorce by 161%. Similarly, parental divorce increases the probability that married offspring of either gender will divorce by nearly 75%. These effect sizes are large by anyone's standards.

Finally, even if many family-of-origin influences are not overwhelming, they appear to pervade virtually every aspect of adult offspring's lives: their standard of living, the size of their social support networks, whether they cohabit prior to marriage, the quality of their marriages, whether their marriages end in divorce, their self-esteem, and their general happiness with life. The overall pattern, therefore, appears to be one of modest but pervasive effects on offspring. Consequently, our study is consistent with a number of previous efforts in demonstrating a degree of continuity between experiences in the family of origin and experiences and circumstances in young adulthood.

A second assumption of the life course perspective is that the timing and sequencing of events is important. Our study provides numerous examples of this principle. For example, a variety of findings suggest that changes in the family of origin between 1980 and 1988 have a greater impact on younger offspring who are still living at home in 1988 than on older offspring who have left home. For example, a decline in parents' marital quality during this period is related to affection for fathers among younger offspring, but not among older offspring. This finding suggests that younger offspring feel less close to their fathers if they observe, at close quarters, increases in discord between their parents. Older offspring, however, are less likely to experience declines in affection, presumably because they have already formed stable relationships with their fathers. We also find that declines in parents' marital quality between 1980 and 1988 are related to less happiness with current dating partners, but only if offspring are teenagers still living at home in 1988. Once again, interparental discord appears to interfere with children's dating relationships, but only if children are sharing a household with parents, and hence, are directly exposed to a problematic interpersonal environment.

Another example refers to changes in parents' economic resources. Improvements in parental income between 1980 and 1988 are associated with increased attainment among younger daughters still living at home in 1988, but not among older daughters who have left home by then. Presumably, these older daughters had already finished school or entered the labor force, and hence, are not able to benefit from improvements in their parents' financial status. Similarly, parents' perceptions of financial decline between 1980 and 1988 are associated with higher psychological distress among daughters still living at home in 1988, but not among those who have already left home.

The consequences of parental divorce also appear to depend on children's age. Early parental divorce is associated with lower affection for both parents—especially fathers. However, later divorces (when most children are adolescents) are associated with declines in sons' affection for mothers and in daughters' affection for fathers. We assume that when divorces occur early in life, relations with both parents are weakened. But by the time children are adolescents, they identify strongly enough with the same-sex parent that divorce does not substantially weaken that relationship. We also find that parental divorces that occur when children are younger (prior to the teenage years) have more negative implications for children's socioeconomic attainment and psychological well-being than do divorces that occur when children are older. This finding may reflect the fact that young children are especially vulnerable and dependent on their families. In contrast, parental divorces that occur when offspring are older (teenagers or young adults) increase the risk of offspring divorce more so than parental divorces that occur when offspring are younger. These results indicate that the consequences of parental divorce depend on children's ages and that the nature of the effect varies with the type of outcome.

The general pattern of findings is consistent with our reasoning in Chapter 1 that it is necessary to consider children's ages and stage in the transition to adulthood when examining *changes* in the family of origin. But it is less critical to take into account children's ages when assessing the impact of relatively stable family-of-origin variables, such as parental education.

A third assumption of the life course perspective is that individuals are active rather than passive. In the present study, it is clear that family-of-origin characteristics do not affect children's lives in a rigidly deterministic manner. Instead, our data indicate considerable variability in the ways in which children react to family-of-origin circumstances. Although many offspring grow up in homes marked by affluence and harmonious relations between parents, they still develop into troubled young adults. And although others grow up in homes marked by poverty and interparental discord, they still develop into competent and happy adults. Offspring are capable of squandering early advantages and of surmounting early disadvantages, depending on the choices they make in adolescence and early adulthood.

Clearly, the family of origin shapes and constrains children's opportunities. But within a given set of opportunities, offspring make choices. For example, parental education and fathers' income increase children's educational choices. Not all offspring with highly educated, affluent parents complete college, of course. And some children with poorly educated, impoverished parents manage to obtain college degrees. However, attending college is an easier choice for the former group than for the latter. Similarly, when parents model egalitarian gender roles and are accepting of unconventional lifestyles, children have a greater range of choices for their own intimate relationships. For example, when mothers earn a high income and when fathers are highly involved in child care, offspring are more likely to cohabit with a partner. Not all offspring with these backgrounds chose to cohabit, of course, and some proceed directly to marriage. Nevertheless, parental behaviors and characteristics shape children's opportunities, and in doing so, make certain behaviors more or less probable.

A view of children as active, rather than passive, also indicates that children are capable of affecting their parents (Ambert, 1992). In this book, we have tended to frame issues in terms of parents affecting children, but some of the findings undoubtedly reflect reciprocal relations between parents and children. For example, our study consistently establishes links between parents' marital quality and long-term problems for offspring. Although interparental conflict undoubtedly makes life difficult for children, poorly behaved, noxious children are also likely to increase the level of strain between parents. Indeed, many child outcomes can best be viewed as the result of circular processes of cause and effect between parents and children.

Finally, the life course perspective considers families in their historical context. Indeed, one of the purposes of our study has been to assess the implications of recent historical changes in family life for youth as they make the transition to adulthood. Although we have had to extrapolate beyond our data somewhat to do so, our findings provide a clearer basis than do most previous studies for drawing conclusions about the links between changes family life and offspring well-being in young adulthood.

Of importance in our study is the recent reversal of a long-term trend for offspring to leave home at progressively earlier ages. It appears that the age at which offspring first leave home is increasing, particularly among young men (Buck and Scott, 1993). This trend involves a large number of youth. Aquilino and Supple (1991) estimate that 74% of persons 19 to 25 years old coreside with their parents for a period of time. As indicated before, parents' socioeconomic status, marital quality, and divorce have a greater affect on youth still living at home than on those who have left. The historical change in the length of coresidence with parents means that the beneficial as well as the adverse effects that we observe are likely to be exacerbated if current trends continue.

Parental Support and Control

Although the life course perspective provides a general macro-level framework for our study, we also relied extensively on a micro-level perspective based on the nature of parent-child interaction. According to this perspective, parental support and control reflect two fundamental dimensions of parental behavior. Previous research consistently shows that a high level of support and a moderately high (but not excessive) level of control are associated with a variety of positive psychological, behavioral, and academic outcomes among children (Lamborn et al., 1991; Maccoby and Martin, 1983; Rollins and Thomas, 1979). Furthermore, parental support and control are related to many contextual family variables, such as social class, economic hardship, parents' marital quality, and parental divorce. For these reasons, many developmental researchers use a *mediation model* in which parental behaviors are assumed to mediate the impact of contextual behaviors on children's outcomes. In the present study, we explored the extent to which parental support and control mediate the estimated effects of parents' socioeconomic resources, gender nontraditionalism, and marital quality and stability on children's well-being.

Our measures of parental support behave in ways that are consistent with previous research. Studies suggest that parental support of children is higher when parents are well-educated and economically comfortable, when mothers are employed (but not for excessive hours), when fathers are highly involved in everyday child care, and when parents have happy marriages. In the present study, offspring's recollections of maternal and paternal support during the teenage years are positively and significantly associated with parental education and income, maternal part-time (but not full-time or overtime) employment, paternal involvement in child care, parents' marital quality, and parents' marital stability (that is, the absence of divorce). Furthermore, offspring's recollections of parental control are significantly higher when parents are well-educated, mothers do not work long overtime hours, fathers are highly involved in housework, parents have traditional attitudes about gender, and parents have a high-quality marriage. These links are precisely the ones we would expect to find if our measures of parental support and control are valid.

Children's recollections of parental support are significantly associated with many of the outcomes in our study. High levels of maternal and paternal support are linked with affection for parents, consensus with parents, frequency of contact with parents, perceived assistance from parents, dating happiness, church attendance, the number of close kin and friends, feelings of community attachment, educational attainment, occupational status, (low) economic adversity, (low) psychological distress, self-esteem, happiness, and life-satisfaction. Correspondingly, parental control is associated in a curvilinear fashion with many outcomes, including affection for parents, consensus with parents, perceived assistance from parents, the number of close friends, feelings of community attachment, psychological distress, self-esteem, happiness, and life satisfaction. In each case, optimal outcomes are associated with a moderately high level of control, whereas poor outcomes are associated with either a low or a very high level of control. This pattern of associations for support and control is entirely consistent with prior research on children and adolescents (Maccoby and Martin, 1983; Rollins and Thomas, 1979)

Because parental support and control are linked with both the independent variables (family characteristics) and the dependent variables (offspring outcomes) in our study, they may play a role in mediating the effects of the former on the latter. In fact, we found a number of instances in which the mediation model is supported. For example, parental support during adolescence mediates about one-half of the estimated impact of parents' marital quality on offspring's current affection for parents. Similarly, parental support mediates many of the associations between measures of parents' marital quality and aspects of offspring's social integration. Parental support also mediates much of the estimated impact of parental divorce proneness (in marriages that remain intact) and parental divorce on offspring's educational attainment, happiness, and life satisfaction.

This pattern of findings suggests that mediation processes are limited to parents' marital quality and divorce, as parental support mediates little of the estimated effects of parents' socioeconomic resources and gender non-traditionalism. This result is due to the fact that parental support is correlated more highly with parents' marital quality variables than with other family-of-origin variables. Our findings, therefore, suggest that many of the problematic long-term effects of marital discord are due to decrements in parent-child relationships. This conclusion is consistent with the interpretations of other observers (Caspi and Elder, 1988; Davies and Cummings, 1994; Emery, 1988). However, few studies have demonstrated long-term patterns using a sample of adult offspring.

In contrast to our findings regarding parental support, parental control does not play a mediating role in our study. We reach this conclusion even though our measure of parental control is related to both our independent and our dependent variables, and even though we allowed for both linear and nonlinear effects in our mediation models. We are not certain why control did not play a mediating role. Perhaps a more detailed measure of control would mediate the observed associations—especially if it included information on specific parental disciplinary practices. Alternatively, it is possible that we used the wrong time period to assess parental control. The level of parental control may be more consequential when children are younger, that is, during middle childhood rather than adolescence. Hence, our focus on parental control during adolescence may have led us to underestimate its importance. Finally, parental support may be so vital to children that it in itself has controlling properties, and the implicit threat of a loss of affection may be sufficient to control offspring's behavior. If this circumstance is true, then the concept of control is already imbedded within our measure of support, and our measure of control may have been superfluous.

Our measures of maternal and paternal support are somewhat problematic, in that the same source (offspring) provided information on these as well as the dependent variables. Consequently, common method variance may have inflated some of the correlations between parental support and offspring outcomes. Although this is a nuisance factor in the present study, we do not believe that it substantially influenced our results for several reasons. First, as noted before, the measures of support (as well as control) are correlated in theoretically meaningful ways with our independent variables—all of which are based on parent data. Second, our measures of support (and control) are not related to many of the outcomes in our study, such as dimensions of offspring dating or marital quality. If a general positivity or negativity bias were operating, then parental support should be correlated with offspring outcomes across *all* domains. Third, the mediation effects that we observed are entirely consistent with previous theory and research on marital conflict and child outcomes. Each of these considerations suggests that our conclusions about parental support are substantively meaningful, in spite of the obvious limitations of using retrospective data.

Gender of Parents and Offspring

PARENTS' GENDER

At various points in this book, we considered the influence of fathers vis-à-vis mothers on offspring. As we pointed out in Chapter 1, Americans are increasingly likely to believe that fathers should be more involved in child rearing. However, fathers still lag far behind mothers in child care, even when mothers are employed full-time. In addition, because of increases in nonmarital birth and divorce, fathers are spending less time coresiding with their children now than in previous eras. Furthermore, many nonresident fathers have relatively little contact with children and pay either no child support or less than they should. In other words, although people are moving toward the idea that fathers should be more involved with children, demographic and social changes have resulted in fathers being less involved with children than perhaps at any time in U.S. history.

Previous research dealing with the importance of fathers is equivocal, with some studies suggesting that fathers are important resources for most children and other studies suggesting that fathers play peripheral roles in the lives of most children. In the present study, we are able to address this issue by considering (a) whether fathers' share of family work when children are growing up is related to offspring outcomes in young adulthood, and (b) whether fathers' education and income are associated with offspring outcomes independently of mothers' education and income.

In relation to the first point, as noted before, fathers' share of family work is associated with a number of positive offspring outcomes, including greater affection for fathers when children are older and greater social integration (more close kin and friends in children's support networks, more organizational memberships, and stronger feelings of community attachment). The picture is not entirely consistent, however, because father involvement in 1980 is related to lower socioeconomic attainment, whereas father involvement between 1980 and 1988 is associated with higher socioeconomic attainment. As we speculated in Chapter 6, it may be that fathers are best able to stimulate young children's achievement by earning a high level of income (and hence, spending few hours at home). In contrast, fathers may best stimulate the achievement of adolescents through providing guidance, advice, supervision, and emotional support (which requires spending longer hours at home). Overall, our analysis suggests that father involvement provides some benefits to children, but the results are far from overwhelming. The relatively small number of significant findings may reflect the fact that few fathers are highly involved in family work and child care. It is possible that if fathers become highly involved in the home in the future, then the links between father involvement and offspring well-being will become stronger.

In relation to parental education, we generally find that mothers' and fathers' educations have similar consequences for children. For example, both maternal and paternal education are associated with the likelihood of residing with parents, the likelihood of marriage, the quality of intimate relationships, daughters' education, aspects of social integration, and dimensions of psychological well-being. However, mothers' education tends to be correlated more strongly than fathers' education with many of these outcomes; for this reason, it is often the case that only mothers' education makes an independent contribution when both are in the regression models together. In two cases, paternal education is the key variable. First, fathers' education, but not mothers' education, decreases the likelihood of offspring divorce. Second, fathers' education is more important than mothers' education in predicting sons' socioeconomic attainment. However, this pattern is the exception rather than the rule. The clearest conclusion would appear to be that although parental education is important, mothers' and fathers' educations are so highly correlated that it is difficult to estimate the separate effects of each.

Given the traditional division of labor in most families, we might expect that fathers' income is a key variable in predicting offspring outcomes. Some evidence supports this assumption. Paternal income, but not maternal income, delays children's marriage. Furthermore, paternal income, but not maternal income, increases offspring's marital quality. Perhaps most importantly, paternal income, but not maternal income, predicts both sons' and daughters' socioeconomic attainment. Indeed, it appears to be in the realm of children's attainment that fathers have the most consistent influence. In contrast, maternal income, but not paternal income, increases the likelihood that offspring cohabit. We assume that this latter finding reflects mothers' nontraditionalism, rather than income, as noted before. These findings suggest that one of the key ways in which fathers affect their children's lives continues to be through the provision of economic support.

Perhaps the most pervasive influence of fathers is indirect. The link between parental marital quality and children's general well-being in adulthood is the most consistent finding to emerge from our study. This suggests that fathers may play their most important role in children's lives as a member of the marital partnership. To the extent that fathers are able to maintain close and supportive relations with children's mothers, children benefit; to the extent that fathers create discord in their marriages, children suffer. Some studies show that supportive behavior on the part of husbands improves the quality of wives' parenting skills (Rutter, 1988). Of course, a similar observation can be made of mothers. That is, mothers play key roles in children's lives through their relations with their husbands. Indeed, our study shows that the quality of the parents' marriage predicts offspring's recollections of supportive behavior from both mothers *and* fathers. These observations suggest that fathers are mainly important to the extent that they are part of a larger mother-father-child triad. Consequently, it may not make sense to ask whether mothers or fathers have a greater influence on children's development. Instead, it may be more meaningful to think about the quality of the mother-father-child triad as being a key predictor of children's outcomes.

SONS VERSUS DAUGHTERS

Previous studies show that parents tend to treat sons and daughters differently. As we noted in Chapter 1, fathers tend to give more attention to sons than to daughters, especially as children age. Parents also use harsher punishment with sons than daughters. In addition, parents expect daughters to do more household chores than sons, and these chores are strongly gender-typed, with sons mowing the lawn and washing the car and daughters cooking and cleaning inside the house. For these reasons, sons and daughters growing up within the same household often have very different experiences of family life.

In the present study, we noted a number of occasions in which family-of-origin characteristics are related to different outcomes for sons and daughters. We assessed this by examining the significance of interactions between family variables and offspring gender in predicting outcomes. In the great majority of instances in which significant interactions emerged, family-of-origin associations were stronger for daughters than for sons.

For example, in relation to socioeconomic factors, indicators of parental financial hardship (unemployment and welfare use) are associated with lower attainment among daughters but not among sons. Similarly, parents' perceptions of financial decline are related to elevated psychological distress among daughters but not among sons. In relation to gender nontraditionalism, mothers' employment increases daughters' but not sons' social integration. Similarly, traditional attitudes on the part of parents are associated with greater church involvement among daughters only. Adopting more liberal gender attitudes appears to improve incomes more for daughters than for sons. In relation to parental marital quality, parental marital happiness is associated with the probability of daughters' but not sons' cohabitation dissolution. Finally, declines in parental marital quality are related to daughters' but not sons' reports of dissatisfaction with dating frequency and difficulty in dating the right people.

In only two instances were family variables related more strongly to outcomes for sons than daughters. First, sons' socioeconomic attainment is highest when mothers were employed part-time in 1980 and lowest when mothers worked long overtime hours. No comparable trend appears for daughters. Second, the estimated effects of low parental marital quality on children's psychological well-being are stronger for sons than for daughters.

Overall, the balance of evidence suggests that family-of-origin characteristics affect daughters more than sons. Such a finding is consistent with previous work by social psychologists suggesting that social processes affect women somewhat more than men (Becker, 1986). It is also consistent with research indicating that women are more sensitive to relationship dynamics than are men (Thompson and Walker, 1991). However, research on attitude and value transmission has not found that parents influence daughters more than sons (Troll and Bengtson, 1979). Consistent with this general trend, the more common finding in our study is a lack of gender differences. Indeed, given that previous work suggests that sons and daughters are often affected differently by family processes, such as economic hardship (Elder, Nguyen, and Caspi, 1985), maternal employment (Hoffman, 1974, 1989), and interparental discord and divorce (Emery, 1982; Hetherington, Cox, and Cox, 1982), it is surprising that gender differences were not more common. Therefore, our general conclusion is one of relatively few differences in the impact of family characteristics on the long-term well-being of sons and daughters.

Policy Recommendations

It is common in books dealing with the family for authors to conclude by drawing implications for public policy. One of the difficulties in doing this is that just about everyone agrees on certain broad objectives, but few agree on the means of achieving them. For example, most people would agree that growing up in poverty is bad for children and that steps should be taken to improve the economic well-being of families with children. However, those on the political left stress the role of government in redistributing wealth to poor families, whereas those on the political right stress the role of the private sector and individual effort. Although the results of basic research such as ours are seldom finely tuned enough to allow precise recommendations as to which approach is more likely to be successful, we can offer several general suggestions that emerge from our study.

EDUCATION AND INCOME

Our study suggests that parental education has numerous positive long-term consequences for offspring, even after taking parental income into account. Indeed, education appears to have effects that generally exceed those of income. Although our study does not reveal numerous long-term effects of economic hardship, we see some evidence that it diminishes offspring's educational attainment and later marital quality. Furthermore, many studies demonstrate that economic strain erodes parents' marital quality and stresses moderately dissatisfying marriages to the point of dissolution. Any policy, therefore, that aims to improve the educational attainment and economic well-being of families is also a promarriage and prochild policy.

Moynihan (1986) documented the difficulties that the federal government has faced in trying to combat poverty. However, if government can do little to eliminate poverty directly, it *can* take steps to maintain the quality of higher education and make it accessible to a diverse group of citizens. The remarkable improvements in educational attainment that occurred earlier in this century were brought about largely through government action. The improvements occurred through the passing of compulsory education laws; expanded public funding of universities, colleges, and junior colleges; the introduction of government-backed student loans; and legislation that increased access to higher education, such as the G.I. Bill. Sampson and Laub (1996), using longitudinal data, demonstrated that young men who took advantage of the G.I. Bill to attend college after World War II experienced substantial enhancements in occupational status, job stability, and economic well-being. This was true even with childhood intelligence and parental socioeconomic status controlled. Furthermore, the benefits of G.I. Bill–training were most pronounced for young men from disadvantaged backgrounds.

But in recent years, government has backed away from its longstanding commitment to education. Public support for education at all levels is stagnant or declining, legislatures are cutting education budgets, administrators are firing teachers, and class sizes—from primary schools to universities—are growing. Disadvantaged youth today reach adulthood without access to large-scale government programs, such as the G.I. Bill, which benefited earlier generations.

Declining support for education is occurring at a bad time. With global restructuring affecting the U.S. economy, high-paying jobs for workers with modest educations are becoming less common. Instead, most of the well-paid jobs being created in the American economy require a college education. This dynamic has played a major role in the growth of economic inequality in the U.S. (Danziger and Gottschalk, 1993). Studies show that postsecondary education provides a major route out of poverty for disadvantaged young adults, even if it means returning to school after a period of unemployment or welfare use (Kates, 1995). Furthermore, employers argue that they need a better educated workforce to meet industry's growing need for technological and managerial skills (Committee for Economic Development, 1996; Holzer, 1996).

Our study suggests that lack of access to higher education not only hurts the current generation of youth but also disadvantages future generations. Given the high long-term payoff of public investment in education, a current policy challenge is to find ways, within existing budgetary constraints, to maintain the quality of institutions of higher education in the United States and to guarantee educational opportunities to students from all income backgrounds. Given the changing structure of the labor market and the fact that individuals may have several occupations over the life course, educational institutions should give special attention to programs that meet the needs of students who are working while attending school, as well as of older individuals (often parents) who are changing their field of employment.

Of course, not all students are willing or able to attend college. Consequently, one useful goal is to increase the proportion of at-risk adolescents who graduate from high school. Incentives, such as cash vouchers or making a first driver's license contingent on staying in school, are worth considering. It would also be desirable to enable high school graduates who do not attend college to obtain additional job qualifications, perhaps through an expanded system of apprenticeships and vocational education (see Galston, 1996, for a discussion of these issues).

In general, we believe that greater attention should be given to the likely impact of government policies on the economic well-being of families with children. For example, there are Congressional efforts to lower or even eliminate the earned income tax credit for the working poor—a program that improves the economic standing of many low-income families with children. Moves such as this are likely to undermine the quality of vulnerable marriages, increase the likelihood of divorce, and disadvantage children. We recommend that those who propose new legislation routinely evaluate and report the probable impact of these changes on families with children, especially those living near or below the poverty line. In this way, the public can weigh the financial costs and savings generated by a given policy against the potential costs and benefits to children and families.

GENDER EQUITY

Our study finds little evidence that nontraditional gender arrangements disadvantage children; children seem to thrive regardless of how parents divide labor at home and in the work place. Instead, our study shows that the best predictor of children's success is the quality of the parents' marriage.

It follows, therefore, that if we want to improve the well-being of youth, then we need to strengthen relationships between parents. We argued earlier that some of the decline in marital quality in the United States has been due to inequitable work and family arrangements resulting from the movement of mothers into the paid labor force. Because of changes in the American economy, most families these days need two incomes in order to raise children in a minimum of comfort. Consequently, workplace policies that make it easier for husbands and wives to share breadwinning and family roles have the potential to improve the quality of marriage and enhance children's well-being.

Our study suggests that greater father involvement in child care results in stronger affection between adult children and their fathers as well as greater social integration in adulthood. Father involvement with children can also decrease strain and tension in dual-earner families, thus improving the marriage and benefiting children indirectly. Policies that facilitate employed fathers' sharing of child care include flextime, compressed-week arrangements, home-based employment, shared jobs, permanent part-time work, and paid family leave—all policies that increase workplace flexibility and parents' control over the conditions of employment. The Family and Medical Leave Act of 1993 was a useful first step in this direction, but it fell short of these broad goals. Given that an increasing number of children are being raised by unmarried parents, these workplace options and incentives should be available to all dual-earner couples, regardless of marital status.

Of course, even in companies that have family-friendly policies, the larger culture of the workplace still discourages men from subordinating their careers to their family lives. Nevertheless, it is necessary to have these progressive policies in place, even if the number of fathers who use them is small. These policies not only make it possible, in principle, for both parents to be involved with their children but also provide an important symbolic recognition of the importance of shared parenting. Gender equity cannot come about as long as structural barriers prevent it, and weakening the structural barriers to sharing work and family roles may be a necessary step in bringing about change in the larger culture.

We believe that a shift toward greater gender equity is likely. Indeed, we have observed considerable change toward more equitable marriages in our sample of parents between 1980 and 1992. For example, 29% of the husbands report an increase in the proportion of household chores that they do, compared with only 14% who report a decrease. At the same time, 33% of the wives report a decrease in their share of housework, and only 19% report an increase. The net gain toward a more egalitarian division of household labor suggests that the number of egalitarian marriages will increase in the future.

FATHERS' RESPONSIBILITY FOR BIOLOGICAL CHILDREN

Although the Family Support Act of 1988 had provisions designed to facilitate the collection of child support from biological fathers, it has had limited effect. One reason for the Act's limited impact is that the burden for implementing enforcement was passed to the states without funds to build the infrastructure necessary to enforce the law. States, already burdened with medicaid and other federally mandated programs, have not had the resources (or have not chosen to use their resources) to implement programs that force fathers to meet their obligations. The original intention of these provisions was to improve the economic well-being of single mothers and their children. However, we believe that if such an infrastructure were in place, then the real costs of divorce would increase, and fewer marriages would dissolve. This would be the case partly because fathers would be more reluctant to initiate divorce. Of course, improved child support collection might also increase mothers' willingness to initiate divorce. However, we think it is likely that if the economic consequences of divorce become more aversive for men, then an incentive would exist for men to invest more time and energy in their marriages, thus helping to resolve the problems that might otherwise lead to divorce in the first place.

The cost of implementing this legislation is small relative to the benefits derived from marriages that remain intact and from single-parent households that have greater financial resources. As funds to implement the policy seem to be a major stumbling block to implementing legislation, we suggest that a system of fines be introduced for nonpayment, similar to those for people who are delinquent on their income taxes or who break traffic rules. The fines could be used to support the infrastructure needed to collect court-ordered support from biological parents.

DIVORCE LEGISLATION

Numerous states are considering legislation that would place restrictions on no-fault divorce. Proponents of this change argue that the two-parent family is the ideal one for raising children; consequently, it is necessary to make divorce harder to get in order to slow down the rate of divorce and increase the number of children living with both parents. Our findings suggest that this view is too simple, as divorce is advantageous for children under some circumstances, that is, when children are in highly conflicted marriages. Our data suggest that between one-fourth and one-third of marriages that dissolve may be in this category.

On the other hand, many couples end their marriages at relatively low thresholds of unhappiness, perhaps to seek greater personal fulfillment with new partners. Our research suggests that many children from these low-conflict divorces experience adverse effects that last far into adulthood. Although we are in favor of policies that encourage moderately unhappy couples to stay married and resolve their differences, we do not advocate measures that force couples to stay together by making divorce more difficult to obtain. We are of this opinion for two reasons.

First, laws making it harder to divorce will keep some children and parents trapped in high-conflict marriages. Similarly, requiring deeply aggrieved spouses to battle each other in court over who is at fault for ending the marriage will further escalate the level of conflict to which many children are exposed. Either way, children will be worse off than if parents are allowed to go their own ways with minimal legal restrictions.

Second, policies that restrict no-fault divorce are unlikely to lower the real rate of marital disruption. The current high rate of divorce is the end point of a trend that started more than a century ago—many decades prior to the introduction of no-fault divorce legislation. Most family scholars do not believe that the introduction of no-fault divorce increased the rate of marital disruption significantly (White, 1991). Although the older fault system limited the grounds for divorce to such things as adultery or mental cruelty, these requirements did not keep unhappily married couples together. Some people wanting to end their marriages simply fabricated evidence, thus making a mockery of the law. Other couples separated permanently without obtaining a divorce.

Introducing new legislation to restrict access to divorce is unlikely to make unhappily married couples *want* to stay together. Rather than restrict divorce, it makes more sense to think about policies that support marriage, such as the educational, income, and workplace policies noted before. Providing greater access to marriage and family counseling is another option.

MARRIAGE AND FAMILY COUNSELING

Marriage and family counseling appropriately focuses a good deal of attention on the marital relationship. However, when children under the age of 19 are living in the household, significant effort should be devoted to make the married couple focus on the children. Our study suggests that the worst situation for children to be in is either a high-conflict marriage that does not end in divorce or a low-conflict marriage that does end in divorce. Consequently, for the children's sake, some marriages should not be salvaged. But in marriages that are not fraught with severe conflict and abuse, future generations would be well served if parents remained together until children are grown.

Although maintaining an unhappy but low conflict marriage entails a degree of sacrifice from spouses, this situation may not be as onerous as some might think. Most adults live more than two-thirds of their lives without children in the household. Spending one-third of one's life living in a marriage that is less than satisfactory in order to benefit children—children that parents elected to bring into the world—is not an unreasonable expectation. This idea is especially compelling, given that many people who divorce and remarry find that their second marriage is no happier than their first (Johnson and Booth, 1996). Furthermore, such an arrangement provides an important benefit for parents that helps to balance the cost: parents—especially fathers—are able to maintain continuous relations with coresident children. Given the pain experienced by most noncustodial parents following separation from their children, this should be an incentive to invest extra effort in the marital relationship.

We believe that marriage and family counselors have an obligation to make sure that parents have a full understanding of the consequences of divorce for offspring, including the fact that low-conflict marriages that end in divorce are particularly stressful for children. We suggest that couples, once they are aware of the consequences of divorce, be encouraged to think about ways in which parent-child relations can be improved in spite of the existence of marital tension. This proposal is consistent with the current emphasis on pragmatic, result-centered approaches that characterizes much of contemporary family therapy (Piercy and Sprenkle, 1990).

Focusing on children diverts the couple from thinking exclusively about themselves. Because most parents are concerned about their children's well-being, they already have an incentive to frame the problem in this manner.

Furthermore, by concentrating on how they (individually and collectively) can improve their children's lives, couples participate in a joint activity that may provide a feeling of individual achievement as well as an appreciation of the contribution of the spouse. Consequently, a shared goal of maintaining children's well-being may increase the chances of reconciliation for couples who are on the brink of divorce. Many self-help organizations and marriage courses have emerged around the idea that reconciliation is a viable and preferable alternative to divorce for unhappy couples.

For these reasons, we recommend that governments, community organizations, employers, courts, and churches work together to ensure that all unhappily married couples have access to counselling that is both affordable and child-centered.

THE ROLE OF INCENTIVES

Finally, the reader will note that many of our policy recommendations involve incentives: incentives for young people to attain more education, incentives for married couples to share work and family roles equitably, and incentives for couples with children to work harder at keeping their marriages together. Effective policies create situations in which people *want* to do what the policy is intended to accomplish. Our final recommendation, therefore, is that family policy, in general, be based on creating incentives for parents to act in the best interests of their children.

Appendix: Tables

Table 2.1 Comparison of 1980 sample of parents who had children eligible for an interview in 1992 with parents of children interviewed in 1992

	Full 1980 sample (N = 1,105)	1980 characteristics of those interviewed in 1992 (N = 471)
Husband's age		
25–34	24	24
35–44	43	45
45+	33	31
Wife's age		
25–34	34	32
35–44	46	48
45+	20	20
Race		
White	88	94
Black	5	3
Hispanic	5	2
Other	2	1
Sex		
Male	40	38
Female	60	62
Household size		
3	21	19
4	41	46
5	25	24
6+	13	11
Home tenure		
Own/buying	87	93
Rent/other	13	7
Husband's education		
Elementary, 0–8	5	2
High school 9–11	9	6
High school 12	33	30
College 1–3	25	28
College 4+	28	34
Presence of children		
12–17 years	57	60
6–11 years	59	58
Under 6 years	23	20
Region		
Northeast	19	19
North Central	28	30
South	23	22
West	30	29
Metropolitan		
Metropolitan	64	59
Nonmetropolitan	36	41

Note: Figures in table are percentages.

Table 2.2   Summary of family-of-origin measures

Variable	Item wording/codes	N	X̄	SD	Alpha
Parental education	Mean years of education (mothers and fathers)	471	13.7	2.1	—
Income 1980	Mother's plus father's income in 1992 dollars	466	$51,464	$22,281	—
Income 1988	(As above)	456	$51,419	$19,352	—
Welfare use 1980–1988	Have you received income from any public assistance program—for example, Medicaid, food stamps, or welfare—since the fall of 1980? (asked in 1983) . . . since the fall of 1983? (asked in 1988) (0 = no, 1 = yes)	471	.09	.29	—
Father's unemployment 1980–1988	Were you (your husband) unemployed for one month or longer since the fall of 1980? (asked in 1983) . . . since the fall of 1983? (asked in 1988) (0 = no, 1 = yes)	471	.29	.45	—
Finances better 1980–1988	During the last few years, has your financial situation been getting better, getting worse, or has it stayed the same? (asked in 1980, 1983, and 1988) (0 = other, 1 = always better)	471	.26	.43	—
Finances worse 1980–1988	(As above) (0 = other, 1 = ever worse)	471	.29	.45	—
Hours 1980	Hours worked by mother in 1980	471	29.4	24.2	—
Hours 1988	Hours worked by mother in 1988	421	26.7	21.3	—
Housework done by fathers 1980	In every family there are a lot of routine tasks that have to be done—cleaning the house, doing the laundry, cleaning up after meals, cooking dinners, etc. How much of this kind of work usually is done by you—all of it, most of it, about half of it, less than half of it, or none of it? (1 = none, 5 = all)	471	2.0	.70	—

Housework done by fathers 1988	(As above)	423	2.1	.66	—
Child care done by fathers 1980	How much of the looking after children is usually done by you—all of it, most of it, about half of it, less than half of it, or none of it? (1 = none, 5 = all)	430	2.4	.63	—
Gender role attitudes	Here are some statements about men's and women's roles. I would like you to tell me whether you strongly disagree (1), disagree (2), agree (3) or strongly agree (4) with each statement. A woman's most important task in life should be taking care of her children. A husband should earn a larger salary than his wife. It should not bother the husband if the wife's job sometimes requires her to be away from home overnight. If his wife works full-time, a husband should share equally in household chores such as cooking, cleaning, and washing. If jobs are scarce, a woman whose husband can support her ought not have a job. A working mother can establish just as good a relationship with her children as a mother who does not work. Even though a wife works outside the home, the husband should be the main breadwinner and the wife should have the responsibility for the home and children. (Score is the sum of all items. A high score indicates a nontraditional attitude.)	471	16.3	3.1	.65
Gender role attitudes 1988	(As above)	471	17.5	2.9	.73
Nontraditionalism index 1980	Wife's hours worked, husband's housework, nontraditional gender attitudes (Score is the sum of Z scores.)	471	-.01	1.9	—
Nontraditionalism index 1988	(As above)	420	.01	2.1	—

(continued)

Table 2.2 Continued

Variable	Item wording/codes	N	$\bar{X}$	SD	Alpha
Marital happiness 1980	I'm going to mention some different aspects of married life. For each one, I would like you to tell me whether you are very happy, pretty happy, or not too happy with this aspect of your marriage. With the amount of understanding you receive from your spouse? With the amount of love and affection you receive? With the extent to which you and your spouse agree about things? With your sexual relationship? With your spouse as someone who takes care of things around the house? With your spouse's faithfulness to you? Taking all things together, how would you describe your marriage? Would you say that your marriage is very happy, pretty happy, or not too happy? Compared with other marriages you know about, do you think your marriage is better than most, about the same as most, or not as good as most? Comparing your marriage to three years ago, is your marriage getting better, staying the same, or getting worse? Would you say the feelings of love you have for your (husband/wife) are very strong, pretty strong, or not too strong? (Items are answered on 3-point scales; score is the sum of all items.)	471	28.3	4.0	.87
Marital happiness 1988	(As above)	417	27.8	4.2	.88

		N			
Marital interaction 1980	I'm going to mention some of the things couples do together. For each one, I would like you to tell me how often you and your spouse do this together. How often do you eat your main meal together? Go shopping together? How often do you visit friends together? Work together on projects around the house? When you go out—say, to play cards, bowl, or see a movie—how often do you do this together? (Items are answered on 4-point scales; score is the sum of all items.)	471	15.7	2.7	.63
Marital interaction 1988	(As above)	424	14.9	2.8	.64
Marital conflict 1980	Do you and your (husband/wife) have arguments or disagreements about whether one of you is doing their share of the housework? How often do you disagree with your (husband/wife)? How many serious quarrels have you had with your spouse in the past two months? In many households bad feelings and arguments occur from time to time. In many cases people get so angry that they slap, hit, push, kick, or throw things at one another. Has this ever happened between your and your (husband/wife)? (Score is the sum of all items.)	471	3.8	2.2	.54
Marital conflict 1988	(As above)	419	3.7	2.2	.47

(continued)

Table 2.2 Continued

Variable	Item wording/codes	N	$\bar{X}$	SD	Alpha
Divorce proneness 1980	Sometimes married people think they would enjoy living apart from their spouse. How often do you feel this way? Even people who get along quite well with their spouse sometimes wonder whether their marriage is working out. Have you ever thought your marriage might be in trouble? Have you ever talked with family members, friends, clergy, counselors, or social workers about problems in your marriage? As far as you know, has your (husband/wife) talked with relatives, friends, or a counselor about problems either of you were having with your marriage? As far as you know, has your spouse ever thought your marriage was in trouble? Has the thought of getting a divorce or separation crossed your mind in the last three years? As far as you know, has the thought of divorce or separation crossed your (husband's/wife's) mind in the last three years? Have you or your (husband/wife) ever seriously suggested the idea of divorce? Recently? Did you talk about consulting an attorney? What about dividing up the property? Have you talked about filing? Have you or your (husband/wife) consulted an attorney about a divorce or separation? Have you or your (husband/wife) filed a divorce or separation petition? (Score is the log of the sum of positive responses.)	471	.28	.33	.91
Divorce proneness 1988	(As above)	423	.26	.35	.89

		N	Mean	SD	α
Stepfamily in 1980	1 = lives with stepparent, 0 = other	471	.10	.30	—
Intact 1980, divorced 1992	1 = parents divorced, 0 = no divorce	471	.09	.27	—
Parents' race	1 = either parent nonwhite, 0 = other	471	.07	.26	—
Mother respondent	1 = mother, 0 = father	471	.62	.49	—
Female offspring	1 = female, 0 = male	471	.51	.50	—
Offspring age	Age in years	471	24.9	4.6	—
Siblings	Counting those who live with you and those who do not, how many children do you have? (Asked of parents in 1992.)	471	2.9	1.4	—
Maternal support	How often did your mother help you with schoolwork? How often did your mother help you with personal problems? How often did you and your mother have talks together? How often did your mother hug you or show affection toward you? Overall, how would you describe your relationship with your mother when you were a teenager? (Items are answered on 3-point scales; score is the mean of all items.)	469	2.28	.48	.78
Paternal support	(As above, except that "father" replaces "mother")	465	1.93	.53	.82
Parental control	How many rules did your parents have for you, for example, rules about staying out late, doing chores, and watching television? How closely did your parents supervise your behavior? How many decisions about things that were important to you were you allowed to make for yourself? Overall, how strict was your family? (Items are answered on 3-point scales; score is the mean of all items.)	471	1.95	.47	.71

Table 3.1 Summary of parent-child relationship measures

Variable	Item wording/codes	N	$\overline{X}$	SD	Alpha
Affection for mother	How well do you feel that your mother understands you? How much do you trust your mother? How much respect do you receive from your mother? How much fairness does your mother show you? Overall, would you say that you are not very close, close, or very close? (Items are answered on 3-point scales; score is the mean of all items.)	463	2.67	.43	.87
Affection for father	(As above)	444	2.44	.54	.90
Consensus with mother	In relation to your general outlook on life, would you say you and your mother share (1) very different views, (2) different views, (3) similar views, or (4) very similar views?	462	2.84	.77	—
Consensus with father	In relation to your general outlook on life, would you say you and your father share . . . (as above)?	442	2.81	.84	—
Lives with mother	0 = does not live with mother 1 = lives with mother	463	.25	.43	—
Lives with father	0 = does not live with father 1 = lives with father	451	.24	.42	—
Lives with parents	0 = does not live with either parent 1 = lives with one or both parents	471	.26	.44	—
Distance from mother	How many miles away from you does your mother live? (log base 10)	347	1.65	.93	—
Distance from father	How many miles away from you does your father live? (log base 10)	340	1.70	.93	—
Distance from parents	How many miles away from you do your parents live? (log base 10)	349	1.67	.91	—

Variable	Description	N	Mean	SD	
Days since mother contact	How many days has it been since you last talked with or had a letter from your mother? (log base 10)	347	.44	.35	—
Days since father contact	How many days has it been since you last talked with or had a letter from your father? (log base 10)	337	.73	.64	—
Perceived help from parents	How likely is it that you would ask your parents for help with transportation; repairs to home or car; other kinds of work around the house; advice, encouragement, moral or emotional support; child care; a loan of $200? ($1 = $ not very likely, $2 = $ somewhat likely, $3 = $ very likely; score is the mean of all items.)	471	2.11	.55	.74
Help from parents	During the past month, have you received the following types of help from parents: help with transportation; repairs to home or car; other kinds of work around the house; advice, encouragement, moral or emotional support; child care? During the past year, have you received a gift or loan of $200 or more from your parents? (Score is the proportion of "yes" responses.)	471	.49	.29	—
Help to parents	During the past month, have you given the following types of help to parents: help with transportation; repairs to home or car; other kinds of work around the house; advice, encouragement, moral or emotional support? During the past year, have you given or loaned $200 or more to your parents? (Score is the proportion of "yes" responses.)	471	.43	.28	—

Table 3.2 Associations between parental education, coresidence with parents in 1992, and distance from parents in 1992

Predictor	Coresidence	Distance
Female offspring	.29	.10
Age of offspring	−.15***	−.12*
Mother respondent	−.15	−.01
Parents nonwhite	.41	−.05
Number of siblings	−.17	−.04
Mothers' education	−.20*	.14*
Fathers' education	−.05	.11#
Constant	6.12***	—
R squared	—	.09***
Chi-square	34.52***	—

Note: For coresidence, table values are logistic regression coefficients. For distance, table values are standardized OLS regression coefficients. For coresidence, the sample consists of 280 offspring who lived with both parents in 1980 and were unmarried in 1992. For distance, the sample consists of 312 offspring who lived with both parents in 1980 and did not reside with parents in 1992. Significance tests are two-tailed.
  #p < .10.   *p < .05.   **p < .01.   ***p < .001.

Table 3.3 Associations between changes in family income between 1980 and 1988 and offspring's assistance from parents in 1992

Predictor	Perceived help	Help from parents
Female offspring	.05	.02
Age of offspring	−.14**	−.15**
Mother respondent	.05	−.02
Parents nonwhite	.05	.02
Number of siblings	.00	.03
Parental education	−.10	−.07
Parental income 1980	−.05	−.08
Parental income 1988	.16*	.11*
R squared	.05*	.04#

Note: Table values are standardized OLS regression coefficients. Sample size for both equations is 384 offspring who lived with both parents in 1980 and never experienced a parental divorce. Significance tests are two-tailed.
  #p < .10.   *p < .05.   **p < .01.   ***p < .001.

Table 3.4 Associations between mothers' hours of employment in 1980 and offspring's relationships with fathers in 1992

Predictor	Affection for fathers	Consensus with fathers	Days since father contact
Female offspring	.01	−.08	.05
Age of offspring	.04	.05	.01
Mother respondent	−.02	−.04	.09
Parents nonwhite	.05	−.01	−.11
Number of siblings	−.04	.01	−.06
Parental education	−.02	.05	.01
Family income 1980	−.02	−.03	.06
Mother employed	.27**	.19#	−.19
Mothers' hours employed	−.27**	−.25*	.23#
R squared	.03	.03	.05

Note: Table values are standardized OLS regression coefficients. For affection for fathers and consensus with fathers, the samples consist of 407 and 405 offspring, respectively, who lived with both parents in 1980. For days since father contact, the sample consists of 303 offspring who lived with both parents in 1980 and did not live with fathers in 1992. Significance tests are two-tailed.

#$p < .10.$ *$p < .05.$ **$p < .01.$ ***$p < .001.$

Table 3.5 Associations between fathers' share of child care in 1980, affection for fathers in 1992, and coresidence with parents in 1992

Predictor	Affection for fathers	Coresidence with parents
Female offspring	.02	−.19
Age of offspring	−.03	−.16***
Mother respondent	−.01	.07
Parents nonwhite	.06	.22
Number of siblings	−.03	−.07
Parental education	−.04	−.21**
Family income 1980	−.01	−.01
Mother employed	.32**	−.73
Mothers' hours employed	−.35***	.01
Fathers' share child care	.15**	−.81***
Constant		6.83
R squared	.06*	
Chi-square		48.25***

Note: Table values are standardized OLS regression coefficients for affection for fathers and logistic regression coefficients for coresidence. For affection for fathers, the sample consists of 407 offspring who lived with both parents in 1980. For coresidence, the sample consists of 280 offspring who lived with both parents in 1980 and were unmarried in 1992. Significance tests are two-tailed.

#$p < .10.$ *$p < .05.$ **$p < .01.$ ***$p < .001.$

Table 3.6 Associations between parents' marital happiness in 1980, divorce proneness in 1980, and dimensions of the parent-child relationship in 1992

Predictor	Affection mother	Affection father	Consensus mother	Consensus father	Perceived help	Help to parents	Help from parents
Parents' marital happiness	.14**	.17***	.07#	.10*	−.03	.08#	.15**
Parents' divorce proneness	−.16**	−.23***	−.08#	−.13*	−.07#	−.06	−.13*

Note: Table values are standardized OLS regression coefficients. All analyses are based on 384 offspring who lived with both biological parents in 1980 and who never experienced a parental divorce, although sample sizes vary slightly across dependent variables. Significance tests are one-tailed. Controls include offspring's gender, offspring's age, mother respondent, parents nonwhite, number of siblings, parental education, parental income, and parents' gender nontraditionalism (mothers' employment, fathers' share of family work, and gender attitudes).

#p < .10.   *p < .05.   **p < .01.   ***p < .001.

Table 3.7 Associations between parental divorce and dimensions of parent-child relationships in 1992

Outcome	Divorce prior to 1980	Divorce between 1980–1992	Any divorce
Affection for mother	−.17*	−.09	−.14*
(Sons)		(−.20*)	
(Daughters)		(.10)	
Mother-child consensus	−.25*	−.05	−.11
Lives with mother	−.72	−1.44**	−1.00**
Distance from mother	−.04	−.25	−.14
Days since mother contact	.10	−.01	.05
Affection for father	−.79***	−.30***	−.54***
(Sons)		(−.13)	(−.35***)
(Daughters)		(−.51***)	(−.73***)
Father-child consensus	−1.02***	−.44**	−.74***
Lives with father	−2.94**	−1.60**	−2.05***
Distance from father	.38*	.15	.27*
Days since father contact	.97***	.42***	.69***
(Sons)		(.15)	
(Daughters)		(.69***)	
Perceived help from parents	−.12	−.15#	−.14*

Note: Coefficients compare offspring who experienced a parental divorce with those who did not. Table values for lives with mother and lives with father are logistic regression coefficients; all others are unstandardized OLS regression coefficients. Coefficients are adjusted for offspring's gender, offspring's age, mother respondent, parents nonwhite, number of siblings, parental education, parental income, and parents' gender nontraditionalism (mothers' employment, fathers' share of family work, and gender attitudes). Significance tests are two-tailed. Separate coefficients are shown for significant interactions between divorce and offspring gender.

#$p < .10$.   *$p < .05$.   **$p < .01$.   ***$p < .001$.

Table 4.1 Summary of intimate relationship measures

Variable	Item wording/codes	N	$\bar{X}$	S	Alpha
Dating					
Steady partner	Are you dating someone steadily now? (1 = yes, 0 = no)	275	.48	.50	—
Dating happiness	Are you very happy, pretty happy, or not too happy with the following aspects of your relationship: The amount of love and affection you receive? The extent to which you and your friend agree about things? Your friend as someone to do things with? Your friend's faithfulness to you? Compared with other relationships you know about, is your relationship better than most, about the same as most, or not as good as most? Taking all things together, would you say that your relationship is very happy, pretty happy, or not too happy? Do you think that you will eventually marry this person?	131	.00	1.00	.82
Dates last month	In the last month, about how many times did you date or go out with someone? (log base 10)	144	.47	.23	—
Dates last year	About how many people have you dated in the past twelve months? (log base 10)	144	.58	.34	—
Satisfaction with number of dates	Would you prefer to date more often, less often, or about the same as you are now? (same = 1, other = 0)	275	.62	.49	—
Difficulty meeting right people	Do you seem to have difficulty dating people with whom you feel you could develop a serious relationship? (1 = yes, 0 = no)	275	.21	.41	—

Marriage/Cohabitation

Happiness	(Same as parents, see Table 2.1.)	164/32	0.0	1.0	.84
Interaction	(Same as parents, see Table 2.1.)	164/32	0.0	1.0	.60
Conflict	(Same as parents, see Table 2.1.)	164/32	0.0	1.0	.65
Problems	Have you had a problem in your marriage/relationship because one of you gets angry easily, has feelings that are easily hurt, is jealous, is domineering, is moody, won't talk to the other, has become less interested in sex, has had a sexual relationship with someone else, has irritating habits, is not home enough, spends money foolishly, drinks or uses drugs, has been in trouble with the law?	164/32	0.0	1.0	.65
Instability	Have you ever thought your marriage/relationship might be in trouble; talked with family, friends, or others about problems in your relationship; thought about breaking up? Has your partner ever thought your relationship might be in trouble; talked with family, friends, or others about problems in your relationship; thought about breaking up? Have you or your partner suggested the idea of breaking up?	164/32	0.0	1.0	.78

Note: Questions on number of dates last month and number of dating partners last year are limited to those not in a steady dating relationship. Dating happiness is limited to offspring dating someone steadily.

Table 4.2 Relationship quality of married and cohabiting offspring

		Married (N = 164)	Cohabiting (N = 32)	t
Relationship happiness	X̄	.02	−.10	.64
	(SD)	(.98)	(1.09)	
Relationship interaction	X̄	.01	−.05	.29
	(SD)	(1.00)	(1.00)	
Relationship conflict	X̄	−.03	.16	−.97
	(SD)	(.97)	(1.15)	
Relationship problems	X̄	−.10	.54	−3.42***
	(SD)	(.93)	(1.18)	
Relationship instability	X̄	−.13	.64	−4.12***
	(SD)	(.97)	(.89)	

Note: Scores are standardized across the sample to have means of 0 and standard deviations of 1. Significance tests are two-tailed.
#$p < .10.$ *$p < .05.$ **$p < .01.$ ***$p < .001.$

Table 4.3 Percentage change in the odds of cohabitation, marriage, and divorce between 1980 and 1995 by parental education and income in 1980

Predictor	Cohabitation	Marriage	Divorce
Female offspring	13	7	3
Age of offspring	−7***	7***	−9*
Mother respondent	10	−24	21
Parents nonwhite	35	−25	−23
Number of siblings	0	2	−12
Stepfamily in 1980	31	−1	61
Mothers' education	−3	−9*	3
Fathers' education	4	−1	−15*
Mothers' income	2*	0	2
Fathers' income	0	−1#	1
Chi-square	28.34**	36.22***	17.93#

Note: Table values are percentage changes in odds associated with each predictor derived from logistic regression analyses: $(\exp(B) - 1) \times 100.$ Cohabitation, marriage, and divorce are based on 3,772, 3,680, and 1,383 person-years, respectively. The time scales for marriage and cohabitation are based on offspring aged between 16 to 35 during any years of the study. Cases of cohabitation are censored if offspring married in a given year. Divorce involves only ever-married offspring, with the time scale reflecting years of marriage from 1 to 14. Mothers' and fathers' incomes are measured in thousands of dollars.
#$p < .10.$ *$p < .05.$ **$p < .01.$ ***$p < .001.$

Table 4.4 Associations between parental education and the quality of offspring's intimate relationships

Predictor	Relationship happiness		Relationship instability		Relationship interaction	
Female offspring	−.14	−.11	.19	.17	−.06	−.04
Age of offspring	−.04*	−.04*	.03	.03*	−.04*	−.04*
Mother respondent	−.19	−.20	.21	.22	−.09	−.09
Parents nonwhite	.00	−.04	.24	.26	.31	.33
Number of siblings	.06	.03	.00	.02	.01	−.01
Stepfamily in 1980	−.05	−.01	.12	.09	.23	.24
Cohabiting	−.22	3.49**	.86***	−1.43	−.22	1.11
Parental education	.03	.09*	−.03	−.07#	.06#	.08*
Par education * cohabiting	—	−.27***	—	.16*	—	−.10
Constant	.93	.34	−.98	−.62	.46	.25
R squared	.05	.10*	.08**	.14***	.06	.07

Note: Table values are unstandardized OLS regression coefficients. The sample consists of 196 offspring (164 married, 32 cohabitating). Significance tests are one-tailed.
#p < .10.   *p < .05.   **p < .01.   ***p < .001.

Table 4.5 Associations between changes in parents' gender nontraditionalism (summary index) between 1980 and 1988 and offspring's dating experiences

Predictor	Number of people dated last year	Difficulty forming relationships	Dating someone steadily
Female offspring	−.16	62*	49
Age of offspring	−.26**	08*	−2
Mother respondent	.04	81	−43*
Parents nonwhite	.01	29	108
Number of siblings	.18*	−1	−5
Stepfamily in 1980	.04	−29	−1
Parental education	.03	−11	9
Parental income	.10	1	−1
Nontraditionalism 1980	.09	8	9
Nontraditionalism 1988	−.21*	−23*	14#
R squared	.14**	—	—
Chi-square	—	20.50*	25.18**

Note: For number of people dated, table values are standardized OLS regression coefficients. For difficulty forming relationships and dating someone steadily, table values are percentage changes in odds derived from logistic regression analyses: $(exp(B) − 1) \times 100$. For number of people dated, the sample consists of 144 offspring who are unmarried, not cohabiting, and not dating anyone steadily in 1992. For difficulty forming relationships and dating someone steadily, the sample consists of 275 offspring who are unmarried and not cohabiting in 1992. Significance tests are two-tailed.
#p < .10.   *p < .05.   **p < .01.   ***p < .001.

Table 4.6   Associations between parents' marital quality in 1980 and offspring's marital quality in 1992

Predictor	Offspring's marital quality in 1992				
	Happiness	Interaction	Conflict	Problems	Instability
Parents' marital happiness	.16*	.01	−.14*	−.15*	−.07
Parents' marital interaction	.06	.09#	−.18**	−.26***	−.21***
Parents' marital conflict	−.06	−.11*	.04	.18**	.01
Parents' divorce proneness	−.17*	.05	.08#	.14*	.17*

Note: Table values are standardized OLS regression coefficients. Coefficients are derived from 20 separate regression equations, in which each independent variable predicts each dependent variable. All equations include controls for offspring's gender, offspring's age, mother respondent, parents nonwhite, number of siblings, parental education, parental income, and parents' gender nontraditionalism (mothers' employment, fathers' share of family work, and gender attitudes). Analysis is based on 146 married offspring who lived with both parents in 1980 and whose parents remained married between 1980 and 1992. All significance tests are one-tailed.

#$p < .10.$ *$p < .05.$ **$p < .01.$ ***$p < .001.$

Table 5.1 Summary of social integration measures

Variable	Item wording/codes	N	$\bar{X}$	SD	Alpha
Church involvement	During the past six months, how often did you attend religious services? How often did you participate in a church social activity? (1 = never, 4 = weekly)	468	2.14	1.02	.76
Organization memberships	Do you belong to any groups or clubs? If so, how many?	471	1.07	1.47	—
Close relatives	Are there relatives whom you feel emotionally close to? If so, how many would that be?	471	3.80	4.11	—
Close friends	Are there people whom you consider very close friends who are not relatives? If so, how many would that be?	471	4.35	4.60	—
Perceived community attachment	Some people feel they have very strong roots in their community, while others could easily move to another area. How attached do you feel to the community? (1 = not attached, 4 = very attached)	470	2.46	1.05	—

Table 5.2   Associations between parental education in 1980 and offspring's social integration in 1992

Predictors	Organizational memberships	Close friends	% Relatives in network
Female offspring	−.06	−.05	.06
Age of offspring	.12**	−.14**	.11*
Mother respondent	<.01	.07	−.05
Parents nonwhite	.04	−.02	.01
Number of siblings	.03	.03	−.01
Stepfamily 1980	−.04	.02	−.03
Parental education	.13**	.10*	−.12*
R squared	.04**	.04*	.04*

Note: Table values are standardized OLS regression coefficients. Sample sizes range from 468 to 471. Significance tests are two-tailed.

#$p < .10$.   *$p < .05$.   **$p < .01$.   ***$p < .001$.

Table 5.3   Associations between maternal employment in 1980 and offspring's social integration in 1992

Predictors	Church involvement		Community attachment	
Female offspring	.10*	−.01	.07	−.10
Mothers' employment hours	.10	.00	.07	−.08
Female × mothers' hours		.16*		.26**
R squared	.04*	.06**	.02	.04*

Note: Table values are standardized OLS regression coefficients. Sample sizes are 468 for church involvement and 470 for community attachment. All equations include controls for offspring's gender, offspring's age, mother respondent, parents nonwhite, number of siblings, stepfamily in 1980, and parental education. Significance tests are two-tailed.

#$p < .10$.   *$p < .05$.   **$p < .01$.   ***$p < .001$.

Table 5.4   Associations between parents' marital quality in 1980 and offspring's social integration in 1992

Predictor	Church involvement	Close relatives	Close friends	Community attachment
Marital happiness	.07#	.07#	.07#	$< -.01$
Marital interaction	.04	$<.01$	.08*	.11*
Marital conflict	$-.08$#	$-.10$*	$-.02$	$-.07$#
Divorce proneness	$-.10$*	$-.14$**	$-.05$	$-.02$

Note: Table values are standardized OLS regression coefficients. Analysis is based on 429 offspring who did not experience a parental divorce between 1980 and 1992. Coefficients are derived from 16 separate regression equations in which each independent variable predicts each dependent variable. Control variables include offspring's gender, offspring's age, mother respondent, parents nonwhite, number of siblings, stepfamily in 1980, parental education, parental income, and parents' gender nontraditionalism. Significance tests are one-tailed.
#$p < .10$.   *$p < .05$.   **$p < .01$.   ***$p < .001$.

Table 5.5   Associations between changes in parents' marital quality between 1980 and 1988 and offspring's social integration in 1992

Predictor	Church involvement	Organizational memberships	Close relatives	Close friends	Community attachment
Marital happiness 1988	.08#	.10#	.05	.16**	.02
Marital interaction 1988	.07	$-.03$	.01	.13*	.05
Marital conflict 1988	$-.04$	.01	$-.03$	$-.09$*	$-.07$
Divorce proneness 1988	$-.07$	$-.10$*	$-.07$	$-.14$**	.01

Note: Table values are standardized regression coefficients, controlling for the 1980 value of each marital quality variable. Analyses are based on 429 offspring who did not experience a parental divorce between 1980 and 1992. Coefficients are derived from 20 separate regression equations in which each marital quality indicator predicts each dependent variable. Control variables include offspring's gender, offspring's age, mother respondent, parents nonwhite, number of siblings, stepfamily in 1980, parental education, parental income, and parents' gender nontraditionalism. Significance tests are one-tailed.
#$p < .10$.   *$p < .05$.   **$p < .01$.   ***$p < .001$.

Table 6.1 Summary of socioeconomic attainment measures of offspring

Variable	Item wording/codes	N	$\bar{X}$	SD
Education	Overall, how many years of school have you completed?	471	14.68	2.17
Occupational status	Pick the category into which your job best fits: technical, official, manager, proprietor or owner, semiskilled worker, clerical worker, service worker, protective worker, farm or ranch manager or owner, farm worker, worker or laborer, professional, and skilled worker or foreman. (Examples of each category were provided. These categories were rank-ordered, with higher scores reflecting higher-status jobs.)	448	5.72	2.23
Income	What was your annual income in the last 12 months? If you are married, count your income only.	435	$21,971	$13,872
Economic adversity	During the past 12 months, how often did it happen that you did not have enough money to afford (a) the kind of food you thought your household should have, (b) the kind of clothes you thought your household should have, and (c) the kind of medical care you thought your household should have? Have you received benefits from any public assistance program, such as medicaid, food stamps, or welfare since 1988? During the last three years, has your financial situation been getting better, getting worse, or has it stayed the same? (Score is sum of items.)	471	.65	.75

Table 6.2 Associations between parental education and daughters'
socioeconomic attainment in 1995

	Education	Income	Adversity
PANEL A: Mothers' education			
Age of offspring	.02	.28***	.01
Mother respondent	−.01	−.03	.12*
Parents nonwhite	−.02	.07	<.01
Number of siblings	−.15*	.02	.06
Stepfamily 1980	−.10	−.05	.10
Mothers' education	.36***	.15*	−.24***
PANEL B: Mothers' education controlling for fathers' education			
Mothers' education	.23***	.11	−.21**
PANEL C: Fathers' education			
Fathers' education	.34***	.12#	−.17**
PANEL D: Fathers' education controlling for mothers' education			
Fathers' education	.22**	.01	−.05
R squared	.20***	.11***	.09**
N	242	214	242

Note: Table values are standardized OLS regression coefficients. Panels B, C, and D
include all control variables. R squared is for the model with all variables included.
Significance tests are two-tailed.
    #$p < .10.$ *$p < .05.$ **$p < .01.$ ***$p < .001.$

Table 6.3   Associations between parental education and sons' socioeconomic
            attainment in 1995

	Education	Status
PANEL A: Mothers' education		
Age of offspring	.04	.11
Mother respondent	−.06	−.01
Parents nonwhite	.04	.03
Number of siblings	−.14*	−.20**
Stepfamily 1980	−.05	−.09
Mothers' education	.24**	.09
PANEL B: Mothers' education controlling for fathers' education		
Mothers' education	.06	−.01
PANEL C: Fathers' education		
Fathers' education	.39***	.18**
PANEL D: Fathers' education controlling for mothers' education		
Fathers' education	.36***	.18**
R squared	.19***	.07*
N	229	220

Note: Table values are standardized OLS regression coefficients. Panels B, C, and D
include all control variables. R squared is for the model with all variables included.
Significance tests are two-tailed.
#$p < .10.$ *$p < .05.$ **$p < .01.$ ***$p < .001.$

Table 6.4 Associations between fathers' income in 1980 and offspring's socioeconomic attainment in 1995

Predictor	Education	Status	Income
Daughters			
Age of offspring	.01	.16*	.33***
Mother respondent	−.01	−.08	−.07
Parents white	.06	.07	.15*
Number of siblings	−.14*	.01	−.01
Stepfamily 1980	−.08	−.07	−.02
Parents' education	.32***	.04	.14*
Fathers' income	.21**	.12#	.13#
R squared	.23***	.07*	.17***
N	235	221	207
Sons			
Age of offspring	.04	.11	.41***
Number of siblings	−.14*	−.20**	−.09
Mother respondent	−.02	.01	−.05
Parents nonwhite	.05	.03	.02
Stepfamily 1980	−.01	−.05	−.06
Parents' education	.35***	.16*	−.07
Fathers' income	.11#	.04	.15*
R squared	.19***	.09**	.21***
N	224	215	216

Note: Table values are standardized OLS regression coefficients. Significance tests are two-tailed.

#$p < .10.$ *$p < .05.$ **$p < .01.$ ***$p < .001.$

Table 6.5 Associations between mothers' hours of employment in 1980 and sons' socioeconomic attainment in 1995

Predictor	Education	Income
Age offspring	.04	.41***
Mother respondent	−.01	−.04
Parents nonwhite	.03	.00
Number of siblings	−.14*	−.10
Stepfamily 1980	.00	−.05
Parental education	.36***	−.06
Fathers' income	.12	.14*
Mothers' employment	.38#	.33#
Mothers' hours employment	−.36*	−.43*
R squared	.21***	.23***
N	224	216

Note: Table values are standardized OLS regression coefficients. Significance tests are two-tailed.

#p < .10.   *p < .05.   **p < .01.   ***p < .001.

Table 6.6 Associations between fathers' share of housework and offspring's socioeconomic attainment in 1995

Predictor	Education	Income	Status	Adversity
Female offspring	.09*	−.22***	.16**	.11*
Age of offspring	.06	.35***	.15**	.06
Mother respondent	−.02	−.05	−.04	.04
Parents nonwhite	.05	.09#	.07	−.01
Number of siblings	−.10*	−.03	−.06	.05
Stepfamily 1980	−.10*	−.03	−.08	.07
Parental education	.35***	.02	.09#	−.10*
Parental income	.11*	.09#	.00	−.12*
Fathers' housework 1980	−.15**	−.14**	−.04	.09#
Fathers' housework 1988	.06	−.05	.14*	−.13*
R squared	.20***	.23***	.08***	.08***
N	384	362	374	395

Note: Table values are standardized OLS regression coefficients. Equations are based on families in which parents remained continuously married between 1980 and 1988. Significance tests are two-tailed.

#p < .10.   *p < .05.   **p < .01.   ***p < .001.

Table 6.7 Associations between parental divorce and offspring's socioeconomic attainment in 1995

	Education	Status	Income	Adversity
Divorce prior to 1980	− .66*	− .60#	− 2,172	.23*
Divorce 1980–1992	− .21	− .29	3,408	.28*
(Sons)		(.35)		
(Daughters)		(− 1.27*)		
Any divorce	− .43*	− .44#	657	.26*
N	471	448	435	471

Note: Table values are unstandardized regression coefficients comparing offspring who experienced a parental divorce with those who did not. Coefficients are adjusted for offspring's gender, offspring's age, mother respondent, parents nonwhite, number of siblings, parental education, parental income, and parents' gender nontraditionalism. Separate coefficients are shown for occupational status because of an interaction between divorce and offspring gender. Significance tests are one-tailed.
#$p < .10$.   *$p < .05$.   **$p < .01$.   ***$p < .001$.

Table 7.1 Summary of psychological well-being measures

Variable	Item wording/codes	N	$\bar{X}$	SD	Alpha
Psychological distress	How often in the last year were you troubled by acid or sour stomach? By headaches or pains in the head? Breaking out in cold sweats? Bothered with nervousness, were you irritable, fidgety, or tense? Felt rather isolated or alone, somewhat apart from others, even among friends? Felt that nothing turns out for you the way you want it to, that your wishes aren't fulfilled? Found yourself wondering if anything is worthwhile anymore? (1 = never, 2 = sometimes, 3 = often.) Would you say you were in very good spirits, good spirits, low spirits, or very low spirits these days? (Score is mean of all items.)	471	1.70	.35	.73
Self-esteem	I feel I have a number of good qualities. I feel that I have much to be proud of. On the whole I am satisfied with myself. I certainly feel useless at times. I feel that I'm a person of worth, at least on an equal plane with others. All in all, I am inclined to feel that I am a failure. (1 = strongly disagree, 4 = strongly agree; score is mean of all items.)	471	3.33	.40	.77
Happiness	Taking all things together, how would you say you are these days? Would you say you are (1) not very happy, (2) pretty happy, or (3) very happy?	471	2.31	.54	—
Life satisfaction	I'm going to mention a number of areas of life. For each one I would like you to tell me about the amount of satisfaction you get. Your neighborhood? Your job or career? Your house or apartment? Your friends? Your hobbies or leisure activities? Your marriage? Your children? The rest of your family? Your financial situation? (1 = no satisfaction, 5 = a great deal of satisfaction; score is mean of all relevant items.)	471	3.86	.53	.65

Table 7.2 Associations between parental education and offspring's psychological well-being in 1992

	Psychological distress	Self-esteem	Happiness	Life satisfaction
Female offspring	.07	.08#	.10**	.03
Age of offspring	−.06	.14**	.08#	.19**
Mother respondent	−.02	<−.01	−.03	−.01
Parents nonwhite	−.07	.03	−.05	−.01
Number of siblings	−.05	−.01	.03	.01
Stepfamily in 1980	.00	−.02	−.08#	−.09
Parental education	−.13**	.10**	.13**	.10**
R squared	.03**	.03**	.04**	.06**

Note: Table values are standardized OLS regression coefficients. Sample size for all equations is 471.
#$p < .10$.   *$p < .05$.   **$p < .01$.   ***$p < .001$.

Table 7.3 Associations between parents' marital quality in 1980 and offspring's psychological well-being in 1992

	Psychological distress	Self-esteem	Happiness	Life satisfaction
Marital happiness	−.13**	.12**	.05	.13**
Marital interaction	−.09*	.05	.09*	.13**
Marital conflict	.09*	−.11**	−.08*	−.12**
Divorce proneness	.11**	−.09*	−.10*	−.10**

Note: Table values are standardized OLS regression coefficients. Analysis is based on 384 offspring who lived with both biological parents in 1980 and never experienced a parental divorce. Controls include offspring's gender, offspring's age, mother respondent, parents nonwhite, number of siblings, parental education, parental income, and parents' gender nontraditionalism (mothers' employment, fathers' share of family work, and gender attitudes). Significance tests are one-tailed.
#$p < .10$.   *$p < .05$.   **$p < .01$.   ***$p < .001$.

References

Acock, Alan C., and David H. Demo. 1994. *Family Diversity and Well-being*. Thousand Oaks, Calif.: Sage.

Acock, Alan C., and K. Jill Kiecolt. 1989. Is it family structure of socioeconomic status? Family structure during adolescence and adult adjustment. *Social Forces* 68:553–571.

Adams, Kenneth S., Anthony Bouckoms, and David Streiner. 1982. Parental loss and family stability in attempted suicide. *Archives of General Psychiatry* 39:1081–1085.

Ahmeduzzaman, Mohammad, and Jai Paul Roopnarine. 1992. Sociodemographic factors, functioning style, social support, and fathers' involvement with preschoolers in African American families. *Journal of Marriage and the Family* 54:699–707.

Allison, Paul D. 1984. *Event History Analysis: Regression for Longitudinal Data*. Beverly Hills: Sage.

Alwin, Duane F. 1984. Trends in parental socialization values: Detroit, 1958–1983. *American Journal of Sociology* 90:359–382.

———. 1991. Family of origin and cohort differences in verbal ability. *American Sociological Review* 56:625–628.

Alwin, Duane F., and Arland Thornton. 1984. Family origins and the schooling process: Early versus late influence of parental characteristics. *American Sociological Review* 49:784–802.

Amato, Paul R. 1986. Marital conflict, the parent-child relationship, and child self-esteem. *Family Relations* 35:403–410.

———. 1987a. *Children in Australian Families: The Growth of Competence*. Sydney: Prentice Hall of Australia.

———. 1987b. Parental divorce and attitudes toward family life. *Journal of Marriage and the Family* 50:453–461.

———. 1988. Long-term implications of parental divorce for adult self-concept. *Journal of Family Issues* 9:201–213.

———. 1990. Dimensions of the family environment as perceived by children: A multidimensional scaling analysis. *Journal of Marriage and the Family* 52:613–620.

———. 1991. Psychological distress and the recall of childhood family characteristics. *Journal of Marriage and the Family* 53:1011–1020.

———. 1993. Urban-rural differences in helping friends and family members. *Social Psychology Quarterly* 56:248–262.

———. 1994. Father-child relations, mother-child relations and psychological well-being in early adulthood. *Journal of Marriage and the Family* 56:1031–1042.

———. 1995a. Explaining the intergenerational transmission of divorce. Paper presented at the Annual Meeting of the National Council on Family Relations, Seattle.

———. 1995b. Single-parent households as settings for children's development, well-being, and attainment: A social network/resources perspective. *Sociological Studies of Children* 7:19–47.

Amato, Paul R., and Alan Booth. 1991a. Consequences of parental divorce and marital unhappiness for adult well-being. *Social Forces* 69:895–914.

———. 1991b. The consequences of divorce for attitudes toward divorce and gender roles. *Journal of Family Issues* 12:306–322.

———. 1995. Changes in gender role attitudes and perceived marital quality. *American Sociological Review* 60:58–66.

Amato, Paul R., and Bruce Keith. 1991a. Consequences of parental divorce for children's well-being: A meta-analysis. *Psychological Bulletin* 110:26–46.

———. 1991b. Parental divorce and adult well-being: A meta-analysis. *Journal of Marriage and the Family* 53:43–58.

———. 1991c. Separation from a parent during childhood and adult socioeconomic attainment. *Social Forces* 70:187–206.

Ambert, Anne-Marie. 1992. *The Effect of Children on Parents*. New York: Haworth Press.

Aquilino, William S. 1990. The likelihood of parent-adult child coresidence: Effects of family structure and parental characteristics. *Journal of Marriage and the Family* 52:405–419.

———. 1991. Family structure and home-leaving: A further specification of the relationship. *Journal of Marriage and the Family* 53:999–1010.

———. 1994. Impact of childhood family disruption on young adults' relationships with parents. *Journal of Marriage and the Family* 56:295–313.

Aquilino, William S., and Khalil Supple. 1991. Parent-child relations and parent's satisfaction with living arrangements when adult children live at home. *Journal of Marriage and the Family* 53:13–27.

Armistead, Lisa, Michelle Wierson, and Rex Forehand. 1990. Adolescents and maternal employment: Is it harmful for a young adolescent to have an employed mother? *Journal of Early Adolescence* 10:260–278.

Astone, Nan M., and Sara S. McLanahan. 1991. Family structure, parental practices, and high school completion. *American Sociological Review* 56:309–320.

Astone, Nan M., and Sara S. McLanahan. 1994. Family structure, residential mobility, and school dropout: A research note. *Demography* 31:575–584.

Attili, G. 1989. Social competence versus emotional security: The link between home relationships and behavior problems at school. Pp. 293–311 in B. H. Schneider, G. Attili, J. Nadel, and R. P. Weissberg (eds.), *Social Competence in Developmental Perspective*. London: Kluwer.

Avery, Roger, Frances Goldscheider, and Alden Speare, Jr. 1992. Feathered nest/gilded cage: Parental income and leaving home in the transition to adulthood. *Demography* 29:375–388.

Axinn, William G., and Arland Thornton. 1993. Mothers, children, and cohabitation: The intergenerational effects of attitudes and behavior. *American Sociological Review* 58:233–246.

Barber, Bonnie L., and Jacquelynne S. Eccles. 1992. Long-term influences of divorce and single parenting on adolescent family- and work-related values, behaviors, and aspirations. *Psychological Bulletin* 111:108–126.

Barber, Brian, Bruce A. Chadwick, and Rolf Oerter. 1992. Parental behaviors and adolescent self-esteem in the United States and Germany. *Journal of Marriage and the Family* 54:128–141.

Barich, Rachel Roseman, and Denise D. Bielby. 1996. Rethinking marriage: Change and stability in expectations, 1967–1994. *Journal of Family Issues* 17:139–169.

Barnes, Grace M., and Michael P. Farrell. 1992. Parental support and control as predictors of adolescent drinking, delinquency, and related problem behaviors. *Journal of Marriage and the Family* 54:763–776.

Barnett, Rosalind C., and Grace K. Baruch. 1987. Determinants of fathers' participation in family work. *Journal of Marriage and the Family* 49:29–40.

Barnett, Rosalind C., L. N. Marshall, and J. H. Pleck. 1992. Adult son-parent relationships and their associations with son's psychological distress. *Journal of Family Issues* 13:505–525.

Batson, C. Daniel, and W. Larry Ventis. 1982. *The Religious Experience: A Social Psychological Perspective*. Oxford: Oxford University Press.

Baydar, N., and J. Brooks-Gunn. 1991. Effects of maternal employment and childcare arrangements on preschoolers' cognitive and behavioral outcomes: Evidence from the children of the National Longitudinal Survey of Youth. *Developmental Psychology* 27:932–945.

Beck, Scott H. 1983. The role of other family members in intergenerational occupational mobility. *Sociological Quarterly* 24:273–285.

Becker, B. J. 1986. Influence again: An examination of reviews and studies of gender differences in social influence. Pp. 178–209 in J. S. Hyde and M. C. Linn (eds.), *The Psychology of Gender: Advances Through Meta-Analysis*. Baltimore: Johns Hopkins University Press.

Becker, Wesley C. 1964. Consequences of different kinds of parental discipline. Pp. 169–208 in Martin L. Hoffman and Lois W. Hoffman (eds.), *Review of Child Development Research* (Vol. 1). New York: Russell Sage Foundation.

Begley, Sharon. 1996. The IQ puzzle. *Newsweek*, May 6.

Bellah, Robert N., Richard Madsen, William N. Sullivan, Ann Swidler, and Steven N. Tipton. 1985. *Habits of the Heart: Individualism and Commitment in American Life*. Berkeley: University of California Press.

Belsky, Jay. 1991. Parental and nonparental child care and children' socioemotional development. Pp. 122–140 in Alan Booth (ed.), *Contemporary Families: Looking Forward, Looking Back*. Minneapolis, Minn.: National Council on Family Relations.

Belsky, Jay, and David J. Eggebeen. 1991. Early and extensive maternal employment and young children's socioemotional development: Children of the National Longitudinal Survey of Youth. *Journal of Marriage and the Family* 53:1083–1110.

Belsky, Jay, and Russell A. Isabella. 1985. Marital and parent-child relationship in family of origin and marital change following the birth of a baby: A retrospective analysis. *Child Development* 56:342–349.

Belsky, Jay, and Emily Pensky. 1988. Developmental history, personality, and family relationships: Toward an emergent family system. Pp. 193–217 in Robert A. Hinde and Joan Stevenson-Hinde (eds.), *Relationships within Families: Mutual Influences*. Oxford: Clarendon Press.

Belsky, Jay, Lisa Youngblade, Michael Rovine, and Brenda Volling. 1991. Patterns of marital change and parent-child interaction. *Journal of Marriage and the Family* 53:487–498.

Bengtson, Vern L., and Katherine R. Allen. 1994. The life course perspective applied to families over time. Pp. 469–498 in Pauline G. Boss, William J. Doherty, Ralph Larossa, Walter R. Schumm, and Suzanne K. Steinmetz (eds.), *Sourcebook of Family Theories and Methods: A Contextual Approach*. New York: Plenum.

Bengtson, Vern L., and S. Schrader. 1982. Parent-child relations. Pp. 154 in D. J. Mangen and W. A. Peterson (eds.), *Research Instruments in Social Gerontology: Vol. 2. Social Roles and Social Participation*. Minneapolis: University of Minnesota Press.

Bernard, Jessie. 1982. *The Future of Marriage*. New Haven: Yale University Press.

Biblarz, Timothy J., and Adrian E. Raferty. 1993. The effects of family disruption on social mobility. *American Sociological Review* 58:97–109.

Blake, Judith. 1989. *Family Size and Achievement*. Berkeley, Calif.: University of California Press.

Blankenhorn, David. 1995. *Fatherless America: Confronting Our Most Urgent Social Problem*. New York: Basic Books.

Blankenhorn, David, S. Bayme, and Jean Bethke Elshtain (eds.). 1990. *Rebuilding the Nest: A New Commitment to the American Family*. Milwaukee, Wis.: Family Service Association.

Blau, Francine D., and Adam J. Grossberg. 1992. Maternal labor supply and children's cognitive development. *Review of Economics and Statistics* 74:474–481.

Blau, Peter, and Otis D. Duncan. 1967. *The American Occupational Structure*. New York: Academic Press.

Blazer, D. G. 1982. Social support and mortality in an elderly community population. *American Journal of Epidemiology* 115:684–694.

Block, Jeanne, Jack Block, and Per Gjerde. 1986. The personality of children prior to divorce: A prospective study. *Child Development* 57:827–840.

Boisjoly, Johanne, Greg J. Duncan, and Sandra Hofferth. 1995. Access to social capital. *Journal of Family Issues* 16:609–631.

Bolger, Kerry E., Charlotte J. Patterson, William W. Thompson, and Janis B. Kupersmidt. 1995. Psychosocial adjustment among children experiencing persistent and intermittent family economic hardship. *Child Development* 66:1107–1129.

Booth, Alan, and Paul R. Amato. 1992. Divorce and psychological stress. *Journal of Health and Social Behavior* 32:396–407.

———. 1993. Divorce, residential change, and stress. *Journal of Divorce* 18:205–213.

———. 1994a. Parental gender role nontraditionalism and offspring outcomes. *Journal of Marriage and the Family* 56:865–877.

———. 1994b. Parental marital quality, parental divorce, and relations with parents. *Journal of Marriage and the Family* 56:21–34.

Booth, Alan, Paul R. Amato, David R. Johnson, and John N. Edwards. 1993. Marital Instability Over the Life Course: Methodology Report for Fourth Wave. Lincoln, Neb.: University of Nebraska Bureau of Sociological Research.

Booth, Alan, David B. Brinkerhoff, and Lynn K. White. 1984. The impact of parental divorce on courtship. *Journal of Marriage and the Family* 46:85–94.

Booth, Alan, and John N. Edwards. 1985. Age at marriage and marital instability. *Journal of Marriage and the Family* 47:67–75.

———. 1990. Transmission of marital and family quality over the generations: The effects of parental divorce and unhappiness. *Journal of Divorce* 13:41–58.

Booth, Alan, and David R. Johnson. 1985. Tracking respondents in a telephone interview panel selected by random digit dialing. *Sociological Methods and Research* 14:53–64.

Booth, Alan, David R. Johnson, and Lynn K. White. 1984. Women, outside employment, and marital instability. *American Journal of Sociology* 90:567–583.

Booth, Alan, David R. Johnson, Lynn K. White, and John N. Edwards. 1985. Predicting divorce and separation. *Journal of Family Issues* 6:331–346.

Bourdieu, Pierre, and J. C. Passeron. 1977. *Reproduction in Education, Society and Culture*. New York: Sage.

Bowen, Gary L., and Dennis K. Orthner. 1983. Sex-role congruency and marital quality. *Journal of Marriage and the Family* 45:223–230.

Bowlby, John. 1977. The making and breaking of affectional bonds. *British Journal of Psychiatry* 130:201–210.

Braungart, Richard G., and Margaret M. Braungart. 1986. Life-course and generational politics. *Annual Review of Sociology* 12:205–231.

Brody, Gene, and Anthony Pillegrini. 1986. Marital quality and mother-child and father-child interactions with school-aged children. *Developmental Psychology* 22:291–296.

Brody, Gene, Zolinda Stoneman, Douglas Flor, Chris McCrary, Lorraine Hastings, and Olive Conyers. 1994. Financial resources, parental psychological functioning, parent co-caregiving, and early adolescent competence in rural two-parent African-American families. *Child Development* 65:590–605.

Bronfenbrenner, Urie. 1958. Socialization and social class through time and space. Pp. 400–425 in E. E. Maccoby, T. M. Newcomb, and E. L. Hartley (eds.), *Readings in Social Psychology*. New York: Rinehart & Winston.

Browne, Irene. 1995. The baby boom and trends in poverty, 1967–1987. *Social Forces* 73:1071–1095.

Bryant, B. 1985. The Neighborhood Walk: Sources of Support in Middle Childhood. *Monographs of the Society for Research in Child Development* 50(3), No. 210.

Buchanan, Christy, Eleanor E. Maccoby, and Sanford M. Dornbusch. 1991. Caught between parents: Adolescents' experience in divorced homes. *Child Development* 62:1008–1022.

Buck, Nicholas, and Jacqueline Scott. 1993. She's leaving home: But why? An analysis of young people leaving the parental home. *Journal of Marriage and the Family* 55:863–874.

Bulcroft, Kris A., and Richard A. Bulcroft. 1991. The timing of divorce: effects on parent-child relationships in later life. *Research on Aging* 13:226–243.

Bumpass, Larry L. 1984. Children and marital disruption: A replication and update. *Demography* 21:71–82.

Bumpass, Larry L., Teresa Castro Martin, and James A. Sweet. 1991. The impact of family background and early marital factors on marital disruption. *Journal of Family Issues* 12:22–42.

Bumpass, Larry L., James A. Sweet, and Andrew Cherlin. 1991. The role of cohabitation in declining rates of marriage. *Journal of Marriage and the Family* 53:913–927.

Burns, Ailsa, and Cath Scott. 1995. *Mother-headed Families and Why They Have Increased*. Hillsdale, N.J.: Lawrence Erlbaum.

Burns, R. B. 1979. *The Self-concept: Theory, Measurement, Development and Behavior*. London: Longman.

Campbell, Angus. 1981. *The Sense of Well-Being in America: Recent Patterns and Trends*. New York: McGraw-Hill.

Campbell, Angus, Philip Converse, and Willard Rogers. 1976. *The Quality of American Life: Perceptions, Evaluations, and Satisfaction*. New York: Russell Sage Foundation.

Campbell, Karen E., and Barrett A. Lee. 1990. Gender differences in urban neighboring. *The Sociological Quarterly* 31:495–512.

Caspi, Avshalom, and Glen H. Elder, Jr. 1988. Emergent family patterns: The intergenerational construction of problem behavior and relationships. Pp. 218–240 in Robert Hinde and Joan Stevenson-Hinde (eds.), *Relationships within Families: Mutual Influences*. Oxford: Clarendon Press.

Chase-Lansdale, P. Lindsay, and Margaret Tresch Owen. 1987. Maternal employment in a family context: Effects on infant-mother and infant-father attachments. *Child Development* 58:1505–1512.

Cherlin, Andrew. 1992. *Marriage, Divorce, Remarriage*. Cambridge, Mass.: Harvard University Press.

Cherlin, Andrew, Frank F. Furstenberg, P. Lindsay Chase-Lansdale, Kathleen Kiernan, Donna Ruane Morrison, and Julien Teitler. 1991. Longitudinal studies of effects of divorce on children in Great Britain and the United States. *Science* 252:1386–1389.

Chodorow, Nancy. 1978. *The Reproduction of Mothering: Psychoanalysis and the Sociology of Gender*. Berkeley: University of California Press.

Christenson, Sandra. 1992. Family factors and student achievement. *School Psychology Quarterly* 7:178–206.

Clark-Stewart, Alison. 1992. Consequences of child care for children's development. Pp. 63–82 in Alan Booth (ed.), *Child Care in the 1990s: Trends and Consequences*. Hillsdale, N.J.: Lawrence Erlbaum.

Clausen, John A. 1993. *American Lives: Looking Back at the Children of the Great Depression*. New York: The Free Press.

Cochran, Moncrieff, and Inge Bø. 1989. The social networks, family involvement, and pro- and anti-social behavior of adolescent males in Norway. *Journal of Youth and Adolescence* 18:377-398.

Cohn, Deborah A., Chardette J. Patterson, and Christina Christopoulos. 1991. The family and children's peer relationships. *Journal of Social and Personal Relationships* 8:315–346.

Coleman, James. 1988. Social capital in the creation of human capital. *American Journal of Sociology* 94:95–120.

Colletta, Nancy D. 1979. The impact of divorce: Father absence or poverty? *Journal of Divorce* 63:27–35.

Committee for Economic Development. 1996. *American Workers and Economic Change*. New York.

Conger, Rand D., Katherine J. Conger, Glen H. Elder, Jr., Frederick O. Lorenz, Ronald L. Simons, and Les B. Whitbeck. 1992. A family process model of economic hardship and adjustment of early adolescent boys. *Child Development* 63:526–541.

———. 1993. Family economic stress and adjustment of early adolescent girls. *Developmental Psychology* 29:206–219.

Conger, Rand D., Glen H. Elder, Jr., Frederick O. Lorenz, Katherine J. Conger, Ronald L. Simons, Les B. Whitbeck, Shirley Huck, and Janet N. Melby. 1990. Linking economic hardship to marital quality and instability. *Journal of Marriage and the Family* 52:643–656.

Conger, Rand D., Xiaojia Ge, Glen H. Elder, Jr., Frederick Lorenz, and Ronald L. Simons. 1994. Economic stress, coercive family process, and developmental problems in adolescents. *Child Development* 65:541–561.

Conklin, Mary E., and Ann Ricks Daily. 1981. Does consistency of parental educational encouragement matter for secondary school students? *Sociology of Education* 54:254–262.

Cooney, Teresa M. 1994. Young adults' relations with parents: The influence of recent parental divorce. *Journal of Marriage and the Family* 56:45–56.

Cooney, Teresa M., Diane M. Leather, and M. Katherine Hutchinson. 1995. Surviving the break-up? Predictors of problematic parent-child relations after parental divorce. *Family Relations* 44:153–162.

Cooney, Teresa, M., Michael A. Smyer, Gunhild O. Hagestad, and Robin Klock. 1986. Parental divorce in young adulthood: Some preliminary findings. *American Journal of Orthopsychiatry* 56:470–477.

Cooney, Teresa M., and Peter Uhlenburg. 1990. The role of divorce in men's relations with their adult children after mid-life. *Journal of Marriage and the Family* 52:677–688.

Coontz, Stephanie. 1992. *The Way We Wish We Were: American Families and the Nostalgia Trap*. New York: Basic Books.

Coser, Rose L. 1964. Authority and structural ambivalence. Pp. 370–386 in Rose L. Coser (ed.), *The Family: Its Structure and Functions*. New York: St. Martins.

Crockett, Lisa J., David J. Eggebeen, and A. J. Hawkins. 1993. Father's presence and young children's behavioral and cognitive adjustment. *Family Relations* 14:355–377.

Crouter, Ann C., M. Perry-Jenkins, T. L. Huston, and S. M. McHale. 1987. Processes underlying father involvement in dual-earner and single-earner families. *Developmental Psychology* 23:431–440.

Cummings, E. Mark. 1987. Coping with background anger in early childhood. *Child Development* 58:976–984.

Cummings, E. Mark, C. Zahn-Waxler, and M. Radke-Yarrow. 1981. Young children's reactions to expressions of anger and affection by others in the family. *Child Development* 52:1274–1281.

Danziger, Sheldon, and Peter Gottschalk. 1993. *Uneven Tides: Rising Inequality in America*. New York: Russell Sage Foundation.

Davidson, N. (ed.). 1989. *Gender Sanity*. New York: University Press of America.

Davies, Patrick T., and E. Mark Cummings. 1994. Marital conflict and child adjustment: An emotional security hypothesis. *Psychological Bulletin* 116:387–411.

Davis, Kingsley. 1984. Wives and work: The sex role revolution and its consequences. *Population and Development Review* 10:397–417.

DeMartini, Joseph R. 1992. Generational relationships and social movement participation. *Sociological Inquiry* 62:450–463.

Demo, David H. 1992. Parent-child relations: Assessing recent changes. *Journal of Marriage and the Family* 54:104–117.

Desai, Sonalde, P. Lindsay Chase-Lansdale, and Robert Michael. 1989. Mother or market? Effects of maternal employment on the intellectual ability of 4-year-old children. *Demography* 26:545–561.

Dodge, Kenneth A., Gregory S. Pettit, and John E. Bates. 1994. Socialization mediators of the relation between socioeconomic status and child conduct problems. *Child Development* 65:649–665.

Doherty, William, and Richard Needle. 1991. Psychological adjustment and substance use among adolescents before and after parental divorce. *Child Development* 62:328–337.

Dornbusch, Sanford, J. M. Carlsmith, S. J. Bushwall, P. L. Ritter, H. Leiderman, A. H. Hastorf, and R. T. Gross. 1985. Single parents, extended households, and the control of adolescents. *Child Development* 56:326–341.

Doyle, Anna Beth, Dorothy Markiewicz, and Cindy Hardy. 1994. Mother's and children's friendships: Intergenerational associations. *Journal of Social and Personal Relationships* 11:363–377.

Draughn, Peggy S., and Mary L. Waggenspack. 1986. Fathers' supportiveness: Perceptions of fathers and college daughters. Pp. 197–212 in Robert A. Lewis and Robert E. Salt (eds.), *Men in Families*. Beverly Hills, Calif.: Sage.

Duncan, Greg, Jeanne Brooks-Gunn, and Pamela Klebanov. 1994. Economic deprivation and early childhood development. *Child Development* 65:296–318.

Duncan, Greg J., and Saul D. Hoffman. 1985. Economic consequences of marital instability. Pp. 427–470 in M. David and T. Smeeding (eds.), *Horizontal Equity, Uncertainty, and Economic Well-being*. Chicago: University of Chicago Press.

Dunlop, Rosemary, and Ailsa Burns. 1988. *"Don't feel the world is caving in." Adolescents in Divorcing Families*. Melbourne, Australia: Australian Institute of Family Studies.

Eggebeen, David J., and Dennis P. Hogan. 1990. Giving between generations in American families. *Human Nature* 1:211–232.

Eggebeen, David J., and Daniel Lichter. 1991. Family structure and changing poverty among American children. *American Sociological Review* 56:801–817.

Eggebeen, David J., and Peter Uhlenberg. 1985. Changes in the organization of men's lives. *Family Relations* 34:251–257.

Elder, Glen H., Jr. 1974. *Children of the Great Depression*. Chicago: University of Chicago Press.

———. 1994. Time, agency, and social change: Perspectives on the life course. *Social Psychology Quarterly* 57:5–15.

Elder, Glen H., Jr., Tri van Nguyen, and Avshalom Caspi. 1985. Linking family hardship to children's lives. *Child Development* 56:361–375.

Elliott, Delbert, David Huizinga, and Scott Menard. 1989. *Multiple Problem Youth: Delinquency, Substance Use, and Mental Health Problems*. New York: Springer-Verlag.

Emery, Robert. 1982. Interparental conflict and the children of discord and divorce. *Psychological Bulletin* 92:310–330.

———. 1988. *Marriage, Divorce, and Children's Adjustment*. Newbury Park, Calif.: Sage.

Faludi, Susan. 1991. *Backlash: The Undeclared War against American Women*. New York: Crown.

Falwell, Jerry (ed.). 1981. *The Fundamentalist Phenomenon: The Resurgence of Conservative Christianity*. Garden City, N.Y.: Doubleday.

Fauber, R., Rex Forehand, A. M. Thomas, and M. Wierson. 1990. A mediational model of the impact of marital conflict on adolescent adjustment in intact and divorced families: The role of disruptive parenting. *Child Development* 61: 1112–1123.

Featherman, David L., and Robert M. Hauser. 1978. *Opportunity and Change*. New York: Academic Press.

Feldman, Roberta M. 1990. Settlement-identity: Psychological bonds with home places in a mobile society. *Environment and Behavior* 22:183–229.

Felner, Robert D., Stephen Brand, David L. DuBois, Angela M. Adan, Peter F. Mulhall, and Elizabeth G. Evans. 1995. Socioeconomic disadvantage, proximal environmental experiences, and socioemotional and academic adjustment in early adolescence: Investigation of a mediated effects model. *Child Development* 66:774–792.

Fine, Mark A., J. R. Moreland, and A. I. Schweibel. 1983. Long-term effects of divorce on parent-child relationships. *Developmental Psychology* 19:703–713.

Fischer, Claude. 1982. *To Dwell Among Friends*. Chicago: University of Chicago Press.

Fischer, Judith L., Donna L. Sallie, Gwendolyn T. Sorell, and Shelley K. Green. 1989. Marital status and career stage influences on social networks of young adults. *Journal of Marriage and the Family* 51:521–534.

Flanagan, Constance A. 1990. Families and schools in hard times. Pp. 7–26 in Vonnie C. McLoyd and Constance A. Flanagan (eds.), *Economic Stress: Effects on Family Life and Child Development*. San Francisco: Jossey-Bass.

Forthofer, Melinda, Ronald Kessler, Amber Stroy, and Ian Gotlib. 1996. The effects of psychiatric disorders on the probability and timing of first marriage. *Journal of Health and Social Behavior* 37:121–132.

Francis, Leslie J., and Lawrence B. Brown. 1991. The influence of home, church, and school prayer among 16-year old adolescents in England. *Review of Religious Research* 33:112–122.

Fullerton, Carol S., and Robert J. Ursano. 1994. Preadolescent peer friendships: A critical contribution to adult social relatedness? *Journal of Youth and Adolescence* 23:43–63.

Furstenberg, Frank F., Jr., and Andrew J. Cherlin. 1991. *Divided Families: What Happens to Children When Parents Part*. Cambridge, Mass.: Harvard University Press.

Furstenberg, Frank F., Jr., and K. Harris. 1992. The disappearing American father? Divorce and the waning significance of biological parenthood. Pp. 197–223 in Scott J. South and Stewart E. Tolnay (eds.), *The Changing American Family: Sociological and Demographic Perspectives*. Boulder, Colo.: Westview Press.

Furstenberg, Frank F., Jr., S. Philip Morgan, and Paul D. Allison. 1987. Paternal participation and children's well-being after marital dissolution. *American Sociological Review* 52:695–701.

Furstenberg, Frank F., Jr., and Christine Nord. 1985. Parenting apart: Patterns of childrearing after marital disruption. *Journal of Marriage and the Family* 47:893–904.

Furstenberg, Frank F., Jr., Christine W. Nord, James L. Peterson, and Nicholas Zill.

1983. The life course of children of divorce: Marital disruption and parental contact. *American Sociological Review* 48:656–668.

Furstenberg, Frank F., Jr., and Julien O. Teitler. 1994. Reconsidering the effects of marital disruption: What happens to children of divorce in early adulthood. *Journal of Family Issues* 15:173–190.

Galambos, Nancy, and Rainer Silbereisen. 1987. Income change, parental life outlook, and adolescent expectations for job success. *Journal of Marriage and the Family* 49:141–149.

Galston, William A. 1996. The reinstitutionalization of marriage. Political theory and public policy. Pp. 271–290 in David Popenoe, Jean Bethke Elshtain, and David Blankenhorn (eds.), *Promises to Keep: Decline and Renewal of Marriage in America*. Lanham, Md.: Rowman and Littlefield.

Gecas, Victor. 1979. The influence of social class on socialization. Pp. 365–404 in Wesley R. Burr, Reuben Hill, F. Ivan Nye, and Ira L. Reiss (eds.), *Contemporary Theories About the Family. Volume 1: Research-Based Theories*. New York: The Free Press.

Gecas, Victor, and Michael L. Schwalbe. 1986. Parental behavior and adolescent self-esteem. *Journal of Marriage and the Family* 48:37–46.

Gecas, Victor, and Monica Seff. 1991. Families and adolescents: A review of the 1980s. Pp. 208–225 in Alan Booth (ed.), *Contemporary Families: Looking Forward, Looking Back*. Minneapolis, Minn.: National Council on Family Relations.

Gelles, Richard J. 1987. *Family Violence*. Newbury Park, Calif.: Sage.

_____. 1989. Child abuse and violence in single-parent families: Parent absence and economic deprivation. *American Journal of Orthopsychiatry* 59:492–501.

Gerson, Kathleen. 1993. *No Man's Land: Men's Changing Commitments to Family and Work*. New York: Basic Books.

Gilder, George. 1986. *Men and Marriage*. Gretna, N.Y.: Pelican.

Glenn, Norval D. 1990. Quantitative research on marital quality in the 1980s. *Journal of Marriage and the Family* 52:818–831.

_____. 1991. The recent trend in marital success in the United States. *Journal of Marriage and the Family* 53:261–270.

_____. 1994. Television watching, newspaper reading, and cohort differences in verbal ability. *Sociology of Education* 67:216–230.

_____. 1996. Values, attitudes, and the state of American marriage. Pp. 15–33 in David Popenoe, Jean Bethke Elshtain, and David Blankenhorn (eds.), *Promises to Keep: Decline and Renewal of Marriage in America*. Lanham, Md.: Rowman and Littlefield.

Glenn, Norval D., and Kathryn B. Kramer. 1987. The marriages and divorces of the children of divorce. *Journal of Marriage and the Family* 49:811–825.

Glenn, Norval D., and Charles N. Weaver. 1988. The changing relationship of marital status to reported happiness. *Journal of Marriage and the Family* 50:317–324.

Glick, Paul C. 1989. Remarried families, stepfamilies, and stepchildren: A brief demographic profile. *Family Relations* 38:24–27.

Goldscheider, Frances K., and Calvin Goldscheider. 1989. Family structure and conflict: Nest-leaving expectations of young adults and their parents. *Journal of Marriage and the Family* 51:87–97.

————. 1993. *Leaving Home Before Marriage*. Madison: University of Wisconsin Press.

————. 1994. Leaving and returning home in 20th Century America. *Population Bulletin* 48:1–33.

Goldscheider, Frances K., and Linda J. Waite. 1991. *New Families, No Families: The Transformation of the American Home*. Berkeley, Calif.: University of California Press.

Gottfried, Adele Eskeles. 1991. Maternal employment in the family setting: Developmental and environmental issues. Pp. 63–84 in Jacqueline V. Lerner and Nancy L. Galambos (eds.), *Employed Mothers and Their Children*. New York: Garland.

Gove, W. R., M. Hughes, and C. B. Style. 1983. Does marriage have positive effects on the psychological well-being of the individual? *Journal of Health and Social Behavior* 24:122–131.

Greenberg, David, and Douglas Wolf. 1982. The economic consequences of experiencing parental marital disruptions. *Children and Youth Services Review* 4:141–162.

Greenberger, Ellen, Robin O'Neil, and Stacy K. Nagel. 1994. Linking workplace and homeplace: Relations between the nature of adults' work and their parenting behaviors. *Developmental Psychology* 30:990–1002.

Greenstein, Theodore N. 1995. Are the "most advantaged" children truly disadvantaged by early maternal employment?: Effects on child outcomes. *Journal of Family Issues* 16:149–169.

————. 1996. Gender ideology and perceptions of the fairness of the division of household labor: Effects on marital quality. *Social Forces* 74:1029–1042.

Grych, J., and Frank Fincham. 1990. Marital conflict and children's adjustment: A cognitive-conceptual framework. *Psychological Bulletin* 108:267–290.

Harnish, Jennifer D., Kenneth A. Dodge, and Ernest Valente. 1995. Mother-child interaction quality as a partial mediator of the roles of maternal depressive symptomology and socioeconomic status on the development of child behavior problems. *Child Development* 66:739–753.

Harris, Kathleen M., and S. Philip Morgan. 1991. Fathers, sons, and daughters: Differential paternal involvement in parenting. *Journal of Marriage and the Family* 53:531–544.

Haveman, Robert, and Barbara Wolfe. 1994. *Succeeding Generations: On the Effects of Investments in Children*. New York: Russell Sage Foundation.

Haveman, Robert, Barbara Wolfe, and James Spaulding. 1991. Childhood events and circumstances influencing high school completion. *Demography* 28:133–157.

Heiss, Jerold. 1972. On the transmission of marital instability in black families. *American Sociological Review* 37:82–92.

Hernandez, Donald. 1993. *America's Children: Resources from Family, Government, and the Economy*. New York: Russell Sage Foundation.

Hess, R. D. 1970. Social class and ethnic influences upon socialization. Pp. 457–558 in Paul H. Mussen (ed.), *Carmichael's Manual of Child Psychology*. New York: Wiley.

Hetherington, E. Mavis. 1972. Effects of father absence on personality development in adolescent daughters. *Developmental Psychology* 7:313–326.

Hetherington, E. Mavis, K. A. Camara, and D. L. Featherman. 1983. Achievement and intellectual functioning of children in one-parent households. Pp. 205–284 in J. Spence (ed.), *Achievement and Achievement Motives*. San Francisco: Freeman.

Hetherington, E. Mavis, and W. Glenn Clingempeel. 1992. *Coping with Marital Transitions*. Monographs of the Society for Research in Child Development, Vol. 57, Nos. 2–3. Chicago: University of Chicago Press.

Hetherington, E. Mavis, M. Cox, and R. Cox. 1982. Effects of divorce on parents and children. Pp. 223–288 in Michael E. Lamb (ed.), *Nontraditional Families: Parenting and Child Development*. Hillsdale, N.J.: Lawrence Erlbaum.

Hill, Martha, and Greg J. Duncan. 1987. Parental family income and the socioeconomic attainment of children. *Social Science Research* 16:39–73.

Hochschild, Arlie. 1989. *The Second Shift*. New York: Avon.

Hoffman, Lois W. 1974. Effects on the child. In Lois W. Hoffman and F. Ivan Nye (eds.), *Working Mothers*. San Francisco: Jossey-Bass.

————. 1989. Effects of maternal employment in the two-parent family. *American Psychologist* 44:283–292.

Hogan, Dennis P., David J. Eggebeen, and Clifford Clogg. 1993. The structure of intergenerational exchanges in American families. *American Journal of Sociology* 98:1428–1458.

Hoge, Dean R., Greg H. Petrillo, and Ella I. Smith. 1982. Transmission of religious and social values from parents to teenage children. *Journal of Marriage and the Family* 44:569–580.

Holmes, T., R. Rahe. 1968. The social readjustment rating scale. *Journal of Psychosomatic Research* 11:213–218.

Holzer, Harry J. 1996. *What Employers Want: Job Prospects for Less-Educated Workers*. New York: Russell Sage Foundation.

Hook, Mary P. Van. 1990. The Iowa farm crisis: Perceptions, interpretations, and family patterns. Pp. 71–86 in Vonnie C. McLoyd and Constance A. Flanagan (eds.), *Economic Stress: Effects on Family Life and Child Development*. San Francisco: Jossey-Bass.

House, James S., Debra Umberson, and Karl R. Landis. 1988. Structures and processes of social support. *Annual Review of Sociology* 14:293–318.

Hoyert, Donna L. 1991. Financial and household exchanges between generations. *Research on Aging* 13:205–225.

Hughes, H. M. 1988. Psychological and behavioral correlates of family violence in child witnesses and victims. *American Journal of Orthopsychiatry* 58:77–90.

Jekielek, Susan M. 1996. The relative and interactive impacts of parental conflict and marital disruption on children's emotional well-being. Paper presented at the Annual Meeting of the American Sociological Association, New York.

Johnson, David R., and Paul R. Amato. 1996. Changes in marital quality: Period and duration of marriage effects. Unpublished manuscript, Department of Sociology, University of Nebraska–Lincoln.

Johnson, David R., and Alan Booth. 1996. Is marital quality a product of environmental or personality factors? Panel evidence from individuals in serial marriages. Unpublished manuscript, Department of Sociology, University of Nebraska–Lincoln.

Johnson, David R., Lynn K. White, John N. Edwards, and Alan Booth. 1986. Dimensions of marital quality: Toward methodological and conceptual refinement. *Journal of Family Issues* 7:31–49.

Johnston, Janet R. 1994. High-conflict divorce. *The Future of Children: Children and Divorce* 4:165–182.

Johnston, Janet R., Marsha Kline, and Jeanne M. Tschann. 1989. Ongoing postdivorce conflict: Effects on children of joint custody and frequent access. *American Journal of Orthopsychiatry* 59:576–592.

Jouriles, E. N., J. Barling, and K. D. O'Leary. 1987. Predicting child behavior problems in maritally violent families. *Journal of Abnormal Child Psychology* 15:165–173.

Kalmijn, Matthus. 1994. Mother's occupational status and children's schooling. *American Sociological Review* 59:257–275.

Karoly, Lynn, and Gary Burtless. 1995. Demographic change, rising earnings inequality, and the distribution of personal well-being, 1959–1989. *Demography* 32:379–405.

Kates, Erika. 1995. Escaping poverty: The promise of higher education. *Social Policy Report. Society for Research in Child Development* 9(1):1–21.

Keith, V. M., and B. Finlay. 1988. The impact of parental divorce on children's educational attainment, marital timing, and likelihood of divorce. *Journal of Marriage and the Family* 50:797–809.

Kelly, Jeffrey A., and David J. Hansen. 1987. Social interactions and adjustment. Pp. 131–146 in Vincent B. van Hasselt and Michel Hersen (eds.), *Handbook of adolescent psychology*. New York: Pergamon Press.

Kessler, Ronald. 1982. A disaggregation of the relationship between socioeconomic status and psychological distress. *American Sociological Review* 47:752–764.

Khoo, S., S. Krishnamoorthy, and A. D. Trlin. 1984a. Attitudes toward sex roles, women's employment and anticipated family size among young unmarried adults. *Australian Journal of Sex, Marriage, and Family* 5:147–158.

_____. 1984b. Maternal employment—does it affect the children when they grow up? *Australian Journal of Social Issues* 19:89–98.

Kiecolt, K. Jill, and Alan C. Acock. 1988. The long-term effects of family structure on gender role attitudes. *Journal of Marriage and the Family* 50:709–718.

Kiernan, Kathleen. 1992. The impact of family disruption in childhood on transitions made in young adulthood. *Population Studies* 46:218–234.

Kiker, B. F., and C. M. Condon. 1981. The influence of socioeconomic background on the earnings of young men. *The Journal of Human Resources* 16:94–105.

King, Valarie. 1994. Nonresident father involvement and child well-being: Can dads make a difference? *Journal of Family Issues* 15:78–96.

Kitson, Gay, and Marvin Sussman. 1982. Marital complaints, demographic characteristics, and symptoms of mental distress in divorce. *Journal of Marriage and the Family* 44:87–101.

Kohn, Melvin L. 1963. Social class and parent-child relationships: An interpretation. *American Journal of Sociology* 68:471–480.

_____. 1977. *Class and Conformity: A Study of Values*, 2nd edition. Chicago: University of Chicago Press.

Kominsky, Robert. 1990. *What's It Worth? Educational Background and Economic Status*. Series P-70, No. 21. Washington, D.C.: U.S. Government Printing Office.

Krein, Sheila F. 1986. Growing up in a single parent family: The effect on education and earnings of young men. *Family Relations* 35:161–168.

Kulka, Richard A., and Helen Weingarten. 1979. The long-term effects of parental divorce in childhood on adult adjustment. *Journal of Social Issues* 35:50–78.

Kurdek, Lawrence A., and Mark A. Fine. 1994. Family acceptance and family control as predictors of adjustment in young adolescents: Linear, curvilinear, or interactive effects? *Child Development* 65:1137–1146.

Ladd, G. W., K. H. Hart, E. M. Wadsworth, and B. Golter. 1987. Preschooler's peer networks in nonschool settings: Relationships to family characteristics and school adjustment. Pp. 61–92 in Suzanne Salzinger, M. Hammer, and J. Antrobus (eds.), *Social Networks of Children, Adolescents, and College Students*. Hillsdale, N.J.: Lawrence Erlbaum.

Lamb, Michael E. 1981. Fathers and child development: An integrated overview.

Pp. 1–70 in Michael E. Lamb (ed.), *The Role of the Father in Child Development*. New York: Wiley.

————. 1987. The emergent American father. Pp. 3–26 in Michael E. Lamb (ed.), *The Father's Role: Cross-Cultural Perspectives*. Hillsdale, N.J.: Lawrence Erlbaum.

Lamborn, Susie D., Nina S. Mounts, Laurence Steinberg, and Sanford Dornbusch. 1991. Patterns of competence and adjustment among adolescents from authoritative, authoritarian, indulgent, and neglectful families. *Child Development* 62:1049–1065.

Langner, Thomas. 1962. A twenty-two item screening score of psychiatric symptoms indicating impairment. *Journal of Health and Social Behavior* 3:269–276.

LaRossa, Ralph. 1988. Fatherhood and social change. *Family Relations* 37:451–457.

Leaky, P., and A. Morgan. 1978. A comparison of movements opposed to nuclear power, flouridation, and abortion. Pp. 143–154 in L. Kriesberg (ed.), *Social Movements, Conflict and Change*. Greenwich, Conn.: JAI Press.

Lee, Gary R., Karen Seccombe, and Constance L. Shehan. 1991. Marital status and personal happiness: An analysis of trend data. *Journal of Marriage and the Family* 53:839–844.

Leibowitz, Arleen, and Jacob A. Klerman. 1995. Explaining changes in married mothers' employment over time. *Demography* 32:365–378.

Lempers, Jacques, Dania Clark-Lempers, and Ronald L. Simons. 1989. Economic hardship, parenting, and distress in adolescents. *Child Development* 60:25–39.

Lennon, Mary Clare, and Sarah Rosenfield. 1994. Relative fairness and the division of housework: The importance of options. *American Journal of Sociology* 100:506–531.

Lewis, Robert A., and Graham B. Spanier. 1979. Theorizing about the quality and stability of marriage. Pp. 268–294 in Wesley R. Burr, Reuben Hill, F. Ivan Nye, and Ira L. Reiss (eds.), *Contemporary Theories About the Family. Volume 1. Research-Based Theories*. New York: The Free Press.

Li, Jiang Hong, and Roger A. Wojtkiewicz. 1994. Childhood family structure and entry into first marriage. *The Sociological Quarterly* 35:247–268.

Lillard, Lee A., and Linda J. Waite. 1995. 'Til death do us part: Marital disruption and mortality. *American Journal of Sociology* 100:1131–1156.

Litwak, E., and I. Szelenyi. 1969. Primary group structures and the functions: Kin, neighbors, and friends. *American Sociological Review* 34:465–481.

Lloyd, Kim M., and Scott J. South. 1996. Contextual influences on young men's transition to first marriage. *Social Forces* 74:1097–1119.

Lobdell, J., and D. Perlman. 1986. The intergenerational transmission of loneliness: A study of college females and their parents. *Journal of Marriage and the Family* 48:589–595.

Logan, John R., and Glenna D. Spitze. 1994. Family neighbors. *American Journal of Sociology* 100:453–476.

Long, N., R. Forehand, R. Fauber, and G. H. Brody. 1987. Self-perceived and independently observed competence of young adolescents as a function of parental marital conflict and recent divorce. *Journal of Abnormal Child Psychology* 15:15–27.

Lueptow, Lloyd, Margaret Guss, and Colleen Hyden. 1989. Sex role ideology, marital status, and happiness. *Journal of Family Issues* 10:383–400.

Lye, Diane N., Daniel H. Klepinger, Patricia Davis Hyle, and Anjanette Nelson. 1995. Childhood living arrangements and adult children's relations with their parents. *Demography* 32:261–280.

Maccoby, Eleanor, and J. Martin. 1983. Socialization in the context of the family: Parent-child interaction. Pp. 1–101 in E. Mavis Hetherington (ed.), *Handbook of Child Psychology: Vol.4. Socialization, Personality and Social Development*. New York: Wiley.

Manski, Charles F., Gary D. Sandefur, Sara S. McLanahan, and Daniel Powers. 1992. Alternative estimates of the effect of family structure during adolescence on high school graduation. *Journal of the American Statistical Association* 87:25–37.

Marini, Margaret. 1978. The transition to adulthood: Sex differences in educational attainment and marriage. *American Sociological Review* 43:483–507.

Marjoribanks, Kevin. 1979. *Families and Their Learning Environments*. London: Routledge & Kegan Paul.

Marsiglio, W. 1991. Paternal engagement activities with minor children. *Journal of Marriage and the Family* 53:973–986.

Martin, Barclay. 1990. The transmission of relationship difficulties from one generation to the next. *Journal of Youth and Adolescence* 18:377–398.

Martin, Teresa Castro, and Larry L. Bumpass. 1989. Recent trends in marital disruption. *Demography* 26:37–51.

Mastekaasa, Arne. 1994. Marital status, distress, and well-being: An international comparison. *Journal of Comparative Family Studies* 25:181–205.

Matsueda, R. L., and K. Heimer. 1987. Race, family structure, and delinquency: A test of differential association and social control theories. *American Sociological Review* 52:826–840.

McLanahan, Sara S. 1985. Family structure and the reproduction of poverty. *American Journal of Sociology* 90:873–901.

———. 1988. Family structure and dependency: Early transitions to female household headship. *Demography* 25:1–16.

McLanahan, Sara S., and Karen Booth. 1989. Mother-only families: Problems, prospects, and politics. *Journal of Marriage and the Family* 51:557–580.

McLanahan, Sara S., and Larry L. Bumpass. 1988. Intergenerational consequences of family disruption. *American Journal of Sociology* 94:130–152.

McLanahan, Sara S., and Gary Sandefur. 1994. *Growing Up with a Single Parent: What Hurts, What Helps*. Cambridge, Mass.: Harvard University Press.

McLeod, Jane D. 1991. Childhood parental loss and adult depression. *Journal of Health and Social Behavior* 32:205–220.

McLoyd, Vonnie C. 1989. Socialization and development in a changing economy: The effects of paternal job and income loss on children. *American Psychologist* 44:293–302.

McLoyd, Vonnie C., Toby Epstein Jayaratne, Rosario Ceballa, and Julio Borquez. 1994. Unemployment and work interruption among African American single mothers: Effects on parenting and adolescent socioemotional functioning. *Child Development* 65:562–589.

McLoyd, Vonnie C., and Leon Wilson. 1991. The strain of living poor: Parenting, social support, and child mental health. Pp. 105–135 in A. C. Huston (ed.), *Children in Poverty: Child Development and Public Policy*. New York: Cambridge University Press.

Menaghan, Elizabeth G., and Toby L. Parcel. 1991. Parental employment and family life: Research in the 1980s. Pp. 361–380 in Alan Booth (ed.), *Contemporary Families: Looking Forward, Looking Back*. Minneapolis, Minn.: National Council on Family Relations.

Mischel, Harriet, and Robert Fuhr. 1988. Maternal employment: Its psychological effects on children and their families. Pp. 191–211 in Sanford M. Dornbusch and Myra Strober (eds.), *Feminism, Children, and the New Families*. New York: Guilford.

Moen, Phyllis, Donna Dempster-McClain, and Robin M. Williams, Jr. 1989. Social integration and longevity: An event history of women's roles and resilience. *American Sociological Review* 54:635–647.

Mott, Frank. 1994. Sons, daughters and fathers' absence: Differentials in father-leaving probabilities and in home environments. *Journal of Family Issues* 15:97–128.

Mott, Frank, and Jean R. Haurin. 1992. Variations in the educational progress and career orientations of brothers and sisters. Pp. 19–44 in Frank Mott (ed.), *The Employment Revolution: Young American Women in the 1970s*. Cambridge Mass.: MIT Press.

Moynihan, Daniel P. 1986. *Family and Nation*. Orlando, Fla.: Harcourt Brace Jovanovich.

Mueller, Daniel P., and Philip W. Cooper. 1986. Children of single parents: How they fare as young adults. *Family Relations* 35:169–176.

Mueller, Charles W., and Hallowell Pope. 1977. Marital instability: A study of its transmission between generations. *Journal of Marriage and the Family* 39:83–92.

Muller, Chandra. 1995. Maternal employment, parent involvement, and mathematics achievement among adolescents. *Journal of Marriage and the Family* 57:85–100.

Murnane, Richard J., Rebecca A. Maynard, and James C. Ohls. 1981. Home resources and children's achievement. *Review of Economics and Statistics* 63:369–377.

Murphy, Kevin M., and Finis Welch. 1993. Industrial change and the rising importance of skill. Pp. 101–132 in Sheldon Danziger and Peter Gottschalk (eds.), *Uneven Tides: Rising Inequality in America*. New York: Russell Sage Foundation.

Newcomer, Susan, and J. Richard Udry. 1987. Parental marital status effects on adolescent sexual behavior. *Journal of Marriage and the Family* 49:235–240.

Newson, J., and E. Newson. 1976. *Seven Years Old in the Home Environment*. London: Allen & Unwin.

Nock, Steven L. 1988. The family and hierarchy. *Journal of Marriage and the Family* 50:957–966.

_____. 1995. A comparison of marriages and cohabiting relationships. *Journal of Family Issues* 16:53–76.

Nock, Steven L., and Paul W. Kingston. 1988. Time with children: The impact of couples' worktime commitments. *Social Forces* 67:59–85.

Norris, F., and S. Murrell. 1987. Transitory impact of life-event stress on psychological symptoms in older adults. *Journal of Health and Social Behavior* 28:197–211.

O'Connell, Martin. 1993. *Where's Papa: Fathers' Role in Child Care*. Washington, D.C.: Population Reference Bureau.

O'Donnell, Lydia, and Ann Stueve. 1983. Mothers as social agents: Structuring the community activities of school aged children. Pp. 113–129 in Helena Z. Lopata (ed.), *Research in the Interweave of Social Roles: Jobs and Families: Vol. 3, Families and Jobs*. Greenwich, Conn.: JAI.

Overall, John E., B. W. Henry, and Arthur Woodward. 1974. Dependence of marital problems on parental family history. *Journal of Abnormal Psychology* 83:446–450.

Parcel, Toby L., and Elizabeth G. Menaghan. 1994. *Parents' Jobs and Children's Lives*. New York: Aldine De Gruyter.

Parke, Ross D., and Navaz P. Bhavnagri. 1989. Parents as managers of children's peer relationships. Pp. 241–259 in Deborah Belle (ed.), *Children's Social Networks and Social Supports*. New York: Wiley and Sons.

Parker, Gordon B., and Bryanne Barrett. 1988. Perceptions of parenting in childhood and social support in adulthood. *American Journal of Psychiatry* 145:479–482.

Parker, Gordon B., Elaine A. Barrett, and Ian B. Hickie. 1992. From nurture to network: Examining links between perceptions of parenting received in child-hood and social bonds in adulthood. *American Journal of Psychiatry* 149:877–885.

Parker, Gordon, H. Tupling, and L. B. Brown. 1979. A parental bonding instrument. *British Journal of Medical Psychology* 52:1–10.

Patterson, Gerald R., John B. Reid, and Thomas J. Dishion. 1992. *Antisocial Boys*. Eugene, Ore.: Castalia Publishing Company.

Paulsen, Ronnelle. 1991. Education, social class, and participation in collective action. *Sociology of Education* 64:96–110.

Paulson, Sharon E., John P. Hill, and Grayson N. Holmbeck. 1991. Distinguishing between perceived closeness and parental warmth in families with seventh-grade boys and girls. *Journal of Early Adolescence* 11:276–293.

Peterson, James L., and Nicholas Zill. 1986. Marital disruption, parent-child relationships, and behavior problems in children. *Journal of Marriage and the Family* 49:295–307.

Piercy, Fred P., and Douglas H. Sprenkle. 1990. Marriage and family therapy: A decade in review. *Journal of Marriage and the Family* 52:1116–1126.

Pina, Darlene L., and Vern L. Bengtson. 1993. The division of household labor and wives' happiness: Ideology, employment, and perceptions of support. *Journal of Marriage and the Family* 55:901–912.

Pleck, Joseph. 1981. *The Myth of Masculinity*. Cambridge, Mass.: MIT Press.

———. 1985. *Working Wives, Working Husbands*. Beverly Hills, Calif.: Sage Publications.

Pope, Hallowell, and Charles W. Mueller. 1976. The intergenerational transmission of marital instability: Comparisons by race and sex. *Journal of Social Issues* 32:49–66.

Popenoe, David. 1988. *Disturbing the Nest*. New York: Aldine de Gruyter.

———. 1993. American family decline: 1960–1990: A review and appraisal. *Journal of Marriage and the Family* 55:527–556.

Popenoe, David, Jean Bethke Elshtain, and David Blankenhorn. 1996. *Promises to Keep: Decline and Renewal of Marriage in America*. Lanham, Md.: Rowman & Littlefield.

Putnam, Robert. 1995. Bowling alone: America's declining social capital. *Journal of Democracy* 6:68–70.

Radin, Norma. 1981. The role of the father in cognitive, academic, and intellectual development. Pp. 379–427 in Michael E. Lamb (ed.), *The Role of the Father in Child Development*. New York: Wiley.

Radin, Norma, and Graeme Russell. 1983. Increased father participation and child development outcomes. Pp. 191–218 in M. E. Lamb and A. Sagi (eds.), *Fatherhood and Social Policy*. Hillsdale, N.J.: Lawrence Erlbaum.

Richards, Maryse H., and Elena Duckett. 1991. Maternal employment and adolescents. Pp. 85–130 in Jacqueline V. Lerner and Nancy L. Galambos (eds.), *Employed Mothers and Their Children*. New York: Garland.

Roberts, Robert E. L., and Vern L. Bengtson. 1993. Relationships with parents, self-esteem, and psychological well-being in young adulthood. *Social Psychology Quarterly* 56:263–277.

———. 1996. Affective ties to parents in early adulthood and self-esteem across 20 years. *Social Psychology Quarterly* 59:96–106.

Rogers, Stacy, and Paul R. Amato. (in press). Is marital quality declining? Evidence from two generations. *Social Forces*.

Rohner, Ronald P. 1986. *The Warmth Dimension: Foundations of Parental Acceptance-Rejection Theory*. Beverly Hills, Calif.: Sage.

Rollins, Boyd C., and Darwin L. Thomas. 1979. Parental support, power, and control techniques in the socialization of children. Pp. 317–364 in Wesley R. Burr, Reuben Hill, F. Ivan Nye, and Ira L. Reiss (eds.), *Contemporary Theories about the Family. Volume 1. Research-Based Theories*. Glencoe, N.J.: The Free Press.

Rosenberg, M. 1965. *Society and Adolescent Self-image*. Princeton N.J.: Princeton University Press.

Rosenthal, Carolyn. 1985. Kinkeeping in the familial division of labor. *Journal of Marriage and the Family* 47:965–974.

Ross, Catherine E. 1991. Marriage and the sense of control. *Journal of Marriage and the Family* 53:831–838.

———. 1995. Reconceptualizing marital status as a continuum of social attachment. *Journal of Marriage and the Family* 57:129–140.

Ross, Catherine E., and Joan Huber. 1985. Hardship and depression. *Journal of Health and Social Behavior* 26:312–327.

Ross, Catherine E., and Chia-ling Wu. 1995. The links between education and health. *American Sociological Review* 60:719–745.

Rossi, Alice, and Peter Rossi. 1990. *Of Human Bonding: Parent-Child Relations Across the Life Course*. New York: Aldine de Gruyter.

Rotundo, E. A. 1985. American fatherhood: A historical perspective. *American Behavioral Scientist* 29:7–25.

Russell, Graeme. 1983. *The Changing Role of Fathers?* St. Lucia, Australia: University of Queensland Press.

Rutter, Michael. 1972. *Maternal Deprivation Reassessed*. Harmondsworth, Middlesex: Penguin.

———. 1979. *Changing Youth in a Changing World: Patterns of Adolescent Development and Disorder*. London: Nuffield Provincial Hospitals Trust.

———. 1988. Functions and consequences of relationships: Some psychopathological considerations. Pp. 332–353 in Robert A. Hinde and Joan Stevenson-

Hinde (eds.), *Relationships within Families: Mutual Influences*. Oxford: Clarendon Press.

Rutter, Michael, and N. Madge. 1976. *Cycles of Disadvantage*. London: Heinemann.

Sampson, Robert J. 1987. Urban black violence: The effect of joblessness and family disruption. *American Journal of Sociology* 93:348–382.

Sampson, Robert J., and John H. Laub. 1994. Urban poverty and the family context of delinquency: A new look at structure and process in a classic study. *Child Development* 65:523–540.

———. 1996. The military as a turning point in the lives of disadvantaged men. *American Journal of Sociology* 61:347–367.

Sandefur, Gary D., Sara S. McLanahan, and Roger A. Wojtkiewicz. 1992. The effects of parental marital status during adolescence on high school graduation. *Social Forces* 71:103–121.

Sarason, Irwin A., Barbara R. Sarason, and Edward N. Shearin. 1986. Social support as an individual difference variable: Its stability, origins and relational aspects. *Journal of Personality and Social Psychology* 50:845–855.

Schafly, Phyllis. 1977. *The Power of the Positive Woman*. New York: Jove, HBJ Books.

Seltzer, Judith A. 1991. Relationships between fathers and children who live apart: The father's role after separation. *Journal of Marriage and the Family* 53:79–102.

Seltzer, Judith A., and Suzanne M. Bianchi. 1988. Children's contact with absent parents. *Journal of Marriage and the Family* 50:663–677.

Sewell, William H., and Robert M. Hauser. 1975. *Education, Occupation, and Earnings*. New York: Academic Press.

Sewell, William H., Robert M. Hauser, and Wendy C. Wolf. 1980. Sex, schooling, and occupational status. *American Journal of Sociology* 83:551–583.

Shaefer, E. 1959. A circumplex model for maternal behavior. *Journal of Abnormal and Social Psychology* 59:226–235.

Simons, Ronald L., Jay Beaman, Rand D. Conger, and Wei Chao. 1993. Childhood experiences, conceptions of parenting, and attitudes of spouse as determinants of parental behavior. *Journal of Marriage and the Family* 55:91–106.

Skinner, Martie L., Glenn H. Elder, Jr., and Rand D. Conger. 1992. Linking economic hardship to adolescent aggression. *Journal of Youth and Adolescence* 21:259–276.

Skolnick, Arlene. 1991. *Embattled Paradise: The American Family in an Age of Uncertainty*. New York: Basic Books.

Snarey, John. 1993. *How Fathers Care for the Next Generation*. Cambridge, Mass.: Harvard University Press.

South, Scott J. 1995. Do you need to shop around? Age at marriage, spousal alternatives, and marital dissolution. *Journal of Family Issues* 16:432–449.

Spanier, Graham. 1991. Cohabitation: Recent changes in the United States.

Pp. 94–102 in John N. Edwards and David H. Demo (eds.), *Marriage and Family in Transition*. Boston: Allyn and Bacon.

Spitze, Glenna. 1988. Women's employment and family relations: A review. *Journal of Marriage and the Family* 50:595–618.

Stacey, Judith. 1990. *Brave New Families: Stories of Domestic Upheaval in Late Twentieth Century America*. New York: Basic Books.

Stack, Caroline B. 1974. *All Our Kin: Strategies for Survival in a Black Community*. New York: Harper and Row.

Staples, Robert, and Leanor B. Johnson. 1993. *Black Families at the Crossroads*. San Francisco, Calif.: Jossey-Bass.

Stephan, Cookie W., and Judy Corder. 1985. The effects of dual career families on adolescent sex-role attitudes, work and family plans, and choices of important others. *Journal of Marriage and the Family* 47:921–929.

Sullivan, Harry S. 1953. *The Interpersonal Theory of Psychiatry*. New York: Norton.

Sutherland, S. L. 1981. *Patterns of Belief and Action: Measurement of Student Political Activism*. Toronto: University of Toronto Press.

Svanum, S., R. G. Bringle, and J. E. McLaughlin. 1982. Father absence and cognitive performance in a large sample of six- to eleven-year-old children. *Child Development* 53:136–143.

Sweet, James A., and Larry L. Bumpass. 1987. *American Families and Households*. New York: Russell Sage Foundation.

Sweet, James A., Larry L. Bumpass, and Vaughan Call. 1988. *The Design and Content of the National Survey of Families and Households* (Working Paper NSFH-1). Madison: University of Wisconsin, Center for Demography and Ecology.

Teachman, Jay D. 1987. Family background, educational resources, and educational attainment. *American Sociological Review* 52:548–557.

Thompson, Linda, and Alexis J. Walker. 1991. Gender in families: Women and men in marriage, work, and parenthood. Pp. 76–102 in Alan Booth (ed.), *Contemporary Families: Looking Forward, Looking Back*. Minneapolis, Minn.: National Council on Family Relations.

Thomson, Elizabeth, Sara S. McLanahan, and R. B. Curtin. 1992. Family structure, gender, and parental socialization. *Journal of Marriage and the Family* 54:368–378.

Thornton, Arland. 1989. Changing attitudes toward family issues in the United States. *Journal of Marriage and the Family* 51:873–894.

———. 1991. Influence of the marital history of parents on the marital and cohabitational experiences of children. *American Journal of Sociology* 96:868–894.

Thornton, Arland, Terri L. Orbuch, and William G. Axinn. 1995. Parent-child relationships during the transition to adulthood. *Journal of Family Issues* 16:538–564.

Tomeh, Aida K. 1973. Formal voluntary associations: Participation, correlates, and interrelationships. *Sociological Inquiry* 42:89–122.

Troll, Lillian, and Vern L. Bengtson. 1979. Generations in the family. Pp. 127–161 in Wesley R. Burr, Reuben Hill, F. Ivan Nye, and Ira L. Reiss (eds.), *Contemporary Theories about the Family*. Glencoe, N.J.: Free Press.

Umberson, Debra. 1987. Family status and health behaviors: Social control as a dimension of social integration. *Journal of Health and Social Behavior* 28:306–319.

———. 1992. Relationships between adult children and their parents: Psychological consequences for both generations. *Journal of Marriage and the Family* 54:664–674.

U.S. Bureau of the Census. 1991. *Money Income of Households, Families, and Persons in the United States: 1990*. Current Population Reports, Series P-60, No. 174. Washington, D.C.: U.S. Government Printing Office.

———. 1992. *Statistical Abstract of the United States. 1992* (112th edition). Washington, D.C.: U.S. Government Printing Office.

———. 1993. *Statistical Abstract of the United States. 1993* (113th edition). Washington, D.C.: U.S. Government Printing Office.

Vandell, Deborah, and Janaki Ramanan. 1992. Effects of early and recent maternal employment on children from low-income families. *Child Development* 63:938–949.

Vannoy-Hiller, Dana, and William W. Philliber. 1989. *Equal Partners: Successful Women in Marriage*. Beverly Hills, Calif.: Sage.

Verba, Sidney, and Norman H. Nie. 1972. *Participation in American: Political Democracy and Social Equality*. New York: Harper and Row.

Voydanoff, Patricia. 1991. Economic distress and family relations: A review of the eighties. Pp. 429–445 in Alan Booth (ed.), *Contemporary Families: Looking Forward, Looking Back*. Minneapolis, Minn.: National Council on Family Relations.

Waite, Linda J. 1995. Does marriage matter? *Demography* 32:483–507.

Wallerstein, Judith S., and Sandra Blakeslee. 1989. *Second Chances: Men, Women, and Children After Divorce*. New York: Ticknor & Fields.

Wallerstein, Judith S., and Joan B. Kelly. 1980. *Surviving the Breakup: How Children and Parents Cope with Divorce*. New York: Basic Books.

Wheaton, Blair. 1990. Life transitions, role histories, and mental health. *American Sociological Review* 55:209–223.

Whitbeck, Les B., Ronald L. Simons, Rand D. Conger, Frederick O. Lorenz, Shirley Huck, and Glenn H. Elder, Jr. 1991. Family economic hardship, parental support, and adolescent self-esteem. *Social Psychology Quarterly* 54:353–363.

White, K. R. 1982. The relation between socioeconomic status and academic achievement. *Psychological Bulletin* 91:461–481.

_____. 1991. Determinants of divorce: A review of research in the eighties. Pp. 141–149 in Alan Booth (ed.), *Contemporary Families: Looking Forward, Looking Back*. Minneapolis, Minn.: National Council on Family Relations.

_____. 1992. The effect of parental divorce and remarriage on parental support for adult children. *Journal of Family Issues* 13:234–250.

_____. 1994a. Coresidence and leaving home: Young adults and their parents. *Annual Review of Sociology* 20:81–102.

_____. 1994b. Growing up with single parents and stepparents: Long-term effects on family solidarity. *Journal of Marriage and the Family* 56:935–948.

_____. 1994c. Stepfamilies over the life course: Social support. Pp. 109–138 in Alan Booth and Judy Dunn (eds.), *Stepfamilies: Who Benefits? Who Does Not?* Hillsdale, N.J.: Lawrence Erlbaum.

White, Lynn K., and Alan Booth. 1985. The quality and stability of remarriage: The role of stepchildren. *American Sociological Review* 50:689–698.

_____. 1991. Divorce over the life course: The role of marital happiness. *Journal of Family Issues* 12:5–21.

White, Lynn K., David Brinkerhoff, and Alan Booth. 1985. The effect of marital disruption on parent-child relationships. *Journal of Family Issues* 6:5–22.

White, Lynn K., and Bruce Keith. 1990. The effect of shift work on the quality and stability of marital relations. *Journal of Marriage and the Family* 52:453–462.

Williams, Edith, and Norma Radin, 1993. Paternal involvement, maternal employment, and adolescents' academic achievement: An 11-year follow-up. *American Journal of Orthopsychiatry* 63:306–312.

Wilson, John, and Darren E. Sherkat. 1994. Returning to the fold. *Journal for the Scientific Study of Religion* 33:148–161.

Wilson, William Julius. 1987. *The Truly Disadvantaged: The Inner City, the Underclass, and Public Policy*. Chicago: University of Chicago Press.

Wolchik, S., I. N. Sandler, S. T. Braver, and B. Fogas. 1985. Events of parental divorce: Stressfulness ratings by children, parents, and clinicians. *American Journal of Community Psychology* 14:59–74.

Wolfe, D. A., L. Zak, S. K. Wilson, and P. Jaffe. 1986. Child witnesses to violence between parents: Critical issues in behavioral and social adjustment. *Journal of Abnormal Child Psychology* 14:95–104.

Yogev, Sara, and Jeanne Brett. 1985. Perceptions of the division of housework and childcare and marital satisfaction. *Journal of Marriage and the Family* 47:609–618.

Young, Christobel. 1987. *Young People Leaving Home in Australia*. Canberra, Australia: Australian National University.

Zaslow, Martha J., Beth A. Rabinovich, and Joan T. D. Suwalsky. 1991. From maternal employment to child outcomes: Pre-existing group differences and moderating variables. Pp. 237–282 in Jacqueline V. Lerner and Nancy L. Galambos (eds.), *Employed Mothers and Their Children*. New York: Garland.

Zill, Nicholas, Donna R. Morrison, and Mary Jo Coiro. 1993. Long-term effects of parental divorce on parent-child relationships, adjustment, and achievement in young adulthood. *Journal of Family Psychology* 7:91–103.

Zill, Nicholas, and Christine W. Nord. 1994. *Running in Place: How American Families Are Faring in a Changing Economy and an Individualistic Society*. Washington, D.C.: Child Trends.

Index

Acock, Alan, 68, 100, 106, 185, 187, 191
Active *vs.* passive model, 4–5, 224–225
Adams, Kenneth S., 195, 203
Adan, Angela M., 17, 50, 185
Adolescent, 37–38, 40, 46, 60, 144
Adulthood, transition to, 1–2
Adult offspring study, 51–52, 61–62, 68–70. *See also* Child study
Adversity. *See* Economic adversity
Affection: and daughters, 46, 222; and parent-child relationship, 46, 49, 226, 227; and sons, 46; and parental control, 49, 226; and education, 51, 56; and socioeconomic resources, 51, 56; and poverty, 52; for father, 62, 63, 67, 69, 73, 222; and maternal employment, 62; and paternal child care, 65, 217, 222, 228–229; and marital quality, 69, 71–72; for mother, 69, 72–73; and parental divorce, 69, 73–80, 81, 223; and remarriage, 80; and parental support, 226, 227; importance of, 227
African Americans: and education, 6, 50, 179; and whites, 6; and unemployment, 7; and marriage, 14; and parent sample, 29; and parental divorce, 109; and social integration, 126; and socioeconomic attainment, 179; and psychological well-being, 187
Age: and life course perspective, 4; at mar-

riage, 14–15, 89, 90, 98, 100, 101, 105–106, 109, 118, 211; of child, 22, 36, 40; and divorce, 73, 75, 77, 79–80, 82, 109, 138, 142, 175, 178, 179, 223; and gender nontraditionalism, 100, 101, 105–106, 171–172, 180, 217; and social integration, 121, 123; and socioeconomic attainment, 171–172, 175; and psychological well-being, 184, 186; and income, 186, 223; and socioeconomic resources, 186, 211, 223; and maternal employment, 217; and marital conflict, 222–223; and family change, 222–224
Ahmeduzzaman, Mohammad, 50
Allen, Katherine R., 3
Allison, Paul D., 20
Alwin, Duane F., 22, 212, 213
Ambert, Anne-Marie, 224
Analytic procedure, 39
Antisocial behavior, 138, 187. *See also* Social integration
Anxiety, and parental divorce, 108
Aquilino, William S., 69, 70, 80, 81, 225
Armistead, Lisa, 60, 163, 192
Assistance: and parent-child relationship, 45, 47, 48–49; and parental control, 49, 226; and socioeconomic resources, 52, 53, 56–58, 59, 82, 91, 99, 214; and parental education, 56; and economic resources, 56–58, 59, 82, 214; and in-